The Politics of Disaster

UNIVERSITY PRESS OF FLORIDA

Florida A&M University, Tallahassee
Florida Atlantic University, Boca Raton
Florida Gulf Coast University, Ft. Myers
Florida International University, Miami
Florida State University, Tallahassee
New College of Florida, Sarasota
University of Central Florida, Orlando
University of Florida, Gainesville
University of North Florida, Jacksonville
University of South Florida, Tampa
University of West Florida, Pensacola

The Politics of Disaster

Tracking the Impact of Hurricane Andrew

DAVID K. TWIGG

University Press of Florida

Gainesville · Tallahassee · Tampa · Boca Raton

Pensacola · Orlando · Miami · Jacksonville · Ft. Myers · Sarasota

22 21 20 19 18 17   6 5 4 3 2 1

First cloth printing, 2012
First paperback printing, 2017

Library of Congress Cataloging-in-Publication Data

Twigg, David K.
The politics of disaster : tracking the impact of Hurricane Andrew /
David K. Twigg.
p. cm.
Includes bibliographical references and index.
ISBN 978-0-8130-4188-9 (cloth: alk. paper)
ISBN 978-0-8130-6455-0 (pbk.)
    1. Hurricane Andrew, 1992—Political aspects. 2. Hurricanes—
Political aspects—Florida. 3. Natural disasters—Political aspects—
Florida. 4. Disaster relief—Political aspects—Florida. I. Title.
HV6361992.F6 T95   2012
363.34'92209759—dc23
2012009927

The University Press of Florida is the scholarly publishing agency for
the State University System of Florida, comprising Florida A&M University, Florida Atlantic University, Florida Gulf Coast University, Florida International University, Florida State University, New College of
Florida, University of Central Florida, University of Florida, University
of North Florida, University of South Florida, and University of West
Florida.

University Press of Florida
15 Northwest 15th Street
Gainesville, FL 32611-2079
http://upress.ufl.edu

This book is dedicated to my wife, Rita, and the rest of my family,
who have supported me in this endeavor
as well as in my previous undertakings.

It is also dedicated to the memories of the victims
and to the survivors of hurricanes and other disasters
and to the many American heroes who came to their aid.

Contents

Figures

Tables

Preface and Acknowledgments

Before dawn on August 24, 1992, Hurricane Andrew smashed into South Florida, particularly southern Dade County, and became the costliest hurricane in U.S. history until Hurricane Katrina displaced it in 2005. Andrew's effects quickly overwhelmed local and state emergency response capabilities and eventually required major federal assistance including regular military units. Although the social and economic impacts of Hurricane Andrew are relatively well researched, much less attention has been given to its possible political effects.

Focusing on incumbent officeholders at three levels (municipal, state legislative, and statewide) who stood for reelection after Hurricane Andrew, this study seeks to determine whether they experienced any political effects from Andrew and explores the possible interaction between the famous "incumbency advantage" and an "extreme event," in this case a natural disaster. The specific foci were campaigns and campaigning (a research process that includes forty-three personal interviews), as well as election results before and after the event.

Given well-documented response problems, my working hypothesis is that incumbents experienced largely negative political fallout from the disaster. The null hypothesis is that incumbents saw no net political effects, but the reverse hypothesis is also considered: incumbents benefited politically from the event.

In the end, this work finds that although the election process was physically disrupted, especially in south Dade County, the disaster largely reinforced the incumbency advantage. Specifically, the aftermath of Hurricane Andrew provided an opportunity for most incumbent officeholders to: (1) enhance constituency service, (2) associate themselves with the flow of external assistance, (3) achieve major personal visibility and media coverage, and yet (4) appear nonpolitical (or at least "above" normal politics). Overall, this combination allowed incumbents to effectively "campaign without campaigning," a point borne out by post-Andrew election results.

I thank for their support, encouragement, and inspiration on the first versions of this work, Betty Hearn Morrow, the late Ralph Lewis, Rebecca Mae Salokar, Virginia Chanley, Kevin A. Hill, the late Paul Mullen, and the members of Florida International University's Political Science Department. I am especially indebted to Richard S. Olson for his encouragement, invaluable advice, and friendship.

I also deeply appreciate the support of John F. Stack Jr. and the staff of FIU's Jack D. Gordon Institute for Public Policy and Citizenship Studies: Hector Cadavid, Jose Cervantes, Carolina Farfan, Chaka Ferguson, Luisa Martinez, and Dario Prepelitchi. David J. Estrin's editorial advice was extremely helpful, as was Paulette Johnson's statistical consultation. At the University Press of Florida, Meredith Morris-Babb, Corey Brady, Catherine-Nevil Parker, and their colleagues have been wonderfully instrumental in guiding me through the intricacies of the academic publishing process.

I have added to, cut, corrected, and adjusted the original, and any remaining errors or omissions are my own. This effort was partly supported by a Florida International University Graduate School fellowship, for which I am especially grateful.

1

Disasters as Political Challenges

Everything was impacted, from air quality to finances. The city was devastated, 22 square miles of devastation. And we had dollars that poured into this city that we were not prepared to deal with. I think probably for a year the air quality was badly, badly contaminated. . . . I think Hurricane Andrew affected every facet of our lives. From the minute it started blowing to today.

1992 elected official from Homestead, Florida, one of the cities hit hardest by Hurricane Andrew, speaking ten years later

Most public officials, especially at the local level, go their entire political lives without having to deal directly with a major natural disaster. Nevertheless, someone must be in office when a disaster strikes, and it is often (if only implicitly) assumed that elected officials will be politically damaged by such an event. This perspective, however, underestimates officeholders, who in most cases worked assiduously to achieve public positions, and it would be more analytically useful to view disasters as political challenges to which officials respond and adapt. This study takes precisely that perspective and focuses on how, why, and with what results local and state public officials in Florida modified their campaigns in the aftermath of Hurricane Andrew. This is therefore the story of the interaction between a major U.S. disaster and the alleged "incumbency advantage" enjoyed by sitting officeholders.

The Incumbency Advantage

Since the 1970s, political scientists have focused on the advantages of incumbents. David Mayhew (1974a; 1974b) and Richard Fenno (1973; 1978) showed that congressional incumbents had the ability to garner publicity—to advertise their experience, knowledge, responsiveness, and sincerity. Congresspersons could claim credit for getting a bill through committee, doing careful casework, and "bringing home the bacon" (such as jobs, contracts, and public works) through bills that benefit their congressional district. They could take positions on issues of value to groups of specific constituents rather than adhere to strict party positions. Congressional offices, committee assignments, and advancement through seniority further supported this advantage, which was brought to bear in the almost permanent quest for reelection. Studies focusing on other incumbents indicate similar advantages.

The Event

Hurricane Andrew ripped into Dade County, Florida, south of the city of Miami, before dawn on Monday, August 24, 1992 (figure 1). The effects were devastating, with "street lights, utility poles, cars and small airplanes . . . tossed like toys" (Garcia and Tanfani, 1992). Structures, particularly mobile homes, collapsed or were blown away, and many roofs were ripped off conventional houses and businesses.

Originally classified as a Category 4 hurricane on the Saffir-Simpson Scale, Andrew was later upgraded, and is now considered one of only three Category 5 hurricanes to strike the U.S. mainland in recorded history (National Oceanic and Atmospheric Administration [NOAA] 2002a). Sustained winds at landfall were estimated to have been 165 miles per hour; unofficial estimates put Hurricane Andrew's wind gusts at 200 miles per hour or more (Tomb 1992). A Category 5 storm, by definition, is expected to cause:

> Complete roof failure on many residences and industrial buildings. Some complete building failures with small utility buildings blown over or away. All shrubs, trees, and signs blown down. Complete destruction of mobile homes. Severe and extensive window and door damage. (NOAA 2002b)

Andrew met or exceeded these expectations. Although the storm only directly killed fifteen individuals in South Florida, estimates of hurricane-related deaths have been as high as eighty-five (Provenzo and Provenzo 2002, 133). Andrew destroyed or severely damaged thousands of businesses and tens of thousands of residences, leaving hundreds of

Figure 1. Composite view of Hurricane Andrew as it approaches, makes land-fall, and moves beyond Dade County on August 24, 1992. (Image courtesy of NOAA, Hurricane Research Division.)

thousands of people homeless. The National Hurricane Center's director at the time, Bob Sheets, described Andrew as leaving in its wake "three hundred square miles of devastation" (in Provenzo and Provenzo 2002, 2).

Throughout southern Dade County, neighborhoods were unrecognizable, even to people who had lived in them for many years. Few people living in the county were unaffected: power was out, water was cut, telephone services were inconsistent, businesses and government offices were closed, and traffic patterns were significantly altered (even after traffic lights began to work again). In the southern portions of the county the damage was particularly severe, with physical and social infrastructures torn apart.

Garbage pickup and disposal and other basic services were overwhelmed by the amount of debris, and the school year could not begin as scheduled because eighty-eight schools suffered damage, some quite severe. In addition, twenty-six schools were being used as emergency shelters for the suddenly homeless.

On the political front, primary elections scheduled for September 1 had to be postponed because polling places had either been destroyed or severely damaged and elections workers were displaced. Economic impacts were equally severe: parks and tourist attractions were closed in an area heavily dependent on tourism, and officials tried to re-attract visitors even as others begged for major assistance. The job market was completely disrupted. Some workers lost jobs and some employers lost workers, but repair and reconstruction opportunities were plentiful, and volunteers and the jobless from elsewhere—often referred to as "disaster gypsies"—flocked to South Florida while locals moved away or could not even look for work due to their losses.

On top of the devastation came problems with the initial relief efforts. The disaster response system in the United States assumes a bottom-up approach, with local governments providing the first level of relief (Schneider 1995). If a disaster is beyond the local government's ability to respond, local officials request state help, and in severe situations, the state requests federal assistance.

Andrew struck the least-populated portion of Dade County, but the damage was so severe that local governments were overwhelmed, with many employees also victims (Schneider 1995). Though the state of Florida moved in quickly with the aid of National Guard troops and other government agencies, it found itself unable to fully meet the challenges. Amidst the destruction, blocked streets, and disrupted communications, basic order began to break down. Crime in the nearly lawless rubble zone left by the hurricane included looting and pillaging of damaged homes and businesses. One local elected official in office at that time recalled a memorable encounter with a young storm victim shortly after Andrew struck:

> When she came back, she had a Glock on the side of her hip. . . . She'd done a complete change of her whole personality, you know. From a nice, vivacious, young married woman she was like a seasoned old, you know, gunslinger. . . . Those people down there evidently had, you know, I guess the thieves . . . running up and down the street. Right down, they lived right down there by Country Walk [a severely damaged neighborhood]. I see her face every time I think about a storm or something like that. . . . My wife and I talk about

that, about how that woman changed so much, from being just like a preppy little girl right out of college to a real old salt. And I'll never forget it, having that gun strapped on her side.

Nine days after Andrew struck, President George H. W. Bush ordered the U.S. military into the area to provide relief and control crime. The Navy airlifted supplies, Army units established tent cities and provided food for displaced storm victims, and Marines cracked down on looters. Military units assisted with emergency repairs to homes, stores, and offices.

All aspects of life in South Florida were affected. Some one thousand prisoners were relocated from two damaged federal prisons to northern Florida and other states (Salokar 1998). Two court facilities were among the many government offices temporarily shut down. Telephone and power lines were down, along with cell phone towers and transmitters. A nightly curfew restricted mobility for over two months in the southern portions of the county.

A year later, schools and businesses in southern Dade County were still not back to normal, with repairs and insurance claims pending (Mailander 1993; Brennan 1993c; Musibay 1993a). Many traffic signals and street signs were still missing (Musibay 1993b). Airports, water and sewage treatment systems, government offices, and parks were only partly operational (Metro-Dade Communications Department 1993). Hurricane Andrew clearly had major physical, economic, and social impacts (see Peacock, Morrow, and Gladwin 2000), but did it also affect politics?

Disaster and Political Opportunities

One possibility is that Hurricane Andrew would have been a shock to the political system. If so, officials would be held accountable by superiors or by voters through efforts to remove them from office. Elected officials could be voted out of office or experience new or stronger opposition. New individuals or groups might enter the political fray. Disasters represent "political dangers" for an official deemed unresponsive or ineffective (Sylves 2008). Some immediate indications suggested Hurricane Andrew was a major political shock, as evidenced by this chapter's epigraph.

Another indication of the political shock the hurricane occasioned comes from Dennis Moss, director of a nonprofit social service agency catering to southern Dade County at the time of Andrew. He decided that he could do more in a position high enough to influence planning and recovery efforts that were beyond the scope of his agency. When the county commission election system changed from county-wide elections to district seats in 1993 (coincidental to the disaster), he decided to run for a commission seat, his first bid for elected office (Moss 2002). His campaign emphasized "Rebuilding and Improving South Dade" (*Miami Herald* 1993c; Brennan and Hartman 1993).

One incumbent county commissioner up for reelection in 1994, Larry Hawkins, faced charges of ethics violations and sexual harassment. Incumbent vulnerability and the recent change to district elections for commission seats brought out eight challengers, including a citizen (Katy Sorenson) with campaign experience who desired to enter politics herself (Sorenson 2002; Filkins 1994a). Two years after the storm, problems associated with the recovery from Hurricane Andrew were among several issues for the crowded field of candidates (Filkins 1994a).

Sorenson received the most primary votes, forcing the incumbent into a runoff (Filkins 1994c, 1994d). The incumbent's campaign focused on his experience; integrity was the challenger's theme (Filkins 1994e). Hurricane recovery issues comprised a major part of Sorenson's duties as commissioner when she won: "There was a lot of work to be done" (Sorenson 2002). In her 2002 reelection bid, Sorenson reminded constituents of her post-Andrew efforts. One mailing to potential voters emphasized rebuilding images, with glossy before-and-after color photographs of structures with significant hurricane damage in 1992 and the same buildings, successfully restored, in 2002, as well as information about her work to strengthen building codes and redevelop the south Dade area (Katy Sorenson Reelection Campaign 2002).

In another such case, state senator Darryl Jones's 1998 reelection bid for his south Dade seat included a mailed advertisement featuring a picture of workers repairing a roof. The ad noted that Jones helped "pick up the pieces after our homes were destroyed" and obtained funding "for a Hurricane Andrew Trust Fund" (Florida Democratic Party 1998). His work on the redevelopment of Homestead Air Force Base, destroyed by Andrew, was also emphasized.

And at a 2002 conference commemorating the ten-year anniversary of Hurricane Andrew, county manager Steve Shiver said in his address that Andrew had prompted him to enter public service. Shiver first sought elected office in 1993, running successfully for the Homestead city council. In 1997 he was elected mayor of Homestead, an office he still held when tapped for the county manager position early in 2001 (Branch 1997;

Finefrock 2001a, 2001b). Incumbent Homestead mayor J. W. "Tad" DeMilly did not seek reelection in 1997 after ten years in office, partly because "what was supposed to be a part-time job [had] become a full-time responsibility" (Etheart 1997a).

Thomas Mann (1987) offered advice to incumbents: maintain the incumbent's reputation, "discourage the strongest potential opponent . . . and avoid mistakes" (265–66). Disasters place new issues on political agendas, often vividly reveal values, and are ripe opportunities for incumbents to make "mistakes" (Olson 2000). A major disaster could cause perceptions of an incumbent to sour, weakening their advantage by encouraging more or stronger challenges.

Potential danger to an incumbent exists if a disaster disrupts the economic well-being of the region and/or the social order. Perceptions of the proper role of public officials may even change with disaster. Wolensky and Miller (1981) found that before a disaster, local elected officials and citizens had the same perception of the proper everyday role of the officials—custodial. After a disaster, however, citizens believed that officials should be more activist, while public officials retained their prior view. Such disjunctions have potential electoral effects: voters do not see officials performing in their proper role because the voters' idea of that role changed more rapidly than that of the officials.

This is clearly one potential outcome of a disaster—political damage to incumbents, or the "negative effects" theory. A catastrophic natural disaster could focus blame on the elected official, encourage opposition, and potentially result in defeat. The incumbent would be—literally in the case of an event like Andrew—gone with the wind. Various anecdotes point to this result of the disaster-politics nexus. John Barnhart (1925) tied severe drought to the rise of the Progressive Party during the late 1800s (see also Reichley 1992); David Truman identified "disturbances" and "disruption of the established patterns of behavior" that might have any number of causes (1951, 106). "Militancy of farmers associations has generally varied inversely with the prosperity of agriculture" (88), and drought in the late 1800s reduced farmers' prosperity.

Existing political tensions in Waco, Texas, flared up after a 1953 tornado caused deaths, injuries, and the destruction of homes and businesses. Progressive citizens attempted "to change the form of municipal government," and accused the older, more conservative elected and financial elites of corruption (Moore 1958, 33). The mayor resigned within a year of the storm "and later left the city" (Moore 1958, 33). Deutscher and New noted that after a 1957 tornado in a Kansas City suburb, "It is probably no coincidence that the man who did the most to help disaster victims (himself a victim) and who represented them at several meetings, decided to run for political office a year after the tornado" (1961 29).

David Godschalk (1988) studied the political response to 1979's Hurricane Frederic in Gulf Shores, Alabama (between Mobile and Pensacola, Florida). There was much contention regarding changes to building codes and other mitigation policies after the storm. The chief executive of the civil defense agency resigned soon after, most incumbent council members and the mayor were defeated in the 1980 municipal elections, and virtually all top appointed officials were replaced by the newly elected leaders. Louisiana's governor was perceived to be weak and ineffective after Hurricane Katrina in 2005. Unable to restore her reputation after the disaster, she chose not to seek reelection.

In his first reelection bid after Hurricane Katrina, New Orleans mayor Ray Nagin had twenty-one challengers, no doubt more than he would have had under normal circumstances. Although voters were scattered, challengers were abundant: Nagin was seen as vulnerable. The local newspaper recommended his challenger, Ron Forman, and endorsements for Nagin were "hard to come by" (Russell, Krupa, and Perlstein 2006). Many donators to Nagin's 2002 campaign switched and gave money to his rivals instead in 2006 (Donze and Meitrodt 2006). The rebuilding of New Orleans was, needless to say, front and center among campaign issues in 2006 (Krupa and Donze 2006).

Mayor Nagin came in first place in the general election, making the runoff along with Mitch Landrieu. The Landrieu name was known throughout Louisiana, and certainly in New Orleans. Mitch Landrieu's father had been mayor of New Orleans, Mitch's sister had just been reelected to her U.S Senate seat in 2004, and Mitch Landrieu had himself been politically successful, serving as Louisiana's lieutenant governor. Landrieu was an extremely strong challenger in the aftermath of the disaster; well-known, with campaign experience, and an elected official.

The opposite potential is that "positive effects" for incumbents may come from a disaster. The incumbent would respond strategically by taking advantage of altered circumstances. In this case, public officials may show how much they care, how willing they are to "tackle tough, difficult problems," and their ability to provide casework and deliver needed resources to help constituents—in short, showing what great leaders they are (Schneider 1995, 16). Political leaders may get more media coverage

Table 1.1. Visibility and vote change

Involvement	Mean Vote Change
Highly Visible	+5.1%
Moderately Visible	+3.0%
Less Visible	+0.3%

Source: May, 1985, Table 6.4, pages 119–20.

and face less criticism if they seem to take charge in a difficult situation (Sylves 2008). They have an opportunity not only to show concern for their constituents, but also to provide them material relief.

Peter May (1985) found that incumbent visibility after disasters correlated with relative election success (margin of increase/decrease) for incumbents in congressional seats, governorships, and the presidency, demonstrating a possibility of increased incumbent advantage (table 1.1). May looked at the first post-disaster elections of a small number of office-holders and the topic was tangential to his main interest (post-disaster relief and reconstruction policy), but this finding is intriguing.

Abney and Hill (1966) specifically explored the hurricane-election nexus, examining the 1965 mayoral election in New Orleans after Hurricane Betsy. They found no specific political effects of the hurricane, but suggested several interesting reasons for this. First, clear responsibility for hurricane protection could not be assigned, so voters did not know who to blame/punish in Betsy's aftermath (thus no negative electoral effects would be seen in such cases). Second, voters saw the incumbent as competent before the disaster and the mayor's relief and recovery efforts were also seen positively, inflating or at least maintaining the perception. Nothing happened that would alter the consistent views of this public official.

After Hurricane Katrina, the *Times-Picayune* had extensive campaign coverage; debates raging before the final balloting centered on recovery and rebuilding issues. Both candidates were quite well-known, but the incumbent was the mayor. His name appeared in the headlines both as campaigner and as official representative—and defender—of the city and its recovery: for example, "City Secures Line of Credit: Nagin: Bankruptcy Option Laid to Rest" (May 16, A-1), "Nagin, Blanco at Odds on Delay in Aid: He Calls State Lethargic; She Points to Congress" (May 16, A-1), "Nagin Unveils Partner Deal with Microsoft" (May 19, one day before the election, B-1, local "New Orleans" section). Just as after Betsy, the official duties added to the visibility of the incumbent and reminded voters that Mayor Nagin was there doing the job. The incumbent captured 52 percent of the vote even though Landrieu had been able to attract nearly six times the financial support for the runoff. Landrieu attempted to portray himself as a better leader than Nagin after the incumbent's initial disaster-related errors, but this effort failed.

Third, in line with public policy literature, Abney and Hill found that most New Orleanians saw Hurricane Betsy as an act of nature or of God, something simply more powerful than mere humankind. Hurricane Betsy was therefore not seen as "a legitimate political issue" in the 1965 election (979–80). This, then, is a third potential: no political effects resulting from disaster, incumbent advantage neither eroded nor enhanced.

These examples must be placed in a larger context. No disaster occurs in a vacuum, and the state of Florida has a long history of demographic and social flux. In South Florida the changes have been especially pronounced since 1960. Any apparent political effects of Hurricane Andrew must be considered in that light. These factors will be explored in chapter 3, but first a summary of the collection and preparation of data presented in this book.

The Study

Hurricane Andrew's legacy of significant damage and social disruption to Dade County, Florida, is well documented, as is the widespread perception of slow and sloppy government response (Peacock, Morrow, and Gladwin 2000; Provenzo and Provenzo 2002). This study focuses on the electoral outcomes for the elected officials in the first and second post-Andrew elections, how and why the hurricane affected incumbent perceptions of reelection chances, and, based on those perceptions, how the incumbents responded in their campaigns.

Power relationships have many permutations, any of which may be affected by a disaster. Hurricane Andrew affected several political jurisdictions, each of which had/have multiple officials, both appointed and elected. Although both appointed and elected officials might be affected by a disaster, this study focuses on elections and incumbent elected officials, including multiple seats from a sample of municipal governments, state legislators, and statewide elected officials.

Methodology is more completely described in the appendix. The basic design of the study was to compare election campaigns and results in

Figure 2. Infrared image of Andrew's eye making landfall, 5 a.m., Dade County, Florida. (Image courtesy of NOAA, Hurricane Research Division.)

three regions of the county, focusing on officials in office at the time of Hurricane Andrew who made contested reelection bids. Each hurricane is unique, but all hurricanes have some things in common. Intense winds circulate around an eye of calm. The strongest winds are found in the eye wall (figure 2); winds gradually weaken out to the edge of the storm system. Andrew moved rather quickly across South Florida, dropping little rain but spawning a sixteen-foot-high storm surge at landfall.

Andrew's eye wall and strongest winds covered an area twenty to twenty-five miles across, throughout the area south of Southwest 112th Street (Clifford 1992, 23A; Mann 1993, 4; Morrow 2000, 4). Large portions of that area suffered severe damage, and the entire area suffered moderate to severe damage. Most residential damage occurred south of Southwest 112th Street (Haag Engineering 1992). The midsection of the county adjacent to the hardest-hit area, north of Southwest 112th Street but south of Southwest 40th Street, suffered predominantly moderate damage with pockets of severe damage. The area north of Southwest 40th Street experienced mild damage (figure 3).

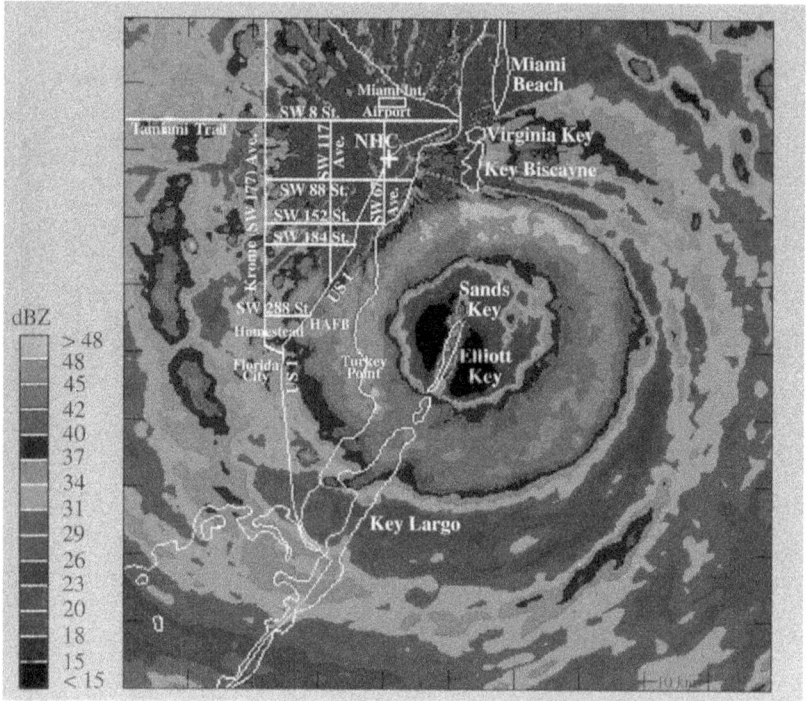

Figure 3. National Weather Service image of the eye of Hurricane Andrew in relation to hard-hit locales in Dade County. This was the last radar picture taken from the National Hurricane Center before the radar was blown off the roof. (Image courtesy of NOAA, Hurricane Research Division.)

Three levels of elected officials were examined, beginning at the municipal level with city commissioners and mayors. Only two municipalities lay completely within the southern/severe section of the county affected by the worst of Andrew's winds (figure 4).

Similarly, only two municipalities were entirely within the middle/moderate hurricane zone. Three additional cities from the northern/mild section of the county were included for comparison with the cities suffering more severe damage. Limiting the study to these seven municipalities provided a manageable scale. Table 1.2 reflects the populations of the seven cities included in this study as of 1990.

Given varying systems of staggered terms, the first reelection opportunity for city officials stretched over several years. Table 1.3 reflects the number of incumbents, across all seven jurisdictions, running for

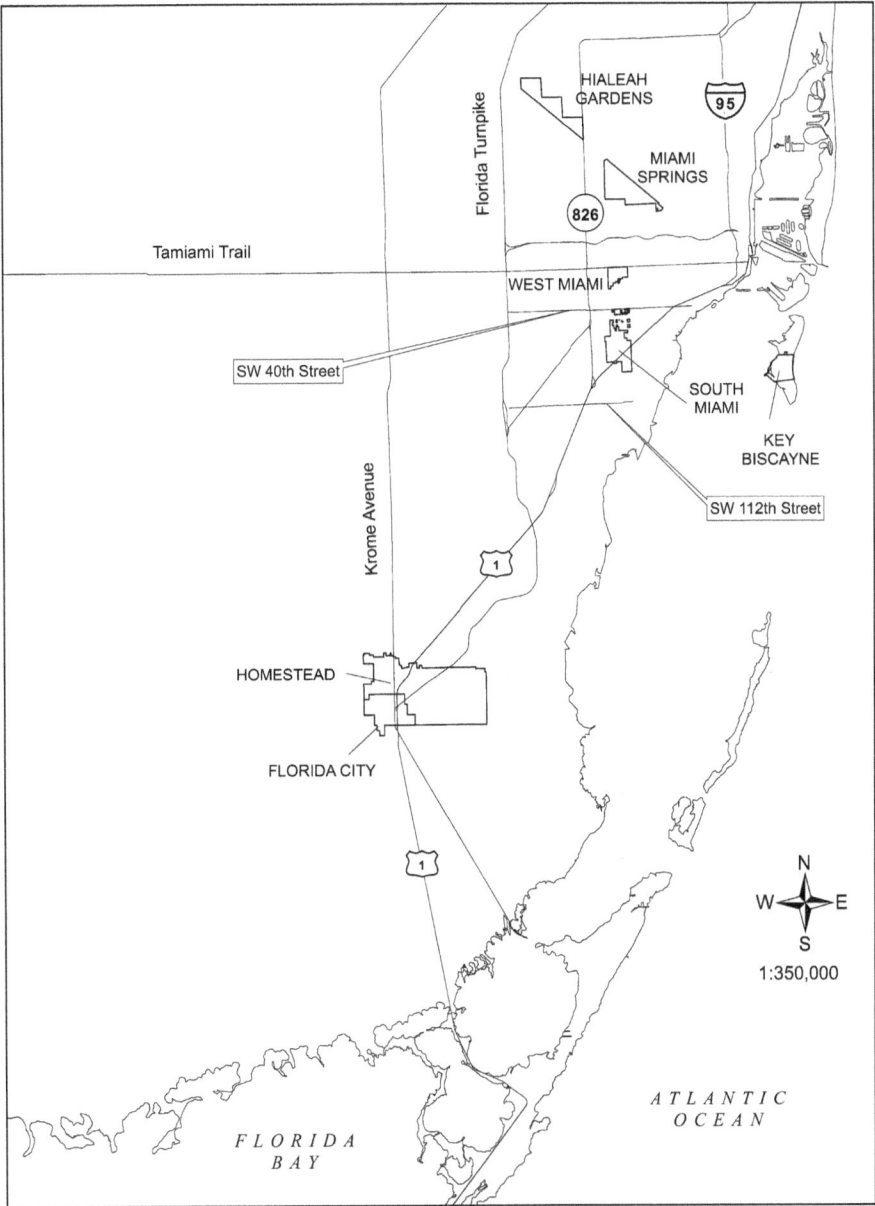

Figure 4. Selected Dade municipalities that experienced mild, moderate, and severe hurricane damage from Andrew. (Map produced by FIU Library GIS Center.)

Table 1.2. 1990 population of selected municipalities, Dade County, Florida

South Zone		Middle Zone		North Zone	
Homestead	26,866	South Miami	10,404	Miami Springs	13,268
Florida City	5,806	Key Biscayne	8,854	Hialeah Gardens	7,713
				West Miami	5,727

Source: Bureau of the Census, 1992, pp. 5–9 (1990 Census data).

Table 1.3. Number of municipal incumbents seeking reelection and first post-Andrew election opportunity

	1993	1994	1995	1996	Total
Florida City		2		1	3
Homestead	3		2		5
South Miami		2			2
Key Biscayne	3	2			5
Hialeah Gardens	3				3
Miami Springs	2				2
West Miami		1		1	2
Total	**11**	**7**	**2**	**2**	**22**

reelection with competition in the first opportunity for reelection after the hurricane, which ranged between March 1993 and April 1996.

State legislative elections were also included in the analysis to determine effects on legislators whose districts included the affected areas. Twenty districts of the state House of Representatives and seven districts of the state Senate were completely or partly located within Dade County in 1992. Eight legislators from districts located from the southern damage zone to the northern zone were challenged in their 1992 reelection bids. Other districts had unopposed incumbents or the incumbents did not seek reelection.

Finally, four statewide races were reviewed to assess any impact of the hurricane on wider constituencies. The targets for interview included the governor/lieutenant governor (who run together on a ticket) and three cabinet positions—all officials who sought reelection in contested races in 1994. Hurricane-affected south Dade was only a small part of the statewide electorate, but the analysis of these races provided important and unexpected results.

To establish trends/patterns, election results and voter turnout from 1980 through 2002 were reviewed at each level, allowing for the identification of post-hurricane changes. Interviews with twenty-six officials and seventeen key campaign supporters (campaign managers or other important staff/supporters) were also conducted. Interviewees were assured, prior to the interviews, that information provided would be used only in the aggregate. Ideal-type candidates and other "respondents" have therefore been created by combining information collected from various similarly placed individuals into one or two aggregated cases within each chapter. Candidates identified herein are for the most part not individuals interviewed for the study; the information comes primarily from public records.

Using *multiple* incumbents expands on the approach of Abney and Hill, who analyzed only *one* race and compared heavily flooded precincts with precincts where no flooding occurred. The inclusion of incumbents from less severely affected areas is also similar to May's comparison of counties affected/not affected by his selected disasters.

Organization

The next chapter (chapter 2) is the story of election adversity in the raw—state legislative elections, the first elections to take place after the hurricane. Campaigns for primary contests were already well under way when Andrew struck. Chapter 3 provides background on Florida's political structure and the demographic changes in the state and in Dade County, setting the story of Hurricane Andrew in context.

The following five chapters tackle the question of hurricane-related political change by reviewing statewide and municipal elections, focusing on the post-Andrew incumbent reelection campaigns. Chapters 4 and 5 explore Andrew's electoral legacy on statewide elected officials. Chapter 4 delves into the Dade County election results of the statewide races, while Chapter 5 explores the responses of statewide elected officials in the aftermath of the hurricane and the recollections and perceptions of political elites involved in those races. This chapter also analyzes the Dade County results of the 1992 U.S. presidential contest, another statewide race—this one for Florida's critically important electoral college votes.

Chapter 6 analyzes the municipal elections in southernmost Dade County, in Homestead and Florida City, which were largely devastated by Andrew. Chapter 7 explores the electoral effects of the hurricane for officials in the moderately damaged city of South Miami and the Village of Key Biscayne, while chapter 8 analyzes the impact of the storm on elections in three mildly affected cities in northern Dade County—Miami Springs, Hialeah Gardens, and West Miami. Finally, chapter 9 summarizes the findings, offers lessons for elected officials, and suggests directions for further study.

2

Florida Legislators

Locally Elected State Officials

[The] mobile home park. . . . was fairly large. . . . And I always made it a point to campaign there. I always made it a point to walk there, and I always made it a point to do that in, usually, the last week of the election cycle. . . . And that year I didn't go there . . . because it was gone. Eight hundred units . . . completely wiped off of God's green Earth. . . . We went to, physically, where it was, and it was gone.

1992 state legislator on campaigning after Hurricane Andrew

The first group of officials in this study to face voters after the hurricane was from Florida's legislature. Elected officials from the municipalities, discussed in later chapters, represent small constituencies, with municipal elections held in small districts completely within one of Hurricane Andrew's damage zones. State legislators' districts are larger, potentially more diverse, and sometimes cross municipal or county lines. Some districts also crossed into more than one of Andrew's damage zones. This chapter explores the experience of state legislators seeking reelection after Hurricane Andrew. Although state legislators are state officials, politically they have localized electoral bases.

Districts entirely or partially in Dade County in 1992 were identified using pertinent county election department maps depicting the bicameral state legislature's House and Senate districts and voting precincts. Outcome data for general elections and primaries (including runoff primaries) from 1980 through 2002 were obtained from the Florida Elections Division and the Miami-Dade County Elections Department, whose data also contain county-only vote totals for districts that cross county borders.

These data proved incomplete; they only provide election outcome information, and many incumbent Florida legislators are returned to office without elections because they have no challengers. It is even possible that a strong, experienced candidate (not an incumbent) would enter a race early and draw no challenger. For example, a state senator, city mayor, or county commissioner with a strong electoral track record might run for a house seat and face no competitors.

Accordingly, the journals of the House and the Senate were reviewed to determine who held office and to gather other potentially relevant information (for example, special elections or change of party identification occurring between elections). The 1980 general legislative session was used as a baseline for a review of the membership of each chamber for each new legislature from 1980 to 2000, at the time of the biennial "Organizational Session." This occurs fourteen days after the November general election and is held to establish committee assignments, officially designate chamber leadership, and establish rules of order. For the 2002 elections, lists of the 2002–4 House and Senate memberships were obtained from the legislature's Web sites. Finally, Miami-Dade County Elections Department data provided precinct-level results for key districts in the years before and after Hurricane Andrew.

Thirteen state House members and two state senators representing parts of Dade County and in office at the time of Hurricane Andrew sought reelection in 1992. All but one were successful (see table 2.1). In 1990, eight of the thirteen had been unopposed; in 1992, four drew no opposition. Only seven of the thirteen sought reelection in 1994, and six were successful, three unopposed. Both senators who sought to retain their seats in 1992 were unopposed. Indeed, only one had a challenger in even the second (1994) election after Andrew, and he won with more than 77 percent of the vote.

The greatest single decline was for one candidate who garnered 83 percent of the Republican primary vote against one challenger in 1992. He saw his 1994 primary vote share drop to 53 percent, but against two challengers, who captured 32 percent and 15 percent of the primary vote. Note also that the 1992 election cycle was well under way before the tropical system that became Hurricane Andrew formed.

The election cycle includes the decision of a candidate to run for office, the formal process of establishing a campaign checking account and filing qualifying papers, fund-raising, the possibility of primary and runoff campaigns, and the general election campaign. In 1992, the decision to

Table 2.1. Proportion of votes pre- and post-Hurricane Andrew: Incumbents in the Florida Legislature

HOUSE

Incumbent	1990 share (%)	1992 share (%)	1994 share (%)
Luis Rojas	100	69.0*	75.8*
Willie Logan	87.7	100	100
Elaine Gordon	62.5*	51.2*	N/A
Mike Abrams	100	100	N/A
Bruce Hoffman	50.3	46.4**	N/A
Rodolfo Garcia	100	77.9	82.4
Carlos Valdes	100	82.8*	53.2*
Luis Morse	100	67	100
Art Simon	71	64.6	N/A
John Cosgrove	100	66.2	61.7
Ron Saunders	100	99.7	N/A
Elaine Bloom	100	100	100
Miguel DeGrandy	80.1*	100	N/A
Average (Mean)	**88.58**	**78.83**	**81.87**
# Unopposed	**8 (62%)**	**4 (31%)**	**3 (43%)**

SENATE

Incumbent	Pre-Andrew vote share	1992; first post-Andrew vote share	Second post-Andrew vote share
Roberto Casas	52.5 (1988)*	100	100.0 (1996)
Howard Forman	61.1 (1990)	100	77.6* (1994)
Average (Mean)	**56.8**	**100**	**88.8**

*Primary election data used; no challenge in general election.
**Runoff primary data used; incumbent lost—no general election.
Source: Florida Department of State, Elections Division; Miami-Dade County Elections Department.

(or not to) run was made by the official July filing deadline, well before Andrew. In fact, Andrew struck South Florida just eight days before the scheduled primary election, and campaigning was well under way for those contests. Still, the hurricane could have affected campaigns and/or the election results in 1992 and/or any stage of the 1994 election cycle.

In that light, the pattern of unopposed incumbents in table 2.1 is interesting for reasons other than the hurricane (but turns out not to be hurricane related). In 1990, eight of the thirteen legislators seeking reelection (62 percent) were unopposed, but in 1992 this dropped to four of thirteen (31 percent). In 1994, the number of unopposed incumbents dropped to three, but with only seven seeking reelection, the proportion rose to 43 percent. Because the decision to oppose an official had to be made before the development of what would become Andrew, the 1992 reduction in unopposed incumbents was no doubt a result of the 1992 redistricting.

Additional analysis of election results is largely inconclusive. To recall, the criteria for including politicians in this study were that they were: (1) in office at the time of Hurricane Andrew; (2) seeking reelection in the first post-hurricane election; and (3) challenged in that contest.

Of the two state senators from Dade County seeking reelection in 1992, neither had opposition in his first bid for reelection. Nine of the thirteen House members from Dade who sought reelection in 1992 had opposition. One (Saunders) was dropped from the study because the district he represented was predominantly in Monroe County (the Florida Keys), and his only opposition was a write-in candidate who garnered just 0.3 percent of the vote.

Eight state legislators, all House members, were included in the study. Three of them were unopposed in 1990, complicating a pre-post comparison. Three of the remaining five incumbents had opposition only in the 1990 primary; all three were from districts entirely in the north section of the county that later suffered only mild damage from Andrew.

The Simon Case

Table 2.2 depicts the 1990 and 1992 results for Art Simon, the only legislator from the group who was opposed in the general elections in 1990 and 1992 and who came from a district that included precincts from the southern (severely damaged) area of the county. Coincidentally, his opponent was the same in 1992 as in 1990. It is an interesting and illustrative case.

One of the purposes of redistricting is to equalize the size of districts. Uneven population growth causes districts to become numerically unequal over time, and redrawing district lines mitigates this inequality by evening out the populations among state legislative districts to comply with the "one person, one vote" principle established by the U.S. Supreme Court in *Reynolds v. Sims* (1964). Thus, Simon's district, a growing part of the county, had a substantial reduction in the number of registered voters between 1990 and 1992, as several precincts were removed from the district during the redistricting process. The county elections department also periodically purges inactive voters from the rolls. One such purge occurred in May 1991.

Table 2.2. Pre- and post-Andrew election results for Representative Art Simon, District 116, Florida House of Representatives

Region[*]	Registered	Total votes[**]	% turnout	Incumbent votes[***]	%	Challenger votes[***]	%
1990							
Middle	41,806	21,213	50.74	14,823	69.9	6,390	30.1
South	8,657	4,760	54.98	3,540	74.4	1,220	25.6
M/S overlap	6,711	3,450	51.41	2,530	74.4	920	25.6
Absentees	0	1,022	—	722	70.6	300	29.4
Total or average	57,174	30,445	53.25	21,615	71.0	8,830	28.9
1992							
Middle	29,325	17,618	60.08	11,237	63.8	6,381	36.2
South	5,716	3,635	63.59	2,454	67.5	1,181	32.5
M/S overlap	3,691	2,582	69.95	1,634	63.3	948	36.7
Absentees	0	1,835	—	1,254	68.3	581	31.7
Total or average	**38,732**	**25,670**	**66.28**	**16,579**	**64.6**	**9,091**	**35.4**

*Region depicts the geographic region of the damage zones created by Hurricane Andrew: The middle, moderate damage zone north of SW 112th Street, the southern, severely damaged zone south of SW 112th Street, and those precincts that overlapped the two zones.

**Ballots, reported in county elections data, are more than the actual number of votes cast for the two candidates. This is due to: (a) individuals casting ballots on which votes for the top offices in the election (that is, the governor in 1990 and the president in 1992) are cast, while votes for offices further down on the ballot (the state legislator) are skipped over; and (b) punch-card ballots not recording votes in some contests because of hanging, pregnant, or dimpled chads. Thus, the "votes" column reflects the total of the votes recorded for this race.

***Percentages of votes shown are calculated from the total number of votes recorded for this race, the lower numbers from the "votes" column. Ballots were cast by 55.81% of registered voters in 1990 and 80.83% in 1992, but there were substantially fewer votes cast for the District 116 races, especially in 1992.

Source: Compiled from Miami-Dade County Elections Department data.

Voter turnout varied significantly between 1990 and 1992. The year 1990 marked a midterm election with the race for governor heading the ballot, but 1992 was a presidential election year, with the independent candidacy of Ross Perot infusing even more excitement into the contest. The percentage of registered Dade County voters actually participating in the November 1992 general election was thus the highest ever recorded, a pattern seen throughout Florida and several other states. Simon received 71 percent of the vote in 1990 and nearly 65 percent in 1992. Although this is a marked reduction, the 1992 vote share still reflects a safe seat for the representative, considering adjustment of the district, the presidential election, and the Perot factor (he brought out many usual nonvoters).

Simon initially announced that he would not seek reelection because of the substantial changes to his district after the redistricting process (Silva and Filkins 1992). The new district was mostly Latino/a, and Simon, despite speaking fluent Spanish, apparently believed that ethnic voting would result in his defeat (Holly and Branch 1992). Legal battles over the redistricting went all the way to the U.S. Supreme Court, however, and resulted in redrawn district lines. With a more even ethnic mix in his district, Simon decided at the last minute to enter the race, which he won handily.

In Simon's case, it should be noted that although the population of his new district was approximately 47 percent Latino/a (Holly and Branch 1992), many of those people were either too young to vote, not yet citizens, or simply unregistered. Indeed, of the district's registered voters as of August 17, 1992 (just one week before the hurricane), 67 percent were non-Latino/a white, while only 30 percent were Latino/a. Partisan registration was nearly evenly divided between Democrats (46 percent) and Republicans (43 percent). Thus, although it was a changing district, Simon, a Spanish-speaking non-Latino white incumbent Democrat, would seem to have been favored against most challengers, absent an issue that would cause the electorate to favor his removal.

An Evolving Region Encounters Disaster

Three of the 1992 state legislative incumbents included in this study were challenged only in the September primary. Four were in contests in the November general election. The only incumbent who lost in 1992, Bruce Hoffman, was a white non-Latino in an increasingly Latino/a area. After the 1992 redistricting, he represented a district that was about 66 percent

Latino/a and faced three Latino/as in the September Republican primary (Garcia 1992a, 1992b; Branch 1992d). He came in second, and the leading candidate in September won in an October runoff (Nickens 1992b; Garcia 1992e). Note that the Cuban-American population in Dade County tends to be heavily Republican, and the Cuban-American challenger reminded voters of his ability to better represent the district. Ethnicity and family values (the incumbent did not have children) were the issues, not the hurricane (Garcia 1992d, 1992e).

Six incumbent legislators were interviewed for this study. In addition, five secondary subjects were identified by the primary subjects as key campaign aids/advisors and interviewed. These eleven interviews included two women and nine men (three white non-Latino/as and eight Latino/as).

The south Dade area was growing at least as fast as the county as a whole before Andrew, and county population growth was substantial. The population was also "highly mobile" (MDC Planning Department 1993, 1994), with the 1990 Census revealing that 54 percent of the county population (56 percent in south Dade) had moved within the previous five years.

Then Hurricane Andrew removed a total of 48,904 housing units—nearly all of that in south Dade, according to property tax data—resulting in the relocation of over 100,000 people. Approximately 57,000 of those moved out of the county (MDC Planning Department 1994). Nearly two years later, the total population of south Dade was still approximately 29,000 people lower than pre-disaster estimates, despite the fact that 76 percent of the housing losses (65 percent in the hardest hit area) had been repaired or replaced (MDC Planning Department 1994).

The more catastrophic an event, the more impact it is likely to have on the affected population and voters. Horrific flooding in New Orleans after Hurricane Katrina in 2005, for instance, disrupted living arrangements even more severely than did Andrew. A pre-Katrina population of approximately 450,000 dropped to about 201,000 a year after the storm, and the population three years later was only 72 percent of what it had been before the floods (Logan 2009). Caution should be used in generalizing about impacts on people in general and voters in particular after what are often referred to as "equal-opportunity destroyers."

Lower income populations generally fare worse, in the long run, than middle- and upper-class demographic groups, and minority populations are often disproportionately poor. A year after Katrina, the white population of New Orleans was reduced by about two-thirds and the black population was reduced by about three-fourths. Demographic analysis is often important in order to understand changes in voting patterns.

Hurricane Andrew struck on August 24 and the primary election was scheduled for September 1, but at least two hundred polling places had been destroyed or severely damaged. Electricity was out, telephone service was weakened, many power lines were down in the south part of the county, transportation was difficult at best, and workers scheduled to staff the precincts (as well as voters) were struggling to find food, water, and shelter.

The day following the storm, the *Miami Herald* reported that the primaries, already predicted to have a low turnout due to their unusual scheduling before the Labor Day holiday, might be "messed up" (Bousquet and Ishoy 1992). On August 27 the newspaper reported that Dade elections officials had requested a postponement of the election, but the governor did not believe that he had the authority to issue such an emergency order (Fiedler 1992a). The governor also heard from Florida's other sixty-six counties that a delay in the scheduled vote would cause them problems. The state arranged to send emergency workers to assist Dade County, but they would arrive the day before the primary—insufficient time to train and place them in a disaster zone, which was in truth more like a war zone (Haner 1992).

Dade County then filed suit (Holly 1992c), and on August 30, two days before the scheduled election, a state court postponed the Dade primary by one week and ordered elections supervisors in other counties not to publish results of races that included Dade precincts before Dade balloting was concluded (Holly and Bousquet 1992). On August 31, just one day before the primary in sixty-six out of sixty-seven counties, the Florida Supreme Court reversed the order requiring the withholding of results from the other sixty-six counties (Fiedler and Silva 1992).

Indeed, one of the primary contests included in this study covered parts of Dade and Collier (west of Dade) counties. That election was thus held on two days: September 1 in Collier and September 8 in Dade. The 1992 primary elections for the state legislature occurred on September 1 and September 8, and the general election on November 3 (eight days, fifteen days, and seventy-two days—approximately ten weeks—after Andrew). If the scheduling of the elections thus appears confusing (and it was), how was campaigning affected?

The 1992 Primaries

The 1992 primary contests included in this study were in districts in the northern, mildly affected part of the county, but because they were scheduled eight days after the hurricane, the physical impact was considerable. Electricity was out in most of the area, trees and debris had to be removed, water quality was affected (county-wide, boil-water orders were in effect), traffic was a nightmare, most businesses were temporarily closed, and emergency relief activities focusing on the southern portions of the county were organizing and becoming operational. It was not, in general, business as usual for the residents of those northern districts. Nevertheless, on Election Day the turnout for these races ranged from 27 percent to 32 percent, surpassing the county average of 24 percent and comparable to the turnout for Broward (30 percent) and Palm Beach (25 percent) counties, north of Dade (Strouse, Filkins, and May 1992; Editorial Board, 1992a).

After Andrew, campaigning essentially came to a halt. By law, fund-raising must stop four days before an election, but mail was temporarily interrupted even in the northern districts. Politicians thus faced a dilemma: what to do with a reelection campaign that was well under way? For incumbents, the answer had two general components: actual campaign activities and duties associated with office.

Florida House districts are relatively small, and campaign tactics include direct mailings, house-to-house canvassing, rush hour street-corner visibility, signage, and broadcast media advertising. Experienced campaigners—and therefore most incumbents—establish timeframes for different activities to ensure timely printing of materials for mailings, fund-raising requests, development of advertisements, and so forth. Although the primary election was postponed, it took most of a week for court decisions to establish that fact. Meanwhile, candidates adjusted their plans based on what they knew, and for six days what they knew was that the election was scheduled for eight days after the hurricane. The incumbent (recall that the responses of all interviewees are aggregated to an ideal-type incumbent figure in this chapter) recounted adjusting the plan for mailings to voters:

> So in the meantime we were still questioning, will there be mail delivery, and will it be timely delivery? And I remember just dumping three mailings at once, which was a waste of money, but I mean

the work had already been done; the investment had already been made. So I remember throwing hundreds of thousands of mail pieces, and people getting three in one day. Some got it on time, and some didn't, but overall, I mean, they got hit with one, at least, and that's all that counted, at that time.

None of those associated with the 1992 primary campaigns noted their own door-to-door canvassing that year; to the extent it was planned, it does not appear to have taken place after the hurricane. The incumbent downplayed the campaign after Andrew as largely unimportant: "I really don't remember the specifics of, you know, your radio or your signs, because the focus was so much on the hurricane, and again, the daily newscast. I mean, there were people who didn't have food. I mean, there were areas where they had to, you know, bring in food."

Here the conflict between campaign activity and official duty is evident, as well as the personal impact of a major disaster on public officials. The legislature was not in session, but as elected officials, state legislators needed to do something to help. While the campaign manager recalled ads that could not air due to electricity outages, the incumbent remembered the confusion and disruption to peoples' lives. Official duties included going on radio to advise people what was being done to provide relief, calming constituents, assuring them that "things are starting to happen . . . exercising some leadership, that, you know, people were doing something." The incumbent also recounted a local drive to collect food, arranging for a military helicopter to deliver donated goods, and going with a local television news helicopter for food distribution:

> And we actually landed and it had such an impact on me, to see people run when, you know, they saw the food there. They were just totally isolated. I mean, I've never seen anything like that. It was like, you know, you couldn't believe that in this country there would be a situation where people were, they had no place to go, they had no running water, they had no electricity, they just had the little shelter, whatever was left. And they'd run when people came with food. . . .
>
> You didn't, why campaign, I mean, you know. What are you going to say? I'm going to run for state rep 'cause; for—'cause why? For what? You know, this was much more important. Again, I think . . . once the hurricane hit, for all practical purposes the campaigns were over. I think that's really the analysis. So I can't

remember, you know, if you did or didn't do radio, where your signs were, just, it was over. I mean, a new event had taken place.

On the other hand, to the extent that the candidate did remember where signs were—before the hurricane—it was for a different reason. Large campaign signs could become missiles in the strong winds of a major hurricane, thereby causing damage and potentially incurring some liability, political if not otherwise. The incumbent expressed pride about memorable and strategically placed signs:

> I always ran very strong campaigns with a lot of signs. I had good signs, but better than having good signs I had great locations. . . . I used to go and just pick my sign locations strategically. And I had big signs. I had the big four by eights. And they were clamped down really good with two by fours. I mean, they were meant to stay. . . . Then the hurricane is heading our way.

Being responsible and/or wishing to avoid liability, the representative recounted spending the day—from five in the morning to midnight—removing signs with a crew of several helpers and a rented truck. The incumbent remembered finding out just how many signs had been placed, how well-installed they were (making them very hard to remove), and receiving unexpected help with their removal:

> Now interestingly enough . . . while I was picking up the signs the night, the day before the hurricane came, some of my signs were being removed and were being used to board up houses. And then people were coming by and asking if they can have the lumber. For sure [I said], take the lumber.

Another aspect of interrupted campaigning was street-corner visibility, which means standing out on street corners at rush hour with signs, waving to passersby. Our incumbent used this effectively during an initial and several reelection campaigns, recruiting retirees and students: "I would ask them, in the afternoon because in the morning they all go to school, that please, if they could join me in the afternoons, standing on the street corners."

This resulted in forty to fifty helpers on some days, perhaps because the incumbent learned to make it a fun activity:

> That was the secret . . . have so much fun . . . I'd have them on all four corners, with a lot of signs. . . . Sometimes I would show up with

five, and by the time two hours, two and a half hours had gone by, I had fifty of them. And they would put on a tee shirt and a sign and a whistle and they would create a lot of noise.

Legislators frequently showed sensitivities about their constituents after Andrew. In this case, the campaign activity was curtailed because, "the lights are off, we don't even have traffic lights. You'd be foolish to try to wave at somebody with a smile on, when the whole town is without lights." However, the duty of acting as public official overshadowed any campaign difficulties. The campaign manager related the immediate switch from candidate to official:

> It was a good time. People came together. And we had a lot of volunteers, people who had worked on the campaign or people just used to coming in. . . . This was a central point for people to come by and say, "Hey, how can I help?" We got a lot of that. We got involved in collecting foodstuff and that kind of thing. . . . A lot of volunteers, we put volunteers at different stores, grocery stores and what have you to collect foodstuff and other items. We did a lot of that.

The incumbent, as a public official, was in meetings with city, county, and other officials. In a time of dire confusion, the incumbent tried to make the best of the situation for constituents, including those of other districts. With limited resource availability between legislative sessions, whatever resources were available were used. One remarkable coincidence occurred when the legislator received a surprise call from someone he had casually met while away on vacation. This casual acquaintance, an owner of a construction business in another state, wanted to help remediate the terrible situation he saw on the news. He sent a crew of workers to Dade County and had them report to the representative. This assistance, gratefully received, was put to good use, the incumbent recalled:

> And I went, as soon as these guys came in, and these guys were here within forty-eight hours, I went out to the radio and I asked . . . if you have a tree on your, that does not allow [access] into your house, you know, call me and I will assist you in removing those trees. We had a lot of trees down, entrances being blocked. Of course, when you go on the radio and you tell them that you're going to lend this service to them, I got bombarded with phone calls. . . . These guys worked hard, this group of people that came, that didn't know me, and did this for the rest of the campaign.

The elimination of the campaign activities was partly the result of physical difficulties with continuing them, but to some extent the idea of partisan politics itself was suspended. This change was evident in several interviews, including one with the campaign manager in the primary campaign, who said, "I just don't remember a lot of politicking at that time. . . . Most of our time was involved with meeting with elected officials. . . . I don't remember a lot of politicking." Then too, to accomplish results quickly officials from different political parties needed to work together, and partisan bickering was not an efficient use of resources and energy.

Elected officials also perceived that their constituents were interested in something besides politics as usual at that moment, as the incumbent recounted: "People no longer really cared about the election. And [that] probably, you know, helped the incumbents. Because people, you know, they weren't focusing on what was being said, direct mail, you know, people wanted to know about the hurricane. . . . It's like trying to run an election in the middle of a war, you know. People don't care."

The primary campaign was nearly over when Andrew struck, and there is no indication that the election itself was drastically affected by the storm. The incumbents were well ahead in terms of fund-raising before the hurricane, and apparently were also well ahead in the minds of voters. The biggest unknown for incumbents was the effect of redistricting, an adjustment that created areas in which they had no electoral experience, especially where clear ethnicity differences existed. Yet the incumbents won overwhelmingly, including one who won with slightly more than 51 percent of the vote against eight challengers.

No one interviewed from this group—or any other—thought the hurricane altered chances of victory. Some were unsure what their challengers were doing, either before or after Andrew. This reflects the low profiles of challenging candidates, who were all campaigning on shoestring budgets, and also incumbents' personal campaign philosophies. Our representative explained it this way:

> I don't remember what he [the opponent] did. I mean, I honestly never pay any attention to any of my opponents. I just do the best thing I can do and let them do what they do. . . . I never had any strong opposition, to be honest with you. . . . I campaign hard. I don't take any opponent lightly. . . . I'm running against Ronald Reagan, the way I look at it, you know? I don't take any opponent

lightly, and I just go out there and mount a full-scale campaign and work hard. That's the way I always did it.

There were no differences that anyone from the incumbents' camps could remember about challenger campaigns after the hurricane. Operating low-key, grassroots campaigns with little funding, the challengers were largely overshadowed by the incumbents and then the hurricane. The campaign manager stated:

> I wouldn't know what he [the opponent] did or didn't do. Again, his campaign existed under the radar screen. My candidate was on the radio. My candidate was in helicopters overseeing the city. My candidate was in private meetings. . . . It may not have benefited, in terms of a campaign, but it, he was more prominent. . . .
>
> As an elected official, the representative was welcomed to be involved in the whole reparation process anyway. It's just by the nature of the office. He was the one being [invited]. I mean, they weren't inviting candidates to city hall to consider what we are going to do about this, they were inviting elected officials. They weren't inviting candidates to get in the helicopter, you know, with the mayor and everybody else to see the damage. They were inviting elected [officials].
>
> And maybe that has an influence. But to be perfectly honest, I don't think that was an influence. It was just, that was the job he was doing at the time, and he did his job. And he was involved and he was interviewed, and everything that was born of that was just part of, you're in the role at the time. I don't think it was political. I think politics kind of stopped at that time.

The 1992 General Election

Four legislators faced challenges in their bids for reelection in November 1992, about ten weeks after Hurricane Andrew. Two of their districts were in the northern damage zone of Dade County, one was in the hardest hit part of the south, and one had a district that overlapped southern and middle damage zones. One was in the somewhat unique position of having the same challenger in 1992 as in 1990.

In the northern districts, incumbents remembered being out in their districts right after the storm, checking on residents, helping to clear streets, and trying to assess the situation. Travel in some areas was impossible, even in the north, due to the number of large trees that had fallen across streets. Further south, officials were much less mobile; one legislator was first contacted several days after the storm by National Guard helicopters, which were actually sent by the governor to see where and how the legislator was.

By Monday afternoon, the same day Andrew hit, our incumbent legislator was on radio and television requesting emergency food and supplies. That appeal—one of many—was so successful that at eleven o'clock that night a convoy of some fifty vehicles was headed south to Homestead. What storage facilities existed at the Homestead City Hall were at capacity, and the convoy moved to farm labor camps, where the legislator recalled with obvious pride, "The very first night we saved a baby there, about midnight. . . . We must have helped over a thousand families that very first night." The incumbent also recalled the need to obtain federal marshal escorts for subsequent trips: "We were shot at the very first night."

The next day, the official was working to obtain temporary replacements for two air rescue helicopters that Dade County Fire Rescue Department officials had housed in hangars at a south Dade airport for safekeeping during the storm. The airport, along with the helicopters, was destroyed by Andrew.

The legislator noted their persistent personal dedication in south Dade, where they sacrificed "close to four months, including living and sleeping down south. I abandoned a lot of different things to be supportive of the people that needed it during the reconstruction." That heavy involvement with relief efforts, the incumbent noted,

> Could be perceived as if I were to be campaigning, but it wasn't in the district, which was a criticism that I received, because I was not as visible in my district as I was where the need was. And so I was criticized for that, and it could have been a campaign issue. Perhaps it should have been a campaign issue, if he felt it were to be an issue, but he didn't make one. He didn't raise that issue.

State legislators, especially members of the Florida House, represent small districts in which they live. Legislators in the southern part of the county had to deal with the effects of the hurricane on their personal lives. It was days before they could get out of their homes or their neighborhoods and turn to the business of being public officials simply because of the immense damage to their own residences and their immediate surroundings. The incumbent remembered, "standing on the corner one time, saying, 'Where am I?' It was a corner where I used to turn, still turn, to go to my home. But I didn't even recognize it." Once families were evacuated, the elected official could turn to other responsibilities:

> Then for me it was every single day out on the street, working with, you know, leaders and trying to get the community back together. Every day, for over a year.... I went with the 82nd Airborne and the 10th Mountain Division, went to their briefings with their generals, and stayed with them a couple of nights just to show, you know, camaraderie and support for what their mission was, and worked with their leadership in setting up feeding, emergency meals in places where people could go, medical care.... Dealing with 90,000 homes and 400,000 people, all of whom were, you know, stranded.... I was out every day. I didn't come here to my office, virtually at all, just walked away from my business, I walked away from everything else and just put full time into helping the community.

Legislators from outside of south Dade found that by the November general election their own districts were back to a relatively normal state. A legislative office that was up and running with telephones and electricity within several days established a hotline system with the Florida Department of Insurance to help homeowners find insurance company representatives; they offered this service to constituents of the district as well as others from affected areas. Further north, insurance issues did not linger as they did in south Dade, and, once the emergency relief period lasting from several weeks to two months was over, no similar special arrangements or activities were noted by any representative or supporter interviewed who was not directly involved in southern activities.

Likewise, the campaigns were unaffected in the north, while the continuing problems in the south made campaigning difficult. To the extent that door-to-door canvassing was a normal campaign activity for southern zone incumbents, it was then difficult or impossible. Our incumbent cited the most poignant example:

> There was a . . . mobile home park. . . . It was fairly large. And it was located just south of [an especially hard hit neighborhood]. And I always made it a point to campaign there. I always made it a point to walk there, and I always made it a point to do that in, usually, the

last week of the election cycle. And I did it because nobody else ever went there. I quickly discovered I was the only elected official ever to go there. . . .

And that year I didn't go there . . . because it was gone. Eight hundred units . . . completely wiped off of God's green Earth. . . . We went to, physically, where it was, and it was gone. All the homes had been destroyed and the whole area . . . cleared.

Subjects interviewed for this study repeatedly noted that people had a lot to worry about after Andrew, things more urgent than elections, campaigns, and voting. The respondent noted, "Who's going to read a piece of [campaign] mail when they're not even maybe living in their house, or who's worried about voting at that time when we've got bigger issues?" Several issues related to campaigning for the November 1992 election were enumerated:

I don't think we even canvassed that year, because it was just so difficult to get around. It was difficult to get people to help you when, you know, they were busy, you know, getting their lives back in order in a lot of cases, so . . . we didn't lean on our volunteers as heavily as we've leaned on them in the past, because we knew they had their own issues. . . .

Even the, you know, the contenders, it was very difficult for them to get their message out. . . . I think you tried through direct mail, if you had the money for it. But the problem with that was that you did not know whether it was getting to the people's houses or not. It was kind of like a shot in the dark. . . . It was probably the toughest year to communicate with the electorate.

And not only that, the electorate just, their minds were someplace else, it wasn't there. . . . We were always very street oriented, you know, canvassing, getting volunteer groups out there, doing that type of stuff. And we basically put a halt to that. So we really did a bare-bones type of campaign.

Legislators remembered few details about fund-raising. All had been involved in numerous campaigns, and 1992 was not exceptional in their memories. The representative thought it was probably more difficult to raise money locally, "Because a lot of people were rebuilding. Everyone was, in fact, in one way or another, or had losses in one way or another." Campaign fund-raising is not limited to the geographic district a candidate is seeking to represent, and the incumbent also believed that Hurricane Andrew brought economic woes to northern districts. Construction had suddenly become more expensive, even for minor home repairs, due to a shortage of supplies and building code changes.

Experienced and successful fund-raisers initiate their activities well before an election, and the elected official estimated raising probably 75 percent of the total contributions before the hurricane hit. The bottom line for campaign finance in 1992 is that the incumbents all raised substantially more than their challengers, as in most elections before and since. Although there were several indications that fund-raising efforts were curtailed because of the destruction and the overall delays in campaigning (at least in the south), the same problems faced challengers, who had difficulty matching their experienced opponents before the hurricane. The elected official, whose expenditures were more than thirty-six times the challenger's, said, "I think I probably would have raised more money, but I don't know what I would have done with it."

No perception of any negative impact from the hurricane on the re-election chances of the incumbents ever appeared. The challengers, some of whom were described as "ghost" or "token" candidates, garnered only 22 to 35 percent of the votes in their districts. There were no debates between candidates, and no hurricane-related issues were apparently raised in the campaign, although such issues were prevalent in the news and in meetings the candidates or their representatives attended at the time of the campaign.

In fact, legislators attended meetings because they were elected officials, and it was the norm for them to be present or be represented at meetings in their districts. That norm was continued, if not expanded, during the hurricane crisis. Our incumbent recalled asking Florida's insurance commissioner to attend a major homeowner association meeting to discuss insurance issues. The ability to deliver the top official to such a meeting, especially when the insurance commissioner was of a different political party than the legislator, clearly indicated to voters both responsiveness and political clout—just what was then needed.

The incumbents were experienced leaders at a time when voters needed experienced leaders, which was a theme used in their campaigns. Campaign difficulties may have been partly offset by a reduced electorate, and were certainly offset by the officials' increased presence and visibility. The respondent noted the benefit:

I guess we were always at chamber meetings and at different meetings, so our focus kind of stayed the same, except for, we didn't do mailings. . . . We focused more at large events. We had a number of different community events, at schools and different auditoriums, and so we'd have hundreds of people there. And it wasn't a campaign thing, it was, he was the rep at the time. So we didn't talk campaign at all, we just talked about what was going [on], what are you facing, you know, what are your needs, kind of thing. But that just, of course, you know, helps.

The personal campaign philosophy of the candidate also affects campaign style. When asked if the hurricane affected the incumbent's perception of 1992 reelection chances, the reply was:

Probably not. Every political person—I guess it's part of the persona—we're all paranoid. Most, I think, political people being paranoid and always, you know, wondering—you just work hard. So I don't recall that it [Andrew] changed my perception. It changed my life, to the extent that I knew that I had a job to do.

Subsequent Elections

The state legislature tackled the issues of rebuilding a significantly devastated but geographically small part of the state, first in a special session from December 9–11, 1992, then in the regular session in February and March 1993. The Dade delegation worked in a largely—and unusually—nonpartisan manner and crafted a mechanism to provide funding for the disaster area. Anticipating a huge increase in sales tax receipts when people began replacing cars, furniture, refrigerators, washers, driers, and other big ticket items, as well as smaller individual purchases, the Hurricane Andrew Trust Fund was designed, at the prompting of the Dade delegation, and approved in the legislature's December 1992 special session. Subjects interviewed often mentioned that the legislative leadership let the Dade members come up with a plan.

The plan was politically palatable to representatives of other areas of the state because it established a mechanism through which a county faced with significant problems after a natural disaster could receive extra emergency funds without taking state resources away from any other districts. A baseline of tax revenue was established from just before the disaster, a normal growth rate added in, and any excess revenues went to a trust fund to be used for Andrew-related reconstruction and recovery efforts. House members and senators from Dade were given the role of developing plans for using those hurricane-generated revenues.

House incumbents used their positions on the Appropriations Committee and the Finance and Taxation Committee to assure that these arrangements were met with approval by their colleagues. Establishing a model that could be used in future emergencies in other parts of the state also helped. The idea of letting Dade County use money generated in Dade County to respond to problems in Dade County was a key selling point to legislators from northern and central Florida. Most of those interviewed spoke of the establishment of the Hurricane Andrew Trust Fund as a significant bipartisan accomplishment. A former House member recalled hearing,

> "This is blood money," by some of the members of the delegation, who considered these issues to be more important than anything they've ever dealt with as a responsibility. I certainly believed that. . . . I don't remember in my history of public service that there would have been anything more important, greater to the county as that one event, and to be able to recapture those dollars and bring them back home, to be able to rebuild.

The incumbent recognized problems with "the gravy train," perceiving that there were, at times, "A lot of entities crying the sky is falling, and I began to have a problem with some of the entities that were tapping into the much-needed revenues." In spite of the "heartburn" this caused, it was also recognized that, "everyone had their own constituency." Proper use of the limited funds was seen as paramount by the representative, who wanted to assure contracts were cut by a state department to oversee the spending and that the auditor general and the governor were involved. The incumbent was proud of the results: "And a lot of it went to a lot of good;" but also realistic: "And some of it, we don't know what part of it, what percentage of it, went to things that weren't really that important." Although interviewees frequently commented on the nonpolitical time after the storm, political issues eventually came back to the foreground, as the incumbent's more critical assessment of the process involved with the Tallahassee efforts makes clear:

> The infighting, between all of the affected interests over how much money they were going to get; it was very, very disconcerting. . . . Our

members just, and the interest groups we dealt with, including local governments, all sorts of nonprofit groups, and others, they were just insatiable, and in my view unreasonable in what they wanted. It was almost like they looked upon . . . the storm as . . . a potential profit center, to see if they could reel in some more funds to improve a golf course, or to build a, some type of a civic center. I mean they wanted, it wasn't just reconstruction. We'd be lucky to get back to where we were, particularly with people leaving the area. They wanted to say . . . we want to be better than what we were, based on some perverted logic that this was how we could attract new people and rebuild the area.

These funds were not for that, and we didn't have enough funds to go around. . . . It created a lot of friction among the House members. It created a lot of friction between the House and the senators, in our own delegation, let alone our delegation compared to the rest of the state. . . . There was a north Dade—south Dade conflict, there was a south Dade versus south Dade, there were senators that had their own ideas.

Hurricane issues lingered for residents of south Dade and their representatives, as can be seen in the extent to which long-term hurricane issues controlled the agendas of the individual legislators as they prepared for the 1993 session. The *Miami Herald* publishes regional "Neighbors" sections twice a week, including in different regional editions items of interest only to local areas. The January 28, 1993, "Neighbors" included a series of articles, specific to geographic regions, highlighting the priorities of the Dade delegation.

The assessment is incomplete, as some legislators did not respond to requests for feedback, but it demonstrates a wider set of priorities for legislators from northern districts than for those from the far southern Dade area (Brennan 1993a; Davis 1993a; Garcia and Muhs 1993; Kidwell 1993; Maass and Kidwell 1993; Muhs and Garcia 1993; Rothaus 1993a). Southern legislators had little on their agendas other than hurricane recovery issues; those from northern Dade County had many non-hurricane priorities.

Besides repairing the damage from Andrew's winds and dealing with increased constituent demands, the legislators also faced a crisis in the insurance industry (Silva 1993). Some insurance companies went bankrupt; homeowners with policies from those companies could not collect. Some insurers that paid out huge sums in claims decided not to write any more policies in Florida or to withdraw their homeowners' insurance programs from the state altogether. Home transactions could not be completed because banks require insurance in order to approve mortgages, and insurance was not readily available: those insurance companies that did not declare bankruptcy or refuse to write homeowner policies in Florida generally doubled or tripled their premiums (Morrow and Peacock 2000; Finefrock 1994a, 1994b, 1994c; Seline 1994)

The insurance commissioner, praised by several of the subjects interviewed for this study and faulted by none, was planning to run for governor in the next statewide general election. The president of the Florida Senate was also preparing his gubernatorial bid, pitting the Senate leader and insurance commissioner, both Republicans, against each other and against the incumbent Democratic governor, a formula likely to create legislative difficulties.

A member of the House Insurance Committee, a senior member of the legislature, he hailed from Dade and was appointed to chair the committee. Originally a reluctant member of the committee, finding its discussions of little interest, this legislator assumed the chairmanship could well be disastrous. With the level of damage and the vast scope of insurance difficulties, reelection prospects seemed dimmed: "I said, 'Oh my God, every single person is going to have a problem with an insurance company, and they're all going to hate me, and I'll never be reelected.'"

With top state leaders potentially at odds over any major political action, the committee chair played a pivotal role in establishing the state's response, negotiating with insurance company executives, and creating new state insurance pools to provide relief to Florida residents, especially those in South Florida (Satterfield 1993; Silva 1993). Examples of the crisis were readily at hand in the district and neighborhood. The incumbent had accepted the position with dismay, but also with determination: "This is the time of crisis, and if he's giving me this leadership opportunity, then I need to do it for the right reasons. And I did, and I got reelected overwhelmingly—in a difficult situation."

By the 1994 elections, the effects of Hurricane Andrew were but a memory in the northern and middle districts of the county. Other than reminding people of resources brought into the district—including resources from the Hurricane Andrew Trust Fund—the incumbents seeking reelection in those areas were back to politics as usual. In the south, however, the constituency was still suffering—or suffering again.

Reconstruction efforts were well under way, but new crises had arisen in the wake of the storm itself, as described by the former legislator:

> I could see people hurting. By that time, we definitely knew about the effects of contractor fraud. We had thousands of people who had paid contractors, who were ripped off. . . . We still had significant problems with insurance companies. We had not only the eleven that went belly-up within a few months of Hurricane Andrew, but by then we had about thirty-eight companies that had just left the state. We had 850,000 policies that were being cancelled. The way I kind of looked at it, I said, a policy—I considered that to be a family.

The insurance problems noted were in fact relevant to Floridians well outside of the south Dade area. Dade, Broward, and Monroe counties were particularly hard hit by these changes, but it had become difficult, at best, for many Floridians to get insurance. The state established a new Catastrophe Fund to provide hurricane insurance, while private insurance companies that were cajoled (and threatened) into remaining in Florida covered other homeowner liabilities. Hurricane issues were not part of other campaigns, but in south Dade, there was little else to discuss.

As in 1992, however, the hurricane did not affect any candidate's perceptions of 1994 reelection chances. The respondent recalled a negative mailing from a challenger which attempted to pin blame on the incumbent for skyrocketing insurance premiums; the charge, however, did not stick. Fund-raising in 1994 was normal in the northern districts, but the incumbent House member from the hardest hit south Dade district nearly doubled their contribution collection in 1994. The 1994 challenger did substantially better than had the 1992 opponent, but the incumbent, then chairing the insurance committee, was still able to raise far more (see table 2.3). The incumbent from that southeast Dade district garnered nearly 62 percent of the votes in 1994, down from a 1992 vote share of over 66 percent, but still a comfortable margin of victory. There were

Table 2.3. Campaign contributions, Florida House District 119, 1992 and 1994

	Incumbent	Challenger
1992	$170,796	$4,240
1994	$326,272	$19,950

Source: Compiled from Florida Department of State, Elections Division, and Miami-Dade County Elections Department data.

slightly fewer votes recorded in 1994 than in 1992 in that district (22,529 in 1994, down from 22,978).

The hurricane experience had little effect on fund-raising, although the critical position chairing the insurance committee seems to have helped one incumbent, who clearly enjoyed an advantage before Andrew. The incumbent, running for reelection again in 1994, explained the incumbent advantage in obtaining contributions:

> When you're an incumbent you know, everybody thinks you're going to win, and you know, you can raise what you need. I basically just sent out a letter, and the money came. I never had problems with raising money. Fund-raising was as difficult as, you know, what you had to do, but as easy as just doing your job. I mean, if I was doing my job right, I would get the support. . . . They were going to have to earn my vote. They were going to have to convince me on the intellectual and on the merits. . . . Once I gave them my word, then I kept it. That was my reputation. So when I would talk to the major business interests and all, I mean, I was on their list. . . . And they would, you know, not give to my opponent.

Rebuilding was well under way in the south by the 1994 elections, but not at all complete. Issues related to fraud, insurance, relocations, and disruptions were still prevalent. Generally, however, such issues were not part of many campaigns. Few were noted by the subjects interviewed here. The former legislator offered these commentaries on issues and campaigns:

> Elections are not about issues anymore. Sad, shouldn't be that way, but elections are not about issues, I found. I've never had an opponent talk about an issue, raise an issue . . . just an attack. It's very difficult to explain an issue in a sound bite, in a thirty-second ad. There are no forums of debate for legislative House races. And the few there are, I mean, they're so controlled, you know, it's one, two questions, but you don't get into any depth on any issue. So campaigns . . . they're about people. It's about who you like.
>
> It's about being reachable, answering every phone call. I mean, I never left my office . . . without returning a phone call. . . . And that's what it's about. It's a people business, and taking care of problems. Issues. I wish it was more about issues. Should be more

about issues. . . . Campaigns are about perception. . . . It's all about perception.

In state legislative districts the district is so small that the campaign becomes very, very personal. Either you know the people in your district or you don't. If you know your people in the district you campaign, you know, you do mail outs, you do radio, most of all you go door-to-door.

So there's no big strategy . . . or a big chief campaign strategist or a chief fund-raiser. . . . It's a small district and it's very much house-to-house, and getting people to see your face, you know, because they vote for the person that they know. And as long as you're not [negatively] in the newspaper—and even some who have been in the newspaper have been reelected—because they know you.

The idea of campaigning as a people business, a "taking-care-of-problems" business, also came through in this answer from a supporter regarding a question about whether Andrew affected perceptions of 1994 reelection chances:

No, because he [the incumbent] was just so loved. . . . He worked us. I mean, we were always everywhere. . . . We answered every letter. We went to all the meetings. . . . He said, every day, you know, while we're in we have to prove why we're here, why the people elected us. We have to serve them. Every phone call is important, every letter, and that was just like his philosophy. . . . He's always been like that. . . .

I think after the hurricane we realized more than ever . . . we just thought, you know, that they probably went through hell, you know, to get to us . . . so maybe just a little extra because we knew, or didn't know, how they were getting to us, and so since they had reached us we were really going to go out of the way, more so than before. . . . His theory was, every day, really, that's how you're campaigning, just by every day, doing that, in and of itself.

The legislators selected as subjects for this study were chosen because they met the criteria established for inclusion (in office at the time of the storm, seeking reelection after Hurricane Andrew with challengers). Three of them sought higher office in subsequent elections. That action by itself is hardly exceptional—experienced politicians frequently seek higher office. The next chapter will show that seven Florida House members did not seek reelection in 1992 because they sought other offices, county commission, state Senate, or U.S. Congress, decisions made prior to the hurricane.

One representative successfully pursued a state Senate seat when term limits forced him out of the House. Two sought statewide office. One of these—with experience on the House Banking and Finance Committee, good credentials for a candidate for the office that regulated state-chartered banks—ran for comptroller in 1994 against the twenty-year incumbent in the Democratic primary. The other remained in the House until 2000 when, forced out by term limits, he ran for insurance commissioner. He had become chair of the House Insurance Committee right after Hurricane Andrew. The decisions to seek higher office were, at least in part, related to their post-Andrew experiences.

Leadership Opportunities

The disaster gave elected officials opportunities to exercise leadership, as has been demonstrated in several of the interview excerpts in this chapter. Legislators went on the radio to assure their constituents that aid was on the way, to request donations, to collect and organize the distribution of emergency relief goods, and to offer help. This was generally beneficial for their reelection efforts, but it rarely paid off in terms of their effectiveness in the legislature. Every year, following the regular session of the Florida legislature, the *Miami Herald* coordinates an assessment of legislator effectiveness. Academics, lobbyists, journalists, and other observers of the legislature rank all House members and senators. The members of each chamber are ranked according to quartiles, with a numeric ranking provided for those within the top quartile (Nickens, 1990, 1991, 1992a, 1993, 1994a; Kidwell 1991; Branch 1992b, 1995; Strouse, 1994a, 1994b; Branch and Bousquet 1995; *Miami Herald* 1990d, 1991c, 1991d, 1992e, 1992f, 1993f, 1993g, 1994d).

Two of the incumbents in this study had higher scores after the hurricane than they did before. The representative of a south Dade district became chairman of the House Insurance Committee immediately following Andrew, when the insurance industry was experiencing a disaster of its own in Florida. He utilized this new position to write and drive legislation through the House that significantly alleviated homeowner insurance problems for Florida residents. The leader of the Hispanic Caucus before Andrew became chair of the Dade delegation in 1992.

One incumbent saw a slight slippage in his ranking after Hurricane Andrew, after he had made the decision to leave the House and seek a Cabinet position in 1994. The longest serving House member during the term after Hurricane Andrew remained at roughly the same level within the top tier. Two others also remained at roughly the same level, whereas another's effectiveness declined slightly.

*　*　*

Incumbents in the Florida legislature have advantages similar to those found in studies of congressional and state legislature incumbency (Jewell and Breaux 1988; Cox and Morgenstern 1993). Both municipal and legislative incumbents received some electoral benefit from their positions and their activities after Hurricane Andrew. None suffered from any blame or other negative repercussions, except in one case where a challenger (unsuccessfully) tried to use the incumbent's hurricane responses against him.

Legislative incumbents, like municipal incumbents, were personally involved in the disaster as much as their constituents, if not more so. They suffered as victims in the southern part of the county, experiencing severe damage to or destruction of their own homes and/or businesses. In areas where the damage was less severe, incumbents still experienced the inconveniences of power outages, water quality concerns, blocked streets, price increases, and lost business. They were involved with relief efforts, collection efforts, and the distribution of emergency supplies. These undertakings exacted personal tolls on many of them and left numerous lasting memories.

Campaign efforts were affected, and normal, planned activities were adjusted. Official duties and appearances offset some of the limitations on campaign activities and alterations of strategies or tactics. Many of these official activities served as surrogate campaigns, providing positive images to constituents without actual campaigning, a pattern we will see with municipal officials as well. Hurricane effects, severe immediately after the storm, declined quickly in the northern and middle areas of Dade County, but did so much more slowly in the southern damage zone.

During disasters, state legislators represent compact constituencies who are fellow victims. We now expand this review to officials elected statewide. These officials did not experience the hurricane firsthand in

Dade County. Tallahassee, the state capital, is approximately five hundred miles and eight hours away by car. Incumbent statewide elected officials do not live in Dade County when they seek reelection, if ever they did. The question to be explored is: Did Hurricane Andrew affect Florida elections at a higher level? First we will review Florida's political structure and the demographic changes in the state and in Dade County, setting the story of Hurricane Andrew in context.

3

The Kaleidoscope of Florida Politics

Florida is a large, elongated state with long distances between urban areas. Early in the twentieth century Florida was mostly rural, with the majority of its population in the northern part of the state. This was the Florida of the Old South—a largely segregationist state (Huckshorn 1991). Florida obtained many military facilities during World War II, and after the war it became a popular destination for veterans and retirees. The influx of veterans and other Northern migrants was bolstered by the implementation of modern mosquito control and air conditioning.

Development of specific sectors like Orlando's Disney World and Cape Canaveral's space exploration also added to the state's attractiveness (MacManus 2004). Doubling several times during the century, Florida's population reached one million during the 1920s, two million in the 1940s, four million in the 1950s, and eight million by 1980 (Dye 1998; Colburn and DeHaven-Smith 1999; see also Black and Black 1987; Carver and Fiedler 1999).

Florida's population—now the fourth largest in the United States—is thus largely not native. It has been described as having "political rootlessness," with traditional ties and loyalties focused on other states and other nations (Dye 1998). Differing ties are largely concentrated in different regions in the state (Carver and Fiedler 1999). Some analysts describe three general regions—north, southeast, and central—whereas others find the state more complex. Hill, MacManus, and Moreno (2004) identify ten media markets, a categorization common for state politicians who have to plan for and buy media time for their campaigns.

Many people register with minor parties or with no party designation, and persistent ticket splitting and inconsistent partisan support are common. Black and Black (1987) found that the state went Republican in 80 percent of presidential contests and 20 percent of gubernatorial elections during 1965–80: a period when it was supposedly Democratic. From 1980 to 2002, Florida backed Republican presidential candidates almost every time and Republican candidates for governor half the time.

The Legislators' Advantage

Florida's bicameral legislature consists of a 120-member House of Representatives and a 40-member Senate. Given the 1990 state population of 12,937,926 (U.S. Census 1990), redistricting in 1992 established 120 House districts of roughly 108,000 residents each; Senate districts are three times bigger. Members of Florida's House are elected for two-year terms, with all members up for reelection in even-numbered years. Senators generally serve staggered four-year terms, but every ten years the Census triggers redistricting, and the new boundaries require a complete election in the "two" years (for example 1972, 1982, 1992, 2002). In these redistricted Senate elections, victors of odd-numbered seats initially receive two-year terms, whereas senators from even-numbered seats receive four-year terms. The entire staggered system then begins anew.

Incumbency has been strong in the Dade delegation to the Florida House (see table 3.1). In over half of the years reviewed, 71 percent or more of the incumbents sought reelection. The exception years include those in which district lines were redrawn (1982, 1992, 2002) and the first year in which term limit restrictions took effect: a constitutional amendment approved by referendum in 1992 was effective in 2000 and many incumbents were eliminated that year. Overall, most incumbents sought reelection, and most were successful. In Dade's delegation to the Florida House between 1980 and 2002, 171 of 183 incumbents (93 percent) were returned to office—74 (40 percent) unopposed.

Likewise, Dade's state senators seeking reelection were generally successful (see table 3.2). Senators sought reelection 38 times between 1980 and 2002 and were returned to office 34 times (almost 90 percent), unopposed in their reelection bids in 18 (over 47 percent) instances.

Masked in these data, however, is an interesting phenomenon. During this period, the Florida legislature was transformed from strongly Democratic to strongly Republican. In 1980, Democrats made up almost 68 percent of each house. In 1992, the Senate had an even split of 20 members from each party, but in 1994, that chamber saw its first Republican majority (53 percent) since Reconstruction. A conservative Democrat

Table 3.1. Challenges to incumbents, Florida House, 1980–2002

Year	1980	1982	1984	1986	1988	1990	1992	1994	1996	1998	2000	2002
# running	17	13	18	15	15	17	13	15	20	17	10	13
% running	58.6	61.9	85.7	71.4	71.4	80.9	65.0	75.0	100	85.0	50.0	65.0
Elected	15	10	16	15	15	17	12	13	20	15	10	13
% success	88.2	76.9	88.9	100	100	100	92.3	86.7	100	88.2	100	100
Lost in general election	1(8)	1(8)	2(8)	0(5)	0(5)	0(6)	0(5)	0(3)	0(4)	0(5)	0(4)	0(8)
Lost in runoff	1(1)	1(1)	N/A	N/A	N/A	0(1)	1(1)	1(1)	N/A	N/A	N/A	N/A
Lost in primary	0(9)	1(12)	0(6)	0(8)	0(6)	0(6)	0(4)	1(5)	0(4)	2(8)	0(3)	0(2)
Unopposed	4	0	7	5	8	9	6	7	12	7	4	5

Notes: Dade seats 1980=29; 1982–1990=21; 1992–2002=20. Numbers in parentheses indicate the number of incumbents in contested elections; for example, in 1980 one incumbent was defeated in the general election out of eight incumbents with opponents in that election.

Sources: Florida Department of State, Elections Division; Miami-Dade Elections Department; *Journal of the Florida House of Representatives*, various years.

Table 3.2. Challenges to incumbents, Florida Senate, 1980–2002

Year	1980	1982	1984	1986	1988	1990	1992	1994	1996	1998	2000	2002
# running	3	5	4	1	3	3	2	5	2	5	1	4
Elected	2	4	4	0	3	3	2	5	2	4	1	4
% success	67	80	100	0	100	100	100	100	100	80	100	100
Lost in general election	0 (2)	N/A	0 (2)	1 (1)	0 (1)	0 (1)	N/A	N/A	N/A	0 (2)	N/A	0 (4)
Lost in runoff	N/A	1 (1)	N/A	N/A	N/A	N/A	N/A	N/A	N/A	N/A	N/A	N/A
Lost in primary	1 (3)	0 (4)	0 (2)	N/A	0 (2)	N/A	N/A	0 (1)	N/A	0 (2)	N/A	0 (1)
Unopposed	0	3	2	0	0	2	2	4	2	1	1	0*

Notes: Dade Seats 1980=8; 1982–2002=7. Numbers in parentheses indicate the number of incumbents in contested elections; for example, in 1980 no incumbent was defeated in the general election out of two incumbents with opponents in that election.
*One incumbent was opposed by two write-in candidates, who each received three votes.

Source: Florida Department of State, Elections Division; Miami-Dade Elections Department; *Journal of the Senate: State of Florida*, various years.

then switched parties, increasing the majority to 55 percent. In 1996, the Republican majority in the Senate climbed to 58 percent, and Republicans in the House achieved a 51 percent majority (Carver and Fiedler 1999). After the 2002 elections, the Republican majority in the Senate climbed to 65 percent, the House to 67 percent.

Incumbents who did not seek reelection frequently remained in politics. In 1992, for example, eight incumbent House members from Dade County did not seek reelection. Seven of the eight, however, sought higher office: four were elected to the state Senate, two were defeated in bids for the same body, and one lost a race for the U.S. House of Representatives.

Florida's Executive

Incumbent advantage is a longtime phenomenon in Florida's executive branch. Speaking of the Florida governor's cabinet in his 1949 classic, V. O. Key described it as: "something of an elective career service. An official dies in office; his successor is appointed by the governor and thereby gets his name before the public. He runs at the next election and is almost invariably reelected so long as he desires to retain the office" (99).

The six cabinet positions in 1992 were attorney general, commissioner of agriculture, commissioner of education, comptroller, secretary of state, and insurance commissioner (a position of multiple responsibilities also referred to as treasurer or state fire marshal). In 1998, Florida voters approved constitutional amendments (effective in 2002) that reduced the cabinet to attorney general, commissioner of agriculture and consumer services, and a chief financial officer (essentially combining the previous posts of insurance commissioner and comptroller).

Statewide Elections, 1980–2002

Incumbent governors typically seek reelection, usually—but not always—with success. Between 1982 and 2002, the only defeated incumbent was Bob Martinez, a Republican and former mayor of Tampa. His 1990 reelection bid was trumped by former three-term U.S. senator Lawton Chiles. Table 3.3 shows the pattern of incumbent success from 1982 through 2002.

Similar patterns of incumbent success are seen in all statewide elected offices, including the six cabinet positions and the U.S. Senate seats (table 3.4 summarizes this history). Roughly 11 percent of the incumbents in

Table 3.3. Incumbents in Florida gubernatorial races, 1982–2002

Year	Incumbent in race?	Challenged?*	Incumbent successful?	Successful incumbent's party
1982	Yes	Primary and GE	Yes	Democrat
1986	No	N/A	N/A	N/A
1990	Yes	Primary and GE	No	N/A
1994	Yes	Primary and GE	Yes	Democrat
1998	No	N/A	N/A	N/A
2002	Yes	GE	Yes	Republican
Total	4	4	3	2 Democrats, 1 Republican

*Indicates whether the incumbent was challenged in party primary and/or in general election (GE).
Source: Compiled from Florida State Department Elections Division data.

Florida's statewide races from 1980 to 2002 were unopposed, consistent with studies that suggest the statewide nature of senatorial contests draws challengers to a greater extent than smaller-district congressional races. The success rate of nearly 86 percent for incumbents in these races is similar to the 81 percent success rate Krasno (1994) found for U.S. Senate races over time. The long dominance of the Democratic Party in Florida is reflected in the fact that 23 out of 30 successful incumbents during this period were Democrats.

Table 3.4. Incumbents in Florida statewide races, 1980–2002

Office	Incumbents in race	Challenges*	Incumbent successful	Successful incumbent's party
Governor	4	4	3	2 Dem, 1 Rep
Insurance Commissioner	5	3	5	3 Dem, 2 Rep
Secretary of State	4	4	3	2 Dem, 1 Rep
Education Commissioner	3	2	2	2 Dem
Agriculture Commissioner	5	5	5	4 Dem, 1 Rep
Attorney General	4	3	4	4 Dem
Comptroller	5	5	4	3 Dem, 1 Rep
U.S. Senate	5	5	4	3 Dem, 1 Rep
Total	**35**	**31 (88.6%)**	**30 (85.7 %)**	**23 Dem (76.7%); 7 Rep (23.3%)**

* Indicates whether the incumbent was challenged, whether in party primary or in general election.
Source: Compiled from Florida State Department Elections Division data.

Opposition was not automatic during this period, but nearly 89 percent of the incumbents seeking reelection to statewide positions faced challengers. Thirty times out of 35 (86 percent), incumbents who sought reelection in these statewide contests were successful. The unsuccessful bids were: (1) Governor Bob Martinez (Republican, 1990), defeated by former three-term U.S. senator Lawton Chiles, as noted above; (2) Secretary of State Sandra Mortham (Republican, 1998), defeated in the primary by state senator Katherine Harris; (3) Commissioner of Education Doug Jamerson (Democrat, 1994), a state senator appointed to fill a vacancy earlier in 1994, defeated by former educator and Martin County superintendent of schools Frank Brogan; (4) Comptroller Gerald Lewis (Democrat, 1994), in office for twenty years and defeated by former Marine general Bob Milligan at a time when limiting terms was a popular cause; and (5) Senator Paula Hawkins (Republican, 1986), defeated by a popular governor, Bob Graham.

The Mark of Andrew

This incumbent dominance is relatively constant in the midst of a complex, changing state population. Colburn and DeHaven-Smith (1999, 4–5) described watching Florida's politics as "like looking through a kaleidoscope, with each twist of the lens producing a new configuration and a new direction." Did anything change after Hurricane Andrew slammed into Florida in 1992? Officeholders seeking reelection were generally successful after the hurricane, consistent with the pattern so far observed. Only one incumbent was defeated in the first election after Andrew. In addition, Lawton Chiles (who died a few weeks before the end of his second term) would have been constitutionally restricted to two terms as governor, and Connie Mack opted not to seek reelection for a third term in the U.S. Senate. Otherwise, incumbents stayed in office.

Including the one defeat here, four of the six incumbents (67 percent) saw their vote shares decrease in the first post-Andrew election, although both U.S. senators received more votes then. Two of the incumbents who experienced this decline in the first election after the hurricane ran again and did better in the second election. The only exception is Senator Bob Graham, a popular former governor who was running for his first reelection as senator in 1992, after the hurricane, and saw a larger margin (65 percent) of victory that year, though he still obtained a comfortable margin (almost 63 percent of the vote) in 1998.

The pattern continued: incumbents seeking reelection were usually (86 percent) returned to office, and the incumbents seeking reelection after a major hurricane were mostly (83 percent) returned to office. In the first post-Andrew election, one incumbent lost and two won by less than 55 percent—Governor Chiles and Agriculture Commissioner Crawford, both with about 51 percent. In the second post-Andrew election, none of the three incumbents running won marginal victories. Does this indicate a temporary post-Andrew dip in support? It is not a strong pattern, nor does it suggest any causal relationship between the hurricane and the reduction of support.

In fact, Florida supported George H. W. Bush, the incumbent in the 1992 presidential contest, giving him over 40 percent of the popular vote (compared to Bill Clinton's 39 percent and Ross Perot's nearly 20 percent) and the state's electoral votes. In 1994, when Republicans gained control of Congress and many Republican candidates used ads in which their Democratic opponents were morphed into Bill Clinton (Nickens and Silva 1994b), the Republican candidate for governor of Florida was Jeb Bush, son of the former president.

Although a political novice, early in the general election campaign Jeb Bush was ahead of incumbent Chiles in the polls (Fiedler 1994; Silva 1994; Silva and Neal 1994b; Nickens, Neal, and Silva 1994; Neal, Nickens, and Fiedler 1994; Nickens, Neal, and Fiedler 1994; Dye 1998). Bush was perceived as a prodigious fund-raiser and something of a celebrity, with the former president and the popular former first lady, Barbara Bush, heavily involved in the campaign.

To combat Bush, the Chiles-MacKay team focused on its "historical base among Panhandle Democrats, Blacks, and condominium voters in Southeast Florida" (Fiedler, Nickens, and Neal 1994b). A successful Democratic formula based on winning in northern Florida, winning big in southeast Florida, and running even in the central corridor between Tampa and Orlando had been the key to victory for governors Reuben Askew, Bob Graham, and Senator Chiles, as well as in the 1972 presidential campaign of Jimmy Carter (Colburn and DeHaven-Smith 1999).

The other close statewide contest in 1994 was the race for commissioner of agriculture. Republican Jim Smith had been attorney general from 1979 to 1986. He was handily elected secretary of state in a 1988 special election with over 63 percent of the vote, and again in 1990 with over 59 percent. He placed second in the Republican gubernatorial primary in 1994, forcing Jeb Bush into a runoff. Smith decided to run for agriculture commissioner because of Bush's substantial lead in the primary (46 percent to Smith's 18 percent), and in order to unify Republicans for the general election.

Agriculture incumbent Bob Crawford had raised only five hundred thousand dollars for his campaign by the time of Smith's switch, and had barely campaigned because he was opposed by a largely unknown consultant from Tallahassee who had never sought public office before (Nickens and Silva 1994a; Nickens 1994b). Crawford's original challenger withdrew, Smith withdrew from the gubernatorial race, and the Republican Party Executive Committee was allowed, under Florida election laws, to name Smith challenger for the agriculture position. Smith's last-minute switch after his concerted efforts at fund-raising (he had raised $2.2 million in his campaign for governor) and campaigning (having spent $1.7 million in television ads) put him well ahead in the polls. He was actually better known than incumbent Crawford (Nickens 1994b, 1994c; Nickens and Silva 1994a).

The 1994 general election marked the point when Democrats dropped below half (49.9 percent) of Florida's 6.55 million registered voters (Fiedler and Silva 1994a). With strong Republican statewide candidates and national predictions of low Democratic turnout (Associated Press 1994), it looked like 1994 would be the year of the Republicans on both the state and national level. That three of the four Democratic incumbents, along with one Democrat in an open race, managed victories at all, regardless of the electoral margin, was a surprise to most observers. In fact, the excitement of the close contests brought out 64 percent of Dade County's voters, "more voters than any gubernatorial election in at least three decades" (Branch 1994), and inspired a turnout 10 percent higher than the 1990 general election (Carver and Fiedler 1999). High turnout tends to favor Democrats.

The vast majority of incumbents seeking reelection between 1980 and 2002 were returned to office, but the political shift in the state legislature noted above also took place in the executive branch during that same period. In 1980, the Democratic Party was dominant in the state: both houses of the state legislature had Democratic majorities, and the governor, all six cabinet members, and both U.S. senators were Democrats. Paula Hawkins broke the partisan barrier that year with her election to the U.S. Senate, giving Republicans one of the nine statewide elected posts.

After the 2000 elections, however, four of the six cabinet officials and the governor were Republicans, giving that party five of the nine seats. In twenty years Florida went from a one-party, Southern Democratic state to a competitive two-party system. By 2002, the Republicans dominated both houses of the legislature, the cabinet, and held the governor's mansion.

The Local Context

Evolving patterns of population and voter registration are important. Major changes to Dade County's demographics, under way well before Hurricane Andrew, continued after the storm. In 1960, the majority of the population—about 80 percent according to the U.S. Census—was non-Latino/a white. Blacks, almost 15 percent of the population, comprised fewer than 7 percent of registered voters according to county elections department figures. Latino/as comprised less than 5 percent of the population (Bureau of the Census 1963). The 1965 Voting Rights Act and Democratic Party policy changes broadened participation in the party by all segments of the population and helped eliminate Southern voting restrictions on African Americans.

Fidel Castro seized power in Cuba in 1959, initiating a continuing exodus of Cuban refugees to the United States. Many settled in Dade County. The 1980 Mariel boatlift brought some one hundred and twenty-five thousand Cubans to the United States within a few months. This unanticipated influx of refugees exacerbated housing shortages and a weak economy, and a small minority of the new arrivals came straight from Cuban jails and mental institutes (Portes and Stepick 1993). A local citizens' initiative requiring county business to be conducted only in English won (Warren, Stack, and Corbett 1986). Cuban-Americans from earlier waves of the Castro-inspired exodus and their children entered politics; many eligible exiles became citizens and registered to vote (Portes and Stepick 1993).

Immigrants from other Latin American and Caribbean countries enriched the county's ethnic mix. The expanding Latino/a population also caused some white non-Latino/as to move from the area. Census figures show that total county population grew steadily, from 935,047 in 1960 to 2,253,362 in 2000, but white flight caused a reduction in the absolute

Table 3.5. Dade County voter registration by ethnicity, selected years

Month/Year	Total	White #	%	Black #	%	Spanish* #	%	Other #	%
10/1955	275,526	260,655	94.6	14,871	5.4	—		—	
10/1960	407,888	380,119	93.2	27,769	6.8	—		—	
10/1965	452,242	403,865	89.3	48,377	10.7	—		—	
08/1970	467,239	409,211	87.6	57,879	12.4	—		149	0.03
10/1975	637,270	544,441	85.4	92,009	14.8	61,213	9.6	820	0.1
08/1980	672,683	563,134	83.7	107,581	16.0	115,646	17.2	1,968	0.3
10/1985	679,489	550,574	81.3	124,444	18.3	164,465	24.2	4,471	0.7
10/1990	673,838	530,246	78.7	133,781	19.9	190,655	28.3	9,811	1.5
10/1992	675,286	527,341	78.1	134,277	19.9	199,177	29.5	13,668	2.0
10/1994	664,219	516,557	77.8	130,531	19.7	217,380	32.7	17,131	2.6
10/1996	853,276	329,282	38.6	171,126	20.1	333,788	39.1	19,080	2.2
10/2000	896,912	280,691	31.3	176,806	19.7	398,573	44.4	40,842	4.6
06/2002	929,818	279,093	30.0	183,775	19.8	418,479	45.0	48,471	5.2

*Until 1996, "Spanish" was defined as a person born in a Spanish-speaking country. Those registered as Spanish also declared a race and were predominantly white. The definition then changed to include anyone who considered him- or herself Hispanic, as a unique ethnic identification. In 1996 and subsequent years, the "Spanish" column is not duplicative of the other ethnic classifications.
Source: Branch, 1997; Miami-Dade County Elections Department, http://elections.miamidade.gov/STATS/regstat.txt.

number of white non-Latino/as, from 778,969 in 1970 to 585,607 in 1990, and 466,446 in 2000.

Ethnic population changes, urban problems, and the soaring cost of housing caused people to relocate. Hurricane Andrew only continued, and possibly accelerated, this trend (Hill and Moreno 2004). Those most able to move permanently from the area were wealthier individuals, mostly homeowners with good insurance settlements—predominantly white non-Latino/as. The hurricane also leveled Homestead Air Force Base, disrupting the living patterns of many military retirees who had settled in South Florida for the warm weather and benefit availability. With the closure of the base and the reduction or elimination of benefits, some military retirees, again mostly white non-Latino/as, also moved.

Destruction of homes and businesses added to the population flux. In November 1992, it was estimated that ninety thousand people would move from south Dade, many outside of the county (Provenzo and Fradd 1995; Provenzo and Provenzo 2002). Even more to the point, before the 1993 Homestead city elections, the city attempted to notify 2,240 registered voters by mail about changes in voting precincts. Over half of those notices were returned because some 1,210 people had moved (Hartman 1993d).

The long-term shift in population is also reflected in the characteristics of registered voters. The proportion of white non-Latino/a registered voters continued to fall between 1992 and 1994 as the proportions of Latino/as and blacks grew (see table 3.5). Note that the "Spanish" column in the table duplicates other ethnicities until 1996, when registration definitions changed. The number of "White" voters decreased after 1980 even though those registering as "Spanish"—born in a Spanish-speaking country—are duplicated (predominantly a duplication between "White" and "Spanish"). This duplication ceased after 1994.

Ethnic Politics

The inclusion of new ethnic groups in local politics is not new, as evinced by Robert Dahl in his 1961 classic, *Who Governs*. It was predictable that Cuban-Americans and other immigrant groups would enter into local South Florida governments and win state legislative seats as their numbers increased and time enabled many of them to become part of the socioeconomic puzzle, then citizens, and finally elected officials. James Madison envisioned "factions" as a positive ingredient in American politics—interests that would form ever-changing coalitions and prevent any one faction from becoming dominant in national politics (Rossiter 1961). Ethnic groups frequently have similar economic interests as well as historical/cultural/language ties that provide a natural cause for affiliation and enable the group to be better represented in the dominant society and power structure.

Issues of ethnicity abound in many areas of the United States, indeed throughout the world, and often impact the political milieu. When Hurricane Katrina hit the Gulf Coast in 2005, the population of New Orleans was 68 percent African American. The city had experienced a succession of Black mayors since 1978 (Bullard and Wright 2009). Mtangulizi Sanyika (2009) provides a detailed analysis of the ethnic tensions simmering in New Orleans as the floodwaters rushed in. To summarize his analysis, Ray Nagin, mayor when Katrina hit and the city flooded, was fourth in the line of Black mayors. But during this nearly thirty-year period, conditions for blacks in the city had not improved substantially, although there were more black city employees, especially in high-level positions, and more black-owned firms were awarded contracts from the city (Sanyika 2009).

Nagin himself was elected in 2002 "with 85 percent of the white vote and 35–40 percent of the black vote, thus leading to" suspicions that he "would favor business and the white population" (89). Resistance to Nagin's leadership and to specific policies increased before Katrina: "Bishop Paul Morton and the (black) Greater New Orleans Coalition of Ministers even called Nagin a 'white man in black skin'" (90). Various assessments noted that blacks controlled the political process but not the economic structure. Power and influence often exist outside of elected office.

Several existing and newly forming social groups were pushing the government to better represent the masses. The African-American Leadership Project (AALP) emerged and spent considerable time and effort developing an African-American Agenda, released shortly before Katrina. Prior to Katrina, a policy of replacing public housing projects was causing significant gentrification, displacing thousands of residents (Bullard and Wright 2009). Ethnicity was at issue in Dade County, Florida, before and after Andrew; just as it was in New Orleans before and after Katrina.

Because New Orleans was unprepared for the flooding after Katrina, thousands of residents had to be evacuated to the Superdome and Convention Center, neither of which had supplies or adequate facilities (Sanyika 2009). Help from outside was slow and overwhelmed for days, reminiscent of the slow and sloppy response to Andrew, but this time with significantly worse results—well over one thousand deaths occurred in New Orleans in the hurricane's aftermath.

Reminiscent of Andrew, a group of business leaders came together and began planning recovery and rebuilding. In this case, serious discussions about reducing the "footprint" of New Orleans considered not rebuilding some low-lying neighborhoods—predominantly black areas—leaving them instead as "flood protection zones or green spaces" (Sanyika 2009). This would have disproportionately reduced New Orleans' Black population. When Mayor Nagin did not immediately reject this notion, black leaders were outraged. Nagin appointed a Bring New Orleans Back (BNOB) Commission; many complained that it represented only business elite interests.

The AALP began grassroots dialogues with residents and evacuees and thereby developed a Citizens' Bill of Rights to assure equitable redevelopment. The AALP worked with and through a city councilwoman;

eventually the city council rejected any footprint reduction and assured an equitable rebuilding of all neighborhoods.

Nevertheless, white elites pushed for several "good government" initiatives that would delete black political power and backed candidates who ran against city commissioners that had voted down the reduced footprint concept. Several white candidates entered the political fray as Nagin stood for reelection; he had less support from business elites since he had not backed some of their initiatives. The state legislature and courts allowed absentee voting only in other parts of Louisiana although many residents were forced to relocate temporarily to other states. This particularly affected blacks, as the worst flooding occurred in predominantly black precincts, and voting turnout reflected that difference in 2006 (Logan 2009).

Ray Nagin's much-publicized comment that New Orleans would be a "Chocolate City" again

> infuriated and alienated significant numbers of white voters but did more to consolidate his support among black voters than any policy speech or debate ever could. For the first time, Nagin had unequivocally and publicly affirmed the political rights of the black majority, thus repudiating the footprint reduction elites, many of whom he had appointed to the planning bodies that had originated the demographic racial-change logic. (Sanyika 2009, 102)

Against 21 challengers, Nagin came in first in the primaries with 38 percent of the overall vote—including 66 percent of the black vote and only 15 percent of the white vote, a significant reversal of his political support from 4 years earlier (102). By 2005, New Orleans was more heavily Democratic than other parts of Louisiana and key to the state electoral success of Democratic candidates for governor and U.S. senator (South End Press Collective 2007).

Ethnic politics often crops up unexpectedly, and mainstream officials and their supporters may fuel the political fires without intending to. Thus, when New Orleans was evacuated and residents fled to other locales, even when it meant living in deplorable conditions, preconceived notions of ethnicity and/or economic class were proffered. On September 5, 2005, former first lady Barbara Bush (mother of then-president George W. Bush) said of evacuees housed in the Houston Astrodome:

What I'm hearing, which is sort of scary, is that they all want to stay in Texas. Everybody is so overwhelmed by the hospitality. And so many of the people in the arena here, you know, were under-privileged anyway, so this (*chuckle*) is working very well for them. (Quoted in Lapham 2007, 10)

These kinds of comments are widely reported and seen by significant portions of ethnic minorities as unsympathetic, if not downright racist. They add to ethnic animosities and organize political cohesion for causes and/or candidates that symbolically represent "the other side."

*　*　*

Ethnic groups may dominate politics in an area or may form coalitions to compete for influence and power. A natural disaster may affect the political balance in various ways, including influencing ethnic coalitions and their support, or lack thereof, for elected officials. In south Dade, the influx of people from other countries and the exodus of local white Americans began well before the hurricane. The influx that continued after Andrew was not all due to the storm, though the exodus may have been hastened by its impact. In any case, the elected officials of the local area reflect the general population, and as the demographics of the population shifted, so did the makeup of those elected to represent it.

Elections in Florida, then, were impacted by significant shifts in population, political affiliation, and ethnic concentrations. Against this backdrop, a powerful hurricane hit the southern part of the state, which contains a small portion of the constituency of statewide elected officials. It might not be expected that this would have an important effect on these officials' election chances two years later. Surprisingly, however, Hurricane Andrew was memorable for these officials and may have played a role in the outcome of the 1994 elections. We turn now to these contests.

4

Executive Branch Effects?

Chapter 2 reviewed the possible effects of Hurricane Andrew on state legislative campaigns and elections. This chapter examines the next level: statewide officers with statewide constituencies. These include the governor (elected for a maximum of two four-year terms, at the presidential midterm, on a ticket with the lieutenant governor), six individually elected cabinet members (in 1992) with four-year terms, and the two U.S. senators who serve six-year terms. Special elections are held for cabinet posts that become vacant during the first half of a term.

Municipal officials of cities and members of the Florida House share similar constituencies—their geographically small districts foster personal relationships with citizens. Statewide constituencies are much larger, stretching over a far greater area, and include different regions, climates, and cultures. Although the working hypothesis for this study was that Hurricane Andrew would generally have negative electoral effects on incumbents, the area affected by the storm was a small portion of a large state, and no electoral impact was expected for this group of officials.

Local Results

To determine whether Hurricane Andrew had any effect on the election results within Dade County, data from the county elections department, which reported votes by precinct, were used, then aggregated by damage zone. Table 4.1 provides an analysis of support for the gubernatorial candidates among the three zones. That support was not equal, but there were similarities for incumbents in 1990 and in 1994, before and after Andrew. As the challenger for governor, Lawton Chiles won in all three

Table 4.1. Results of Florida gubernatorial elections in Dade County, Florida, pre- and post-Andrew, by damage zone

1990	Zone	Challenger Chiles	Chiles's share (%)	Incumbent Martinez	Martinez's share
	North	149,196	62.7	88,871	37.3
	Middle	33,179	59.8	22,304	40.2
	South	34,160	66.8	17,009	33.2
	County total or average	232,542	62.7	138,417	37.3

1994	Zone	Incumbent Chiles	Incumbent share (%)	Challenger J. Bush	Chiles's % change '90–'94
	North	137,303	50.8	132,771	-11.9
	Middle	30,439	48.1	32,812	-11.7
	South	31,447	61.8	19,471	-5
	County total or average	215,276	52	198,371	-10.7

Note: County totals include precincts that overlapped two damage zones, and thus do not reflect column totals.

Source: Compiled from Miami-Dade County Elections Department data.

zones in 1990, with the most support in the south zone and the least in the middle zone. In 1994, Chiles, then the incumbent governor, did worse in all three zones. He maintained his highest support in the south, where the erosion of support was half as much as in the rest of the county. His area of lowest support in 1990, the middle zone, remained weakest in 1994, and is the only area in which he lost. This probably indicates a change due to the strong challenge.

Table 4.2 provides a similar analysis for the cabinet positions that had pre- and post-Andrew elections. Two cabinet members in office at the time of the hurricane ran for governor in 1994, while another had been appointed earlier in the year to fill a vacancy. Three cabinet positions are included in the table: agriculture commissioner, attorney general, and comptroller. Only these positions had incumbents in office when Andrew struck who were running for reelection in the first election after the hurricane with opposition—the criteria established for selecting incumbents for this study.

Of particular interest is that in three of the four cases, governor/ lieutenant governor and two cabinet offices, incumbents lost support throughout the county, but the change in the south zone is substantially less than in the two other zones.

Table 4.2. Florida Cabinet incumbent success by damage zone, pre- and post-Andrew

AGRICULTURE COMMISSIONER

Zone	1990 Crawford votes	% Vote share	1994 Crawford votes	% Vote share	Incumbent % change
North	137,662	63.7	122,975	51.5	-12.3
Middle	30,570	58.9	27,301	46.7	-12.2
South	32,947	68.3	29,085	61.1	-7.2
County total or average	**215,318**	**63.3**	**193,247**	**51.9**	**-11.4**

COMPTROLLER

Zone	1990 Lewis votes	% Vote share	1994 Lewis votes	% Vote share	Incumbent % change
North	39,579	65.9	125,316	53.0	-12.9
Middle	31,873	61.4	26,723	46.0	-15.4
South	33,137	69.2	28,126	59.6	-9.6
County total or average	**219,385**	**65.4**	**194,273**	**52.7**	**-12.7**

ATTORNEY GENERAL

Zone	1986 Butterworth votes	% Vote share	1994 Butterworth votes	% Vote share	Incumbent % change
North	154,114	67.3	138,848	56.6	-10.7
Middle	43,048	55.1	33,313	55.9	+0.8
South	32,799	55.1	33,790	70.1	+15.0
County total or average	**244,647**	**64.4**	**222,631**	**58.5**	**-6.1**

Note: County totals include precincts that overlapped damage zones and thus do not reflect column totals.
Source: Compiled from Miami-Dade County Elections Department data.

Support for incumbents remained highest in the south. In the gubernatorial contests, the change in Chiles's vote share in the south zone (-5.0 percent) was less than half that for the county as a whole (-10.7 percent). The decrease in the south for agriculture commissioner (-7.2 percent) was well below the county's decrease (-11.4 percent), and the drop in the comptroller's races was also smaller in the south (-9.6 percent) than for the total county (-12.6 percent).

There is a difference in the attorney general races. Here the 1986 election is compared to 1994 because the incumbent was unopposed in 1990. In 1986, Robert (Bob) Butterworth was elected attorney general for the

Table 4.3. Florida Cabinet incumbent success by damage zone, second election post-Andrew

AGRICULTURE COMMISSIONER VOTE SHARE (%)

Zone	1990	1994	1998	Change from 1990	Change from 1994
North	63.7	51.5	63.9	0.1	12.4
Middle	58.9	46.7	58.0	-0.9	11.3
South	68.3	61.1	72.8	4.5	11.7
Average	63.3	51.9	63.7	0.4	11.8

ATTORNEY GENERAL VOTE SHARE (%)

Zone	1986	1994	1998	Change from 1986	Change from 1994
North	67.3	56.6	63.6	-3.7	7.0
Middle	55.1	55.9	58.2	3.1	2.3
South	55.1	70.1	71.7	21.6	1.6
Average	64.4	58.5	63.4	-1.0	4.9

Source: Compiled from Miami-Dade County Elections Department data

first time. His support in the north part of the county was highest, possibly because he had held elected offices in Broward County, immediately north of Dade County, including a county judgeship. In 1994, he lost support in the north (-10.7 percent), held nearly even in the middle zone, and gained significantly (+15 percent) in the south. Thus the 1994 support for Butterworth was 70.1 percent in the southern zone versus 58.5 percent countywide.

A Pearson Chi-Square analysis of these results found no statistical significance, possibly because of the limited number of cases. The changes can potentially be attributed to the effects of the hurricane, but at least one alternative explanation should also be considered. If the closer 1994 gubernatorial contest brought out more Republicans, the rising tide carried all boats. Republicans gained three seats in the cabinet despite having their candidate for governor lose, finishing a close second.

To determine whether this latter explanation is partly borne out, the success of the two incumbents who ran for reelection a second time after the hurricane was also analyzed (table 4.3). Both the agriculture commissioner and the attorney general increased their county-wide vote share in 1998 compared to 1994. The south zone support in both cases, however, remained substantially higher than the total for the county. Voter

Table 4.4. Florida gubernatorial races, 1990 and 1994, Gold Coast region, by county

County	1990 Democrat	1990 Republican	1994 Democrat	1994 Republican
Palm Beach	154,085 (59.22%)	106,110 (40.78%)	198,638 (61.34%)	125,208 (38.66%)
Broward	217,422 (65.45%)	113,869 (34.28%)	261,368 (65.35%)	138,333 (34.64%)
Dade	232,542 (62.69%)	138,417 (37.31%)	215,276 (52.04%)	198,371 (47.96%)
Monroe	11,179 (61.38%)	7,034 (38.62%)	13,232 (56.64%)	10,086 (43.17%)

Note: Percentages do not total 100 in several of the elections, because this table does not reflect all votes cast in these races: write-in tickets garnered a small number of votes in some cases. In each case, however, the contest was between the Democratic and Republican tickets, the results of which are given here.
Sources: Elections departments for Palm Beach, Broward, Miami-Dade, and Monroe Counties.

turnout dropped throughout the county in 1998, registering at 57 percent in 1990, 64 percent in 1994, and 48 percent in 1998. Later in this chapter further questions about voter registration and turnout will be explored. For now, the possibility of a sustained hurricane-related increase in support for incumbents remains open for consideration.

Carver and Fiedler (1999) analyzed the results of the 1990 and 1994 gubernatorial elections by five geographic regions. The Democratic incumbent ticket of Chiles and MacKay lost support in all regions, managing to maintain a majority in only one—the Gold Coast. The Gold Coast in Carver and Fiedler's analysis consists of Palm Beach, Broward, Dade, and Monroe counties on Florida's southeast coast. These counties each provided majorities for Chiles and MacKay in 1994, with Dade County, home of the Republican challenger, Jeb Bush, showing the slimmest margin, just over 52 percent (table 4.4).

Miami-Dade County Elections Department data for the 1990 and 1994 November general elections, the elections for governor and cabinet immediately before and after Hurricane Andrew, were analyzed using precinct data aggregated to match the three damage zones created by the storm. A straight precinct-by-precinct analysis was not feasible because redistricting in 1992 changed how precincts fit into legislative districts, adjusted the boundaries of existing precincts, and created new precincts. Maps of the county depicting precinct boundaries were reviewed to determine which precincts fell into the three zones. Copies of precinct maps for 1994 and 1990 were compared to identify precincts within the three storm zones for each of the two years.

The south zone had the lowest turnout of any zone in all three elections pre- and post-Andrew (table 4.5). Voter registration decreased in

Table 4.5. Voter turnout by damage zone, November 1990, 1994, 1998, Dade County, Florida

	Registered*	Ballots**	(Turnout)
1990			
North	455,348	246,542	(54.14%)
Middle	99,019	56,559	(57.12%)
South	98,227	52,486	(53.43%)
County total or average	**673,838**	**383,166**	**(56.86%)**
1994			
North	454,012	277,929	(61.22%)
Middle	101,715	64,279	(63.20%)
South	89,444	51,801	(57.91%)
County total or average	**664,218**	**425,124**	**(64.00%)**
1998			
North	564,819	261,414	(46.28%)
Middle	125,722	57,934	(46.08%)
South	120,680	51,434	(42.62%)
County total or average	**834,234**	**397,624**	**(47.66%)**

*County registered voter totals include precincts that overlap damage zones and are not column totals.

**Available absentee ballot data, included for purposes of totals only, are not identifiable with specific precincts and, therefore, neither with zones. Ballots columns do not add to the totals, which include absentees and precincts that are partly in more than one zone.
Source: Compiled from Miami-Dade County Elections Department data.

the county as a whole between 1990 and 1994, with the largest drop in the southern zone. However, the elections department periodically purges the voter lists of individuals who have not voted in several elections. Two such purges occurred between the November elections of 1990 and 1994, one before and one after Andrew. Although it may be speculated that the post-Andrew purge was partly due to victims of the hurricane moving or not being able to vote for various reasons, the pre-Andrew purge resulted in a more substantial reduction.

Two separate precinct-level reports are available for most elections from the county's election department. One is the canvas report, depicting the results of voting for individual candidates by precinct. This report separates absentee ballots from vote results within precincts, and no information is available to match absentee ballots with specific precincts. A second report, generated later, provides an analysis by precinct of registered voters and ballots cast, including absentees, by party registration, ethnicity, and gender for some years. Using this report, the registration changes were analyzed by damage zone.

Although Hurricane Andrew caused a substantial number of people to move from the southern part of Dade County, the proportional distribution of voters did not change appreciably. Neither voter registration nor voter turnout provides any clear evidence of hurricane effect. Democratic registration decreased in all zones, whereas registration in the Republican Party, minor parties, and "no party affiliation" increased. In the south, the Democratic decrease and the Republican increase were lower than in the other two zones, but this was a minor difference.

The 1994 county turnout of 64 percent was higher than the 57 percent turnout in 1990, and the 1998 turnout was lower, at 48 percent, than 1990. In fact, the November 1992 presidential election saw the highest voter turnout in history, with over 80 percent of Dade County's registered voters casting a ballot—only two and a half months after Andrew (although the southern zone turnout was low). Presidential elections always draw higher turnouts than midterm (and Florida governor) elections.

Candidate enthusiasm is credited with the high 1992 turnout, especially with Ross Perot making it a serious three-way contest. The 1994 Florida governor's race was clearly more interesting to voters than that of 1990. In the earlier race, the incumbent Republican, Bob Martinez, was running behind a popular former U.S. senator in the polls leading up to the election. Martinez had backed a controversial services tax proposal after campaigning as a "no new taxes" candidate. He then had dropped his support, after convincing his party's legislators to back the tax, and had been defeated in efforts to restrict abortions in the state (Carver and Fiedler 1999).

In 1994, however, Republicans were energized because their candidate—Jeb Bush—was ahead in the polls for a while and appeared to have a good chance of winning. That also energized Democrats behind the popular Chiles-MacKay ticket, and the close race no doubt brought out more independents than usual. A slight decrease in turnout in 1994 among registered Democrats in the middle zone, the only counter trend that year, may reflect the fact that Republicans had achieved a plurality among registered voters in that zone. Hurricane Andrew was not seen as an issue in the governor's race, nor in any cabinet race (Carver and Fiedler 1999), except possibly insurance commissioner.

The 1994 incumbent agriculture commissioner made his opponent's last-minute switch in races his main issue, the comptroller's race was

Table 4.6. Pre- and post-Andrew elections absentee ballots, gubernatorial and selected Cabinet races

	1990	1994	Change
Ballots	15,634	19,278	3,644
GOVERNOR			
Chiles (D)	8,552	8,747	195
Martinez (R)	5,964		
Bush (R)		8,978	3,014
AGRICULTURE COMMISSIONER			
Crawford (D)	7,474	7,533	59
Bronson (R)	5,583		
Smith (R)		8,716	3,133
COMPTROLLER			
Lewis (D)	7,932	8,025	93
Comstock (R)	5,380		
Milligan		7,990	2,610
ATTORNEY GENERAL			
Butterworth (D)	unopposed	9,067	N/A
Ferro (R)		7,379	N/A

Source: Compiled from Miami-Dade County Elections Department data.

framed as one of experience versus integrity, and the attorney general was challenged by a former judge tainted by ethics violations (*Miami Herald* 1994e).

Florida's insurance industry experienced huge adjustments after Hurricane Andrew. The incumbent insurance commissioner resigned to run for governor, using Hurricane Andrew images in some of his campaign advertising but coming in third in the Republican primary (and second in his home county, Dade).

An increase in the number of absentee ballots cast in 1994 translated mostly into votes for the Republican challengers (see table 4.6). Partisan changes are also important in these statewide races. Between 1990 and 1994, the number of registered Democrats decreased by 29,450, whereas the number of registered Republicans increased by 9,204.

Finally, even within the cities included as part of this study, there was no clear pattern of change in voters between the 1990 and 1994 elections. Table 4.7 depicts the seven selected municipalities by damage zone, providing a view of particular pockets within the aggregated areas. Registration increased 7 percent in the northern zone cities, decreased slightly

Table 4.7. 1990 and 1994 November voter turnout by damage zone, selected municipalities, Dade County, Florida

	Registered		Ballots		Turnout (%)		Change		
							Registration	Ballots	Turnout
	1990	1994	1990	1994	1990	1994			
NORTH ZONE									
Hialeah Gardens	1,882	2,518	892	1,577	47.4	62.63	636	685	15.23
Miami Springs	6,013	5,979	3,686	4,015	61.3	67.15	-34	329	5.85
West Miami	2,330	2,399	1,497	1,727	64.25	71.99	69	230	7.74
Subtotal or average	**10,225**	**10,896**	**6,075**	**7,319**	**59.41**	**67.17**	**671**	**1,244**	**7.76**
MIDDLE ZONE									
Key Biscayne	4,236	4,054	3,056	2,928	72.14	72.23	-182	-128	0.09
South Miami	5,211	5,079	3,337	3,412	64.04	67.18	-132	75	3.14
Subtotal or Average	**9,447**	**9,133**	**6,393**	**6,340**	**67.67**	**69.42**	**-314**	**-53**	**1.75**
SOUTH ZONE									
Florida City	2,612	1,895	1,047	770	40.08	40.63	-717	-277	0.55
Homestead	7,482	5,650	3,331	2,713	44.52	48.02	-1,832	-618	3.5
Subtotal or average	**10,094**	**7,545**	**4,378**	**3,483**	**43.37**	**46.16**	**-2,549**	**-895**	**2.79**

Source: Compiled from Miami-Dade County Elections Department data.

Table 4.8. 1990 and 1994 November voter turnout, southern damage zone, Dade County, Florida

	Registrations			Turnout		
	1990	1994	Difference	1990	1994	Difference
Florida City	2,612	1,895	-717 (-27.5%)	40.08	40.63	0.55
Homestead	7,482	5,650	-1,832 (-24.5%)	44.52	48.02	3.5
South Zone	98,227	89,444	-8,783 (-8.9%)	53.43	57.91	4.48
Dade County	673,838	664,218	-9,620 (-1.4%)	56.86	64	7.14

Source: Compiled from Miami-Dade County Elections Department data.

(-3 percent) in the cities of the middle zone, and decreased substantially (-25 percent) in those in the south. Voter turnout, however, went up in all three zones, in all seven cities, and fluctuated within zones.

Much of that fluctuation may be explained by socioeconomic and partisan differences. In the northern zone, West Miami and Miami Springs were largely developed communities in 1992, whereas Hialeah Gardens was still growing. Both West Miami and Hialeah Gardens were heavily Republican (60 percent and 68 percent, respectively) in 1994, whereas Miami Springs was fairly evenly divided between the two major parties (49 percent Democrat, 42 percent Republican). Hialeah Gardens had the greatest increase in turnout between 1990 and 1994, but the lowest absolute turnout in both elections.

In the middle zone, Key Biscayne had the lowest increase in turnout, but the highest turnout of all jurisdictions in both elections—over 72 percent in each case. Here the population is the wealthiest of all the jurisdictions and heavily engaged in civic affairs. People of higher socioeconomic status tend to participate in elections at a greater rate. As we will see, the citizens of Key Biscayne were involved in creating their own city in 1990, which generated fairly strong movements for and against significant local issues.

The southern zone cities lost over one-fourth of their registered voters (table 4.8). This was not an even loss and not entirely representative of the southern zone as a whole. Florida City lost slightly more voters than Homestead (28 percent versus 25 percent); the entire southern zone lost only 9 percent of its voters. Florida City is the poorest city included in the study. People of low socioeconomic status show the least participation in voting.

*   *   *

Historically and currently, Florida politics are dynamic but atomized, yet incumbent statewide officeholders are likely to be returned to office when they seek reelection, conforming to national patterns. Hurricane Andrew was a localized disaster and affected only a small area. A local issue has minimal impact on statewide elections in Florida partly because of this atomization.

In the four statewide races selected for inclusion in this study there was unusually strong support for incumbent officeholders in the southern damage zone of Dade County in 1994. This support was partially offset by an increase in turnout due to a strong Republican gubernatorial challenger, resulting in a smaller decrease in votes for three incumbents (and an increase for the attorney general) in the southern zone than in other parts of the county. The difference, however, was not enough to swing the results of any of these four statewide contests. Nevertheless, it is a curious phenomenon and potentially important if these changes in electoral behavior were to be tied to a major natural disaster.

This phenomenon is not explained by the loss of population in the wake of Hurricane Andrew, because that loss appears to have affected the voting population in the southern damage zone equitably across ethnic and partisan divisions. The questions remain then: What is the reason for this unusually high level of incumbent support in southern Dade County? Did the hurricane affect voters' perceptions of the incumbents? One way to determine that is to see if the hurricane affected the incumbents' strategies or perceptions of reelection chances. The next chapter addresses that question.

5

Andrew's First Cavalry

State Officials Respond

"Where the hell is the cavalry on this one?" was probably the most politically explosive—and certainly the most nationally quoted—question posed in the immediate aftermath of Hurricane Andrew (see, for instance, Averch and Dluhy 2000). The speaker was Kate Hale, Dade County Emergency Management director in 1992, and it was raised to the press in a moment of "Day Three" frustration, when local and state officials became conscious of their almost complete inability to supply food and shelter, control looting, or even reach and account for many victims of the storm (Slevin and Filkins 1992; see also Averch and Dluhy 2000; Provenzo and Provenzo 2002; Fiedler and Merzer 1992; Swarns 1992; Donnelly 1992; Wallace 1992a).

In the midst of a national presidential campaign, Hale's question triggered federal action: President George H. W. Bush ordered two thousand regular federal troops into the area to assist the forty-five hundred National Guard troops already on the scene. That effort grew as the U.S. military eventually moved en masse into South Florida with tents, food, and equipment. At least as important was their visible backup to law enforcement personnel restoring order. Indeed, the response to Andrew was the then-largest domestic military relief operation in history.

Although overshadowed for a time by Andrew's impact and the arrival of federal troops, state officials had moved in quickly, with one cabinet official arriving in south Dade only hours after Andrew's winds abated. Others soon followed, and responding to Andrew became a central part of state officials' lives over the next several months.

Five individuals—three cabinet incumbents, the governor, and the lieutenant governor—met the criteria for inclusion in this study (incumbent elected officials in office at the time of the hurricane, running for reelection with competition in the first election after the storm). Four of these five were interviewed (one had passed away). In addition, six campaign managers or individuals otherwise closely connected to the selected campaigns, as identified by the incumbents, were interviewed. A total of ten interviews focusing on four statewide campaigns were conducted. All interview subjects were male. One was Latino; the other nine were white non-Latinos.

In their study of the New Orleans mayoral race after Hurricane Betsy, Abney and Hill (1966) suggested that one reason for the observed non-effect of the disaster was that it was difficult to place blame on any one official for various problems. Florida's multiheaded executive branch, with six separately elected cabinet officials, governor, lieutenant governor, legislators, and municipal and county governments, also made it difficult to assign blame (or take credit for positive responses).

The first post-Andrew statewide elections were held in 1994, two years after impact. Although Dade County was (and remains) the most populous county in the state, the severe, long-lasting problems associated with Andrew afflicted only the southern part of the county, which includes roughly half of Dade County geographically, but less than one-third of its population. With sixty-six other counties in Florida, no effects from the hurricane were expected in the 1994 statewide contests, although parts of Monroe County to the south, Collier County to the west, and Broward County to the north did experience some level of hurricane-force winds (sustained winds over seventy-four miles per hour, one minute or more in duration). Precinct analyses discussed earlier, however, suggested some effect in the area that suffered the greatest impact—south Dade County.

The Response by Statewide Officials

Each cabinet member had his own matters to deal with. The commissioner of education saw a public school system—the fourth-largest in the country—that could not begin on time, that had numerous damaged or destroyed facilities (with others being used as shelters), that had its regular construction program interrupted (with funding therefore jeopardized due to missed deadlines), and whose students and employees were severely affected in various ways. The secretary of state was responsible for elections, and primaries were scheduled for just a week after the storm hit. The state comptroller was facing a "throwback" economic situation: Andrew had transformed south Dade into a cash-only—but cash-scarce—society. Credit was unavailable and no banks were operational, including state-chartered banks regulated by the comptroller. The problems were not just operational—security was a major concern.

Agriculturally, Dade County was the third-largest producer in Florida, with virtually all the farmland in its southern portion. Avocado, lime, and lemon groves were decimated—trees had been literally ripped out of the ground. Winter vegetable farmers were preparing to plant their crops, but Andrew had destroyed the state-owned-and-operated Homestead Farmers' Market, which operated under the umbrella of the commissioner of agriculture. Farmers would not plant without knowing whether they would have a facility to pack and ship their produce. This dilemma rapidly made its way up to the commissioner.

The attorney general had looting, price gouging, and (somewhat later) construction and insurance fraud issues to contend with. These were fraught with potential political consequences, as were the problems confronting the insurance commissioner, who was facing immobilized policyholders unable to collect from bankrupt companies and the near statewide elimination of new homeowners' policies as traumatized companies reassessed their Florida exposures.

The governor had a dual responsibility. First, he was the "symbol" of state response. Second, he had ultimate responsibility for everything not covered by the various and separately elected cabinet members, as well as for state interfacing with FEMA and other federal relief efforts.

In this context, statewide elected officials not only went to Dade County after the hurricane, but most also shifted significant resources from other parts of the state to south Dade and stayed on site for months, directing their offices' duties. In theory this was unnecessary. Although Tallahassee, the state capital, is approximately five hundred miles from Dade County, modern communication and transportation capabilities made it possible to manage staff—and therefore the response—from the comforts and facilities of home. State officials, however, recognized that this was not merely an organizational or managerial situation. The respondent (all incumbents, campaign managers, and other political insiders will be referred to here as "the respondent(s)" to maintain anonymity), familiar with Governor Chiles' post-Andrew efforts, offered the following:

[Andrew] politically galvanized Chiles and the administration. Chiles literally, at the moment that it occurred, moved to South Florida. Literally took an interagency team of agency heads, and I'm not talking about senior management, I'm talking about the agency heads themselves, and established, in effect, a governor's office in South Florida. And he, probably for the better part of two or three months, spent almost full time down there. And he spent full time working with the feds, working with FEMA, working with the locals, working with the We Will Rebuild committee to see how to put the infrastructure back in place.

The governor's example suggested the proper approach:

We got on it right away because of all the damage. The governor, you know, got right on it. And we'd never seen anything like this in our lifetime. . . . I think the governor made a very good response. I mean, you know, he moved his office down there and set up headquarters, and we did virtually the same thing—spent a lot of time down there, assessing the situation, trying to help the federal initiatives. . . . Even though I was elected separately I had a great deal of respect for Governor Chiles. The fact that he was spending so much time down there told me that I needed to spend that much time down there too.

The respondent who was in Broward County, immediately north of Dade, during the hurricane rushed to the heavily stricken south Dade area that same day, arriving in Florida City, where he recalled, "I ran into no city. There was nothing, basically, no houses standing." Indeed, "nothing" sums up several realities, including laws controlling problems or authorizing needed responses. Chaos assumed a multidimensional meaning, including organizational, regulatory, and legal.

The state comptroller had no authority to waive rules or to allow state-chartered banks to set up temporary emergency facilities, nor did federal regulators have any flexibility with the congressionally mandated rules for federally chartered banks. As insurance settlements came in, however, huge amounts of money were being deposited into banks. The influx of deposits suddenly put banks out of compliance with laws regulating how much capital they were allowed to have on hand.

The commissioner of agriculture and consumer services had no legislative (or budgetary) authority to rebuild the critical Homestead Farmers'

Market. Nor were there any laws controlling price gouging on essential goods, including ice, water, plywood, and generators. The state legislature was not scheduled to convene for months, and legislative elections were required before that, with the primaries slated for only eight days after the hurricane hit. Thus, no quick legislative fix was possible for any of these issues.

In response to these dilemmas, what may be politely deemed extralegal solutions were found and implemented. The comptroller coordinated with his federal counterpart to establish emergency temporary banking rules for both state- and federally chartered banks (see also Adams 1992). Completely without authorization, they proceeded under the idea that, as the respondent said: "If we go to jail, we go to jail together. . . . We needed to do it and worry about getting the authority later. Maybe promulgate a rule that may not be valid, but. . . ." In other words, action had potential risks, but taking no action was apparently unthinkable.

Also on the financial front, Florida banks from outside the affected area furnished mobile ATM machines: "they called it the Buck Truck," the respondent recalled (see also Garcia 1992c). Help came from outside Florida as well, he recalled: "A Texas-based institution had an even larger kind of a mobile branch . . . something the size of a Winnebago." Even in the banking industry, innovation was the order of the day, as he recalled: "In one instance a bank set up an outdoor facility. They had armed guards to protect the money . . . because that's all the bank had . . . a bench." It is interesting to note that Congress and the state legislature both eventually ratified the emergency actions, but it turned out to be a harder sell than the "risk-takers" probably anticipated at the time: Hurricane Andrew was the first major disaster to come after the saving and loan and bank failures of the 1980s, so state and federal legislators were sensitive to issues of oversight and rule relaxation.

Overseeing the Florida Department of Agriculture and Consumer Services, the commissioner of agriculture was involved with the farm and landscape nursery industries, where Andrew's damage came in at approximately one billion dollars (*Miami Herald* 1992h, September 28). He was also facing price gouging and other consumer issues. The Division of Forestry, located within the Agriculture Department, had water tank trucks and bulldozers (normally used in firefighting and forest management). Equipment was brought in to clear debris and supply water to residents who needed it (a boil-water order was in effect countywide; some areas had no potable water at all). Given the extent of the damage in south Dade, this was a lengthy process.

Hundreds of Agriculture Department employees moved into Dade County for the cleanup activities and stayed for several months. The Farmers' Market issue had to be addressed, and the respondent recounted:

> Our first challenge was: how fast can we rebuild the facility, and it was probably about a thirty million dollar loss. . . . We totally got it rebuilt in ninety days, less than ninety days, which for government was [normally] impossible. And basically, we just built it, and we bypassed every state regulation on the books because of the emergency we were in, and got it built. . . .
>
> Just after we had completed it . . . we had gone back to the legislative staff in Appropriations . . . and they were saying, "We might have to do something in the legislature so that you all will have the authority to rebuild it." And we said, "No, we've already rebuilt it." We just did it, you know. We did it properly, but we had to waive a lot of rules and regulations and procedures.

In his area, the attorney general faced a lack of laws prohibiting price gouging on essential goods and services. People tend to become temporarily more civic minded after a disaster, and voluntarily reduce demand and hold down prices (Dacy and Kunreuther 1969). Exceptions to this norm produced public outrage over gouging, which was captured by the news media along with public officials' outrage. The attorney general first resorted to threats and jawboning, calling national and international corporate headquarters and telling them that the current practices of their branch operations would not be tolerated. It had the desired effect.

Regarding the Department of Justice's operation post-Andrew, the respondent explained: "We went after them with nothing, other than the bully pulpit and going on every single radio station and TV station and national TV, just trying to humiliate businesses that would actually steal from those who had just been beaten up pretty bad."

Local county commissions quickly passed laws against price gouging, and resources from throughout the state were used to bolster the enforcement efforts of the local state's attorney. The offices of the state's attorney, attorney general, and Department of Agriculture and Consumer Services worked together, issuing subpoenas (sometimes "with TV cameras in tow") and threatening to bring charges against perpetrators (Silva and Barciela 1992). In the end, companies caught price gouging rolled back prices, offered refunds, and donated money to hurricane relief funds (Strouse 1992).

Andrew's lessons provoked other actions. The state legislature subsequently passed a law expanding the governor's emergency powers, so that if a Florida governor declares an emergency when a hurricane approaches or declares a disaster after impact, price gouging regulations automatically kick in, with public announcements through the news media and advance warnings to companies about the practice and its consequences.

Construction fraud also surfaced in the storm's aftermath. Unscrupulous contractors required large deposits, then absconded with the money. Others, including many unlicensed contractors, charged high prices for substandard or incomplete work. Many jobs were done without permits or inspection (see, for instance, Keating 1993).

Homeowners wanted to protect themselves from these abuses by checking credentials, but the Florida Department of Professional Regulation was prohibited by law from sharing information about complaints made against contractors. In response, the attorney general and the Dade County state's attorney established a joint task force to front the Department of Professional Regulation, so that citizen complaints to the law enforcement hotline became a matter of public record, then were forwarded to the regulatory department for appropriate action.

The attorney general's task force of employees pulled from other parts of the state was heavily involved in Dade County for at least six months, with Attorney General Butterworth himself on site for at least two months. The respondent connected the relief efforts to his reelection campaign, but only in a limited way:

> We actually had a task force dispatched to [Dade] from various offices of the Attorney General's Office and they worked with the local State's Attorney's Office and local law enforcement. It wasn't so much a situation that we were making arrests or prosecutions, but once our presence was known, you know, the abuse sort of went away. And, obviously, in the election, you know, that was one of the many issues that, you know, that he could articulate, that in his career—his tenure—these are the many things that he had taken a lead on. And obviously that was an issue, but it was only part of an overall. It wasn't like it was a single issue; it was just one of the many things he had accomplished while in office.

The governor himself was in South Florida for most of the first two months after Andrew, the most chaotic period. The respondents remembered notable news coverage, some of which was good, "Lawton Chiles got a lot of press, walking barefoot—that was pretty stupid—in knee-deep water, going to various houses." Some, however, was bad: "There was looting and things going on, he was riding around and the press saw him. He actually had a bulletproof vest on. That didn't go over well at all. It was like, 'What, are we in a war zone?' . . . That was a bad PR day for the governor and for the effort."

Occasional publicity faux pas aside, the governor is the top elected official of the state. He may be limited in his actual authority, as Chiles was with six separately elected cabinet officials responsible for significant functional areas of the executive branch that in turn shared power with the legislative and judicial branches of government. The governor is nevertheless the unquestioned titular and ceremonial head of the state government, and his actions cemented the perception that the state government cared and tried to help. This combination was explained by the respondent, who was involved with political campaigns throughout the state:

It basically comes down to a perception of leadership, as opposed to any specific issue. Those folks saw Chiles on the news every night. They saw Chiles walking in the neighborhood. They saw Chiles eating at the soup kitchen with the families, and [involved] with the reconstruction. They saw him out there inspecting the buildings. They saw him with the federal officials. They saw the helicopters, when they landed, come in.

And all of those were covered night and day—radio, television, newspapers. I mean, there were special editions, neighborhood editions. So . . . you've got the Homestead neighborhood section of the paper with a picture of Chiles, three blocks down from someone they knew. And so they were right away saying, "This guy cares. He's here. He's the governor. He could be doing a lot of other things, but he's here and he's in my neighborhood."

That perception of leadership, I think, carried a lot of the, if you want, the failures of the state and federal government to be as prepared as they should have been. That aftermath and that reaction and that caring hand were almost more important than the actual conduct of the results at the end. And it showed in the polls. You know, it showed.

Statewide Officials and the Local Interface

Within days of the August 24 storm, Chiles was reaching out to South Florida business leaders to enhance governmental efforts. Two respondents credited the governor for bringing together the local business and civic leaders who formed "We Will Rebuild," a private-sector initiative that raised funds and provided grants to businesses and organizations to help where governments could not. News reports document an August 27 telephone conference call involving eighteen "state business leaders and economic development directors," the governor, and the secretary of the Florida Commerce Department (Birger 1992). The purpose was to provide long- and short-term help to south Dade businesses and, through them, to the entire South Florida economy, already sluggish before Andrew.

The United States was in national recession in 1992, but the Dade County economy was faring particularly poorly. Miami International Airport had been home to Eastern Airlines' corporate structure and was a major flight hub and maintenance center for that airline. Eastern struggled to recover from a crippling strike, but finally declared bankruptcy in January 1991. Over ten thousand local jobs were lost as a result. In December of the same year, Pan American Airways declared bankruptcy, putting nearly the same number of South Florida employees out of work. Several other airlines were in one or another form of bankruptcy status, tourism was down, and the area's unemployment rate was particularly high. Then came Hurricane Andrew.

On Saturday, August 29, 1992, a meeting of "about 30 of Dade's leaders and Gov. Lawton Chiles" planned for the next day was noted in the *Miami Herald*, "to help the business community focus its charity efforts" (Tanfani 1992). "More than 60 of Dade's most powerful leaders" reportedly attended the meeting, including the governor and Jeb Bush, a local real estate developer and son of President George H. W. Bush (Chardy and Corzo 1992). At that meeting, the leaders explained their response to Hurricane Andrew—which mostly comprised dealing with crises in their own organizations and among their own employees, and working to regain full operational status—and discussed what else would be needed for the community. On Tuesday, September 1, President Bush toured south Dade for the second time since the storm. Later, he addressed the nation about the needs of South Florida. He asked for, among other things, assistance to the American Red Cross "or a new group called 'We Will Rebuild' being formed by South Florida business leaders" (Brennan, Fiedler, and Merzer 1992). On September 4, the formal kickoff of We Will Rebuild was announced in the *Miami Herald*: "over 100 of Dade's most powerful community and civic activists will head a national campaign to rebuild South Dade" (Crockett 1992). This article reported that President Bush "summoned the task force and personally asked [local businessman Alvah] Chapman to head it."

Whether this was a case of political one-upmanship or merely a case of coincidental parallel processes is unclear, but all the statewide officials meeting the criteria for inclusion in this study were Democrats, and interestingly, no one interviewed actually credited President Bush for this group's formation. One respondent spoke of business leaders coming together "immediately" and taking charge through We Will Rebuild. Another credited the governor and lieutenant governor for setting up We Will Rebuild: "That was a political act because the county [government] was unable to react politically to this thing."

In a state the size of Florida, the governor cannot focus on one problem to the exclusion of all others for long, but the scope of this disaster required extended attention. Florida's system, however, provides a lieutenant governor with a function similar to the vice president's in the federal system: a heartbeat away from the top job but with virtually no responsibilities other than those that the highest elected official deigns to assign. After Andrew, Governor Chiles assigned Lieutenant Governor Buddy MacKay to head up the governor's office in South Florida and oversee the ongoing state disaster response, which caused MacKay to essentially move to Dade County for six months or so.

MacKay's assignment put him in close contact with local leaders, including We Will Rebuild, for a significant amount of time. Politically, it also put a North Florida politician in South Florida, the Democratic stronghold of the state, during the period immediately leading up to the 1992 presidential elections. Coincidentally, Lieutenant Governor MacKay was also the Florida chairperson of the Clinton for President Campaign.

The emergence of citizen groups is common in the wake of a disaster (Wolensky and Miller 1981, 1983; Wolensky and Wolensky 1990), sometimes to the extent of constituting "an ephemeral governing structure, different in form, action, and capability," arising to deal with "great and unexpected demands" made in the wake of the disaster (Taylor, Zurcher, and Key 1970, 128–29). We Will Rebuild had the potential to become just such an "ephemeral government" because, according to the respondent, it grew out of and included the Dade Non-Group.

The Non-Group had existed in Dade County for decades and was made up of influential business leaders who met periodically over dinner and discussed local issues (Slevin 1994; Fields 1996; Balmaseda 1994). When the Non-Group decided to address an issue or back a cause, its members marshaled their considerable corporate forces, contacted elected and top appointed officials, financed media campaigns, and created and/or joined official governing boards (if they were not already members). Unofficial and unelected, the group was exempt from Florida's open government laws, but it was known as a force to be reckoned with. Hardly a democratic body, however, the Non-Group was subject to criticism, if not suspicion, and We Will Rebuild, one of its projects, was not without conflict.

The respondent related that financial donations to We Will Rebuild were seen by some as "preempting" fund-raising by traditional aid organizations that would otherwise benefit from an outpouring of support, such as the United Way and the Red Cross. Largely a white, non-Latino, male group in an increasingly majority-minority community, the Non-Group represented exclusive old power in a diversifying area. Not coincidentally, it would seem, the Mesa Redondo ("Round Table" in Spanish), billed as a Cuban Non-Group by the respondent, also began to exert its considerable influence with elected officials. Likewise, Women Will Rebuild was formed because the nearly all-male We Will Rebuild made decisions that were perceived as ignoring the urgent needs of affected families (Enarson and Morrow 2000).

The situation was obviously becoming complex, and two respondents talked about local elected officials' concerns with who was making which decisions: "This is crazy," one remembered hearing. "We're the people elected to resolve this, and we're being cut out completely."

It is not unusual for elected state officials to work with local leaders, elected or not. New relationships frequently form, usually temporarily, in the wake of a disaster. Leaders run "ephemeral" relief and recovery operations, issuing orders to those under their official command and influencing organizations and individuals involved in disaster-related activities over whom the leaders exercise no official authority. The Non-Group was a known entity, and its leadership was neither questioned nor controlled. Two respondents emphasized its importance, the first noting:

The government structure down there [in Dade County] is not a marvel of efficiency or clarity, and this [Non-Group] ability to get together quickly and decide what was going to happen, with

Republicans and Democrats who were basically in very pivotal positions, focusing on it is probably one of the great strengths Dade County had for twenty years or so. And it was a great strength in Andrew. It just had this contradictory impact.

The second offered:

Nothing was happening because county government was so slow in getting to the federal government and all the other things. . . . We Will Rebuild, the community leaders, organized, and they took over. They did a superb job of responding to the vacuum—it was a complete vacuum. I thought they overdid their role by leaving out public officials from their ruling junta, and minority groups, unions, women. . . .

They just did what they usually do, the head of Burdines, the head of the chamber. They got twelve guys together and made decisions, because that's what they're accustomed to doing in the private sector. So I thought they had overdone [it], but nonetheless, they did the job. [After all], the [local] political system completely failed to respond.

Statewide officials helped behind the scenes by mediating some of these issues within the local community. Women and minorities were added to the We Will Rebuild board, and later to the Non-Group itself, although not in proportion to their incidence in the local population. Other conflicts or resentments continued, in particular over assistance and reconstruction priorities. They were resolved only after state leaders subtly exerted their influence to convince We Will Rebuild leaders to establish a time frame for the organization's operation and termination.

The Statewide Official-Federal Interface

A full explanation of the post-Andrew interface between Florida's statewide officials and federal officials and organizations would require a separate and extended study, but suffice it to say that state officials occupy that middle ground between local and federal officials, and FEMA's response to Andrew had raised much local ire that statewide officials tried to convey. One respondent recounted an apparently private appeal to the top similar to the one that began this chapter: "There was one huge argument right on the [airport] tarmac between President Bush and [Governor] Lawton Chiles, where Lawton had requested federal assistance, and had requested it in writing, but the letter had gone to the wrong place. So nothing had happened for a week. And Lawton was hot."

Frustration with the speed of federal response was widely shared by local and other state officials and may have caused the extended on-site involvement of state officials. One respondent who lived in Dade County at the time remembered:

> The lieutenant governor was here more than I was. You know, every time you looked around Buddy was here, meeting with We Will Rebuild, meeting with the chambers, meeting with everybody. Buddy MacKay was the person here. I don't know how much time he spent in Tallahassee—he was here all the time.
>
> So the governor was, you know, intimately involved in whatever had to be done to recapture the city, physically, and Buddy did that. And people responded to Buddy, people in office. So Buddy, it was important to have him here, symbolically. You call Tallahassee, you get fourteen secretaries. You never get the governor because he's doing something else. Buddy was here and did a wonderful job.

Effects on Incumbents?

The initial response to the hurricane, as has been noted, was disjointed and inadequate. Many local residents were angry with the government— a term that, when used generically, encompasses many layers of organization. Once the response kicked in, people began to appreciate what was finally being done. A respondent linked monetary assistance to a partial redress of incumbent shortcomings:

> It certainly helped the incumbents, the fact that there was enormous federal and state money that came in that helped ameliorate the disaster problem, which, in some areas, was very drastic, particularly in the south end of Dade County. . . . In Homestead and . . . south [Dade], it took years for that to be rebuilt, and the presence of federal and state money was very significant in making the public, even those who didn't live in that area . . . know that help was on the way. Succor was on the way.
>
> And so that developed a sense of security, which is very important for politicians. The public doesn't feel when an emergency crisis occurs that they're being ignored. But it was the federal money,

and state money, and the private sector made a strong contribution. So all the weaknesses of the officeholders were overcome by the money. It wasn't quite overcome, but I don't think too many people lost elections subsequent to that because of the ravages of Hurricane Andrew.

Like municipal and state legislative officials, those state executive officials involved were personally affected by their experience. "It was a life-changing experience for me," one respondent noted. It may be that at the time there was little consideration for personal reelection chances, especially because the statewide officials' terms would not end for another two years. Retrospectively, however, it was perceived to have a positive influence on reelection chances by at least some of the statewide officials, as one respondent stated eleven years after Andrew:

I think that was, it was probably one of the key political drivers in Chiles' popularity going forward. That when there was this crisis, it wasn't micromanaged from Tallahassee, you know, that Dade County didn't feel like the stepchild that they feel a lot, that the rest of the state hates Miami-Dade. [After Andrew] the government came to them and was interested in a day-to-day 24/7 basis trying to solve their problems. So politically he acted in the right way. Government reacted, I think, in the right way too. But I don't believe we ever, ever had a full understanding of what the impact would be of a storm that size and the impacts of the outer years [long term]. And we probably still don't. We probably still don't.

Most of the respondents interviewed for this study, including all of the statewide incumbents, believed that people in south Dade were still very much affected by the hurricane at the time of their reelection bids in 1994. They still visited the area in their capacities as state officials and for campaign and fund-raising appearances. Campaign professionals also utilized polls to gauge the important, but unique, issues in the area. As one respondent explained:

If you looked at polling back then, obviously, you know, insurance was [so high it was] off the radar down there, you know, the construction standards, building standards, growth management, those issues in that area of Dade were obviously at the top of the spectrum. But as you moved on, you know, it dissipated. . . .

Florida's this kind of state of many mega-states, you know, that you've got a central Florida region, and a Tampa Bay region and a, you know, northwest Florida, and a northeast Florida. You get this kind of chauvinistic view [in each region], you know, we take care of our own. And they're skeptical of Miami-Dade anyway, because of its size, and because it demands so many resources just because of its size, and the peculiar populations, and because of the immigration problem. I mean, it draws a tremendous amount of state resources down there. . . .

As you campaigned, you had to campaign on general issues that were of importance statewide, but when you went south, you had to be particularly careful about how you framed the issues and which ones you moved forward on.

Hurricane Andrew caused little change in campaign fund-raising in 1994. Two years after the storm, most of the state, and much of Dade County, was back to normal. Hurricane reconstruction was well under way. Cabinet officials typically received significant portions of their contributions from individuals, corporations, associations, and political action committees connected to the industries that they regulated: for example, the insurance commissioner received money from insurance executives, the comptroller received money from bankers (a fact singled out in 1994 as proof of a too-cozy relationship), and the agriculture commissioner received money from farmers, ranchers, and landscape nursery owners.

As noted above, southern Dade County was a major agricultural center, and fund-raising events were held there in 1994. Some of the farmers from the area, who had lost their citrus groves and avocado orchards in Andrew's winds, had decided not to replant and had gone out of business. One respondent spoke of former supporters conspicuous by their absence from a fund-raiser: "I remember one big fund-raiser we had in the Homestead area, and I do remember a number of people who didn't come because they were basically out of business because of the storm."

Other dynamics were at play in the agriculture commissioner race, however. After Jim Smith, secretary of state, dropped out of the race for governor and sought the agriculture seat, the incumbent agriculture commissioner was suddenly the underdog. Contributions were then more difficult for the incumbent to collect statewide.

On another front, incumbent fund-raising in the comptroller's race was seen as difficult by one respondent not due to the hurricane, but because the Republican opponent was collecting far less than the incumbent. The comptroller, a twenty-year incumbent, was overconfident—"The poster boy for overconfidence," one respondent suggested—because the challenger was a political novice and unable to compete in fund-raising. The challenger had little money to launch a media campaign. Two respondents noted that the incumbent did not produce new television ads, preferring to save money by running those from four years before.

The governor's race had fund-raising challenges as well, but again not because of the hurricane. Lawton Chiles had run successful populist campaigns for years. In 1970, as an unknown state senator running for the U.S. Senate for the first time, he had captured the media's fancy by walking the length of the state to talk to people and find out what they really thought about issues. "Walkin' Lawton," as he became known, ran shoestring campaigns (financially speaking), but his popularity carried him through two reelection campaigns for the U.S. Senate against weak challengers.

In 1990, when Chiles decided to run for governor, however, he raised over five million dollars, a personal record. Nevertheless, this was about half as much as the incumbent collected, but Chiles again played the populist theme by limiting contributions to one hundred dollars per donor. That limit was continued in 1994, which "drove a whole bunch of people crazy," one respondent recalled, but this time he was the incumbent and the challenger was Jeb Bush, whose national fund-raising campaign and family support—including from his father, the former president—raised over fourteen million dollars. Chiles again raised only about half of his opponent's war chest, but still set a new personal campaign record of over seven million dollars, including public financing.

Raising a lot of money in small bits requires many contributors. The Democratic base is in South Florida, including Dade County. The hurricane experience and the extensive government efforts put into the area enabled then-governor Chiles and Lieutenant Governor MacKay to attain a new level of comfort with and understanding of the county and its unique culture. That gave the feeling, according to one respondent, that they "were identified with Dade County," and not just "a couple of rednecks from Lakeland and Ocala."

People from We Will Rebuild thus looked at the pair as friends and not as Democrats. Public employee unions, normally essential for Democratic candidates and "normally pretty cynical," knew that the incumbents "had been down there and had stood up for them" in a time of need. One respondent framed this involvement as "total devotion" during the first six months after the storm. Support from Dade County constituents was therefore perceived as strong.

Three hurricane-related issues were noted in campaign appearances or through the news media. The governor was questioned at one point about storm shelters' restrictions against pets. Refugees from an impending storm evacuate from their homes to spend hours or days inside school gymnasiums or other large buildings that can accommodate large groups. Shelters are crowded, most provide no food or beds, and once a storm hits, they may be without electricity and air conditioning. Rules prohibiting pets are intended to protect against health and personal problems.

Nonetheless, some people will not evacuate from potentially dangerous areas because they do not wish to leave their pet alone in what may be a vulnerable situation. A respondent remembered this issue as one Governor Chiles had argued needed to be addressed. A similar issue regarding lack of adequate protection for livestock had come up in the agriculture commissioner race. However, these questions apparently were not raised by opponents and never became actual campaign issues.

One respondent recalled an issue raised by the attorney general's opponent. The media contacted the incumbent's campaign regarding a suggestion that the attorney general may not have done a good job: many questions were raised about shoddy building practices adding to the amount and severity of damage in Dade County, but no one went to jail. The campaign office mitigated public relations damage by explaining that building codes are local laws and therefore not under the attorney general's jurisdiction. The media were apparently satisfied with the explanation, and the issue died quickly.

As with legislative interviews discussed previously, partisanship was not generally seen as prominent in the aftermath of the hurricane. One respondent explained, "The disaster issue really wasn't a political issue at all. It was a bipartisan issue. People didn't care what party you were. Everybody just pitched in."

Most importantly in the governor's race, Jeb Bush, from Dade, was unable to carry his own county. He had raised traditional conservative Republican charges: for example, Governor Chiles was soft on crime and too liberal, government was too large, and so forth. One respondent noted that if it had been perceived that Chiles and MacKay "had been unconcerned [about the hurricane response]," "had blown it," or "hadn't been sensitive to what they [the victims] were going through," it would have been political death, at least in Dade County. After all, Chiles and MacKay, the respondent specified, "were running against a person from Dade County, and that would have been his issue, [but] it was just not an issue."

Nor was it a main campaign issue for incumbents. The response in Dade County was noted as an accomplishment for incumbents, primarily when campaigning in Dade County. It was buried within other accomplishments, however, especially outside of the south Dade area. One respondent connected to the Chiles-MacKay campaign said:

> There was no criticism of the administration by the other party about the hurricane. And there was no criticism on either side against the other. It just seemed to be a nonpolitical issue, the hurricane. I just don't recall it ever coming up in one way or the other, either subliminally or actively or otherwise. . . . If Hurricane Andrew had been an issue . . . it would have even helped in a very positive way. But because it wasn't a proactive issue, if you will, it really had no effect on the election. . . .
>
> However, the fact that they responded so well, and government worked so well, from Tallahassee, vis-à-vis Dade County's government, and Florida City's government, and Homestead, the fact that it worked almost flawlessly, may have had a bearing on people's votes. They were running for reelection, so the folks in south Dade said, "Hey, they were here when we needed them." I don't remember any criticism. I'm talking as a voter now, I don't remember any criticism of Tallahassee that we ever had. They did the best they could. We got supplies. Everybody responded.

The regional factionalism of Florida politics described in chapter 3 deserves consideration here. Incumbents spent a lot of time and effort in Dade, which played well there. In other areas of Florida, that could have been a political liability, could have been seen as too much time and effort spent in one place, especially when it was in Dade County. A respondent explained the state's relationship with its most populous county:

> People in the state of Florida . . . when you go two counties up . . . especially in Tallahassee, people do not believe that Dade County is part of Florida. They think that it's just like some foreign entity, whereas the rest of the world thinks Miami is Florida. Ironically

enough, Florida does not accept Miami as being part of Florida. So really, something happening in Dade County will not have an effect statewide.

Campaigns, especially the governor's campaign, justified this extended attention to South Florida when campaigning in other areas. Many of the individuals interviewed for this study, including all of the former elected officials, commented that the state learned from Andrew that it was unprepared to handle a major catastrophe. Other entities were criticized—the Red Cross, the county, FEMA—but so was the state. It had problems, too.

The state's actions after Hurricane Andrew to address its own deficiencies were seen by all the elected officials and several of the close supporters interviewed as very important. Recounting those actions and the lessons learned from Andrew while campaigning in Dade County could remind people what state officials did after Andrew and assure voters that next time things would go better.

Outside of Dade County, the same discussion could be used as justification for the attention given to Dade and to remind people that hurricanes and other natural disasters can strike elsewhere. The message was that if they did, the state would be ready—thanks largely to Andrew's lessons. The Dade spin is seen in the words of one respondent, a former elected official; the outside-Dade justification in the words of another respondent, this one a manager from a statewide campaign. First, the elected official:

> We set up a commission . . . that studied our disaster preparedness. It turned out that not only was FEMA a disaster, but Florida's disaster management was a disaster. And the reason was, it was never funded. . . . We now have the finest disaster management in America. And because we were well funded, we were able to hire the best disaster managers. My recollection is that they came from North Carolina. We sort of hired their leadership, lock, stock, and barrel. I think we got credit in South Florida for having been responsive and for having put together a governmental reform that was the best in the country. We certainly talked about it.

The campaign manager offered:

> As a result [of Andrew], I mean, we completely redid the emergency preparedness. I mean, if you go up here [in Tallahassee] to

the bunker now, it doesn't look anything like the room that existed prior to that. I mean, it is a wired room now, you can get immediate weather, you can get immediate contact with, you know, all the first-responders everywhere. . . . We bring in the feds, we bring in every agency head, and it is, it is a very coordinated room now. . . . And so you can campaign on that, that "Don't worry if you live in southwest Florida, you know, we've been taught an ugly lesson down here, and we're responding on that basis, and here's what we're doing with the cat[astrophe] fund or here's what we're doing with emergency management, or here's what we're doing with consumer protection, or here's what we're doing with, you know, with human resource response. So that we're better prepared. So, don't worry about living in Fort Myers, Naples, or Tampa, or Broward and getting wiped out, and being in a similar situation. We're working on that. . . ."

There was always this undercurrent of, I don't want to say fear, but kind of trepidation in the back of the minds of voters, to say, "Whoa, what would I do if it blew my house away, and blew my job away? What would I do? Or if I was a retiree, where would I go? Or if I were in adult congregate living, you know, how would I do? If I were in a hospital?" So all of those things were played out by the agencies, to try and kind of take care of those issues, and try to speak to those issues, in terms of preparedness and also how it's being taken care of down there. And I think that helped to kind of soothe, and keep that issue from becoming a statewide issue. It never really became a statewide issue at all.

Campaigns for statewide office are primarily media campaigns—especially reliant on television advertising—as more than one respondent pointed out during interviews. The governor's 1994 campaign, however, did adjust its tactics in south Dade due to Hurricane Andrew. Many people in the south Dade area had not finished rebuilding their homes by the fall of 1994. Many victims had used insurance money to buy or lease large campers, parked them in their yards, and supervised the rebuilding process daily. In these cramped quarters, many did not subscribe to newspapers, some may not have had telephones installed, and other normal living conditions were temporarily suspended. A campaign professional with the 1994 Chiles/MacKay reelection team explained their response to the dilemma:

You really had no contact with those voters. I mean, it was such that they didn't have phones, you couldn't call them. And you couldn't go door-to-door. . . . We were hesitant to go door-to-door in those areas as a full-blown campaign, mainly because we didn't want [them] to think that, you know, here we are, that we're pandering to a group of people, you know, who were really going through a tremendous blow, and oh, by the way, elect us and we'll make everything all better again, you know. Chiles was, he didn't like that kind of voter contact; I mean, he was more straightforward in everything he did.

And so we did do some of that, we did go to community meetings and groups, and we had people there. As we found clubs that were organized or community groups, we'd have contact with them. We'd use the traditional advertising; we used radio a lot more in south Dade than we did in other parts of the state because it was about the only thing that everybody tuned in to. They wouldn't even get their damn papers. I mean, they'd go to the grocery store or something and pick up the paper and flip through, but it wasn't like the paper was delivered to their house and they read the paper.

So you relied on kind of local leadership, local word of mouth, local groups, radio, to carry that message, and then endorsements of kind of local leaders who said, you know, "Chiles is the one, he's been here helping us," and, you know, those kind of things. So it did, it changed the tactic for that area.

It appears that the statewide incumbents generally believed that they benefited from state government's response to Hurricane Andrew, and it is intriguing that three of the four 1994 races were particularly close: Chiles pulled out a victory with 50.8 percent of the vote, Crawford won with 51 percent, and Lewis lost with 49 percent. The analytic problem is that the south Dade area did not have enough voters to make a large difference amidst four million votes cast statewide; then again, small differences can be important. Again intriguing, Comptroller Lewis, alone among the four incumbents, did not stay in South Florida for months after Andrew. And he lost.

On a different level, respondents from all four incumbent campaigns spoke of how the experience affected them personally, how they saw the public responding, or how they believed other campaigns may have been affected. Thus their words provide the key to answering the question that remained at the end of chapter 4: Did the incumbents perceive differences in south Dade support after Hurricane Andrew? A venerable scientific axiom is that you affect something by merely observing it, and this study appears to have stimulated new reflections among its subjects. Here is the first reflection:

They had a number of functions down there they invited us to. I think politically, even [Insurance Commissioner] Tom Gallagher and I were very visible down there, and people seeing us made a difference. That word spreads pretty quickly. I think that all of us that were involved in it, as staying down there a lot like Tom and I did, I think it helped us in that area of Florida. But we never even, until this time I never even considered it that way. But when we went down there a year or so later, we were given heroes' welcomes. . . .

I would go down to south [Dade] County. After Hurricane Andrew, I was treated much differently than I was before. They always treat a statewide officeholder with respect who goes into rural communities. But I was treated differently after Hurricane Andrew. . . . I think probably that disaster had more of an effect on me, as a public servant, I think, than anything else . . . in a positive way. In a very, very positive [way]. Negative, too, from how I'd see people trying to take advantage. . . . Just to see how people, what they did was just heroic, flat out heroic. And people go and do what they have to do. It's amazing. It was really something. . . . My whole office really got involved in it. We probably had sixty, seventy people that spent full time, full time, dealing with that issue. And it left them changed also. I hope we don't forget it. . . .

The real professional pollsters thought that Florida was going Republican in 1990, but they say what stopped that was Lawton Chiles. So when Lawton ran again in '94, sure, the difference could have been down there. I mean, he really cared about that disaster. I mean, he was there; I mean, he did things that most governors would not do.

The second reflection:

It was a life-changing experience for me. . . . I think it played on our side because it was a feeling of goodwill that we had come in at a time when things were totally unprepared and . . . had hung in there. . . . You know, we were on the ground, and we were there day in and day out.

The third:

> So politically, just drawing some conclusions, it actually, I think, was a very positive thing, politically, for me and for the governor. And then the other dimension of that was that we learned so much from the disaster that the governor went back to the legislature, as well as I did too in my budget, and built a bigger response team effort, in the Office of Emergency Management. All that became really, kind of, the state of the art.
>
> So in addition to the immediate response of dealing with people's problems and the damage that was done, then there was a very long-term response, and I think that was judged very well too. And so I guess the bottom line is, very much like Rudy Giuliani, if you respond well to crisis, it can be a political plus. [But] if you don't respond well, it could be terrible. . . .
>
> I think, if anything, as I said, it probably enhanced it [the reelection chance]. Additional media coverage down there during the storm, I think the favorable reaction to our ability to move several hundred employees in there. . . . We had probably two or three hundred employees from my department assigned to that area . . . so I think we got a really good reception, and that was a very positive thing.

And the fourth:

> I think Tom Gallagher did a good job and he got good media from it. . . . He went down there, he was down there all the time. He spent a lot of time. And he's not dumb. They filmed a lot of footage of him walking through the rubble and doing whatever, and he later used that, legitimate public service announcements . . . "Make sure that you have the coverage you need on your house." . . . And then he later used it in campaigns . . . that he was there, on site, taking care of things. . . . The visual was very impressive.

Only rarely in the interviews was there any indication that actions had been taken after Hurricane Andrew with any political (that is, reelection) motives. The disaster was "too real." State officials, like municipal officials and state legislators, did what they could to aid their citizens in a very challenging situation. Interview questions raised the election linkage, however, and organizing responses then triggered retrospection, which enabled a more complete analysis, as indicated by one respondent's remarks:

> I do believe that I was tested there. And when people would intro-
> duce me at various functions, maybe I didn't think it was as im-
> portant because I just did my job, I thought. But whenever I was
> introduced by somebody, and it was not even on my résumé, they,
> during that election, they would highlight the role that myself and
> my office played in the Homestead disaster. . . . Other people saw it
> as more significant, I think, than those of us that were involved in
> it. Because when you're at ground zero, you do your job. But other
> people, who were not there, see that maybe you went the extra mile.

In sum, at least until these interviews, respondents did not apparently see the electoral connection of responding to Hurricane Andrew in the south Dade area. This makes sense, because other aspects of the state-wide campaigns were not affected by the hurricane. Given the geogra-phy of Florida, the distance between major metropolitan areas, and the diverse regional populations, statewide campaigns are largely media events, centered within major media markets. Statewide campaigns are thus different than those for small municipalities or state House seats.

Andrew's Legacy

Two of the incumbents studied here ran for reelection again in 1998. The limited effect seen in 1994 was basically gone six years after the storm. An incumbent's hurricane response may still have been noted in introduc-tions for personal appearances, especially in Dade County, but by then only within a longer list of accomplishments. Other hurricanes (with weaker winds), serious floods, and devastating fires had afflicted Florida in the interim. Andrew was a distant memory. Even so, there was some indication of a residual effect from Hurricane Andrew in south Dade, as one respondent recalled:

> I think people still remembered what I did, what my office did. There
> was still a positive residual there. Because of the hurricane, I'm not
> sure, but I think it's because of how we responded to the hurricane.
> I had a number of town hall meetings down there after the hurri-
> cane, as to how we can do better. . . . I had many town hall meetings.
> I had some of my top employees probably live down there for three

months. So, you know, that stuff probably rubs off. I never really questioned it much, but yeah.

Policy and Executive Legacy

The administrative legacy of Hurricane Andrew within Florida appears to have outlived the electoral legacy. Three of the respondents noted that part of Andrew's legacy was stronger building codes. One spoke of issues that came before the Florida Cabinet—including a proposal to weaken Monroe County's code, which had been considered before Andrew but had not been brought up after—and of political opposition that formed due to cabinet members' positions on environmental design and building codes. Another specifically mentioned a recent strengthening of building codes in a central Florida county shortly before the interview——eleven years post-Andrew. This enhancement to the local code was a result of a new statewide code approved by the legislature in 2000 (the implementation of which was delayed by the 2001 legislature). As a third respondent noted: "The state took over a stronger role, they got rid of these local options, and they put some hurricane standards in for coastal areas, and it's, there's a lot stronger control on that building control mechanism from the state. . . . We're talking, you know, over ten years now, but all of that still plays out."

Finally, numerous references were made to the Emergency Management Center—the state-of-the-art "bunker," as one respondent described it—created because of the state's inadequacies in the Andrew disaster. Subjects also spoke of the new state laws restricting price gouging in the wake of future disasters and providing more authority to the governor in declaring a state of emergency before a storm hits. Insurance pools and the state's insurance catastrophe fund were listed as results of Andrew as well.

In his classic 1995 book, John Kingdon describes the public policy milieu as a "policy primeval soup" that changes as new elements of policy alternatives are added and old elements form new combinations (117). Policy communities have interest in certain areas. Sometimes existing problems become highly visible and arise to the governmental agenda for consideration of policy action. Among other possible reasons for sudden high visibility are natural disasters, which focus media attention and force the public and policymakers to pay closer attention to the issue (95). Such a focusing event may open a policy window and enable policy entrepreneurs to push their alternatives into legislative initiatives (165). Certainly Andrew was such a focusing event. Media coverage focused on the aftermath of the disaster, the significant property destruction, the misery of the victims, the looting, and the remarkable relief efforts as first-responders from other parts of Florida, other states, and eventually the U.S. military moved in to help. Grand jury reports focused local attention on their building codes, which were strengthened; the Dade County emergency management structure was revamped. The county government eventually built a new emergency center to better coordinate resources before, during, and after an emergency.

Florida officials created laws that gave the governor more authority to declare an emergency in preparation for an expected disaster and prohibited price gouging, they revamped emergency procedures, and they built a new emergency operations "bunker." Efforts to adopt the stronger South Florida building code for the entire state ran into major resistance. The backlash was so strong that South Florida officials became concerned that the statewide code would weaken the local one. Hurricane Floyd threatened South Florida in 1999, following a path very similar to Andrew's. But then Floyd, several times larger than Andrew, turned north and skirted the coast, causing millions of people to evacuate from the Florida Keys through Virginia—coastal areas in five states. Floyd refocused Florida legislators, the statewide building code was passed, and the stronger South Florida code was grandfathered in for South Florida, although parts of the Florida Panhandle were allowed weaker code guidelines, as Birkland (2006) notes.

The federal response after Andrew, of course, was also seen—rather immediately—as disastrous. Congressional hearings were held and studies were undertaken. The Federal Emergency Management Agency's Office of Inspector General's 1993 performance audit report found that the Federal Response Plan needed "substantial refinements to deal with a disaster of such extraordinary magnitude, particularly in the first few days when broad assistance was so vitally needed but slow in arriving" (1). The plan had been initiated after a review of responses to Hurricane Hugo and the Loma Prieta earthquake determined "that the Federal Government may be the principle responder when a catastrophic disaster overwhelms the State and local governments' ability to respond" (1).

The performance audit found that, after Andrew, federal agencies perceived that they lacked authority to respond without state requests, and state and local officials were so overwhelmed that "they could not identify their requirements for federal assistance" (FEMA 1993, 2). Andrew was symptomatic of the federal problem, but hardly unique. Within a three-week period, Andrew hit Florida and Louisiana, Typhoon Omar struck Guam, and Hawaii was victimized by Hurricane Iniki. During the 1992 federal fiscal year, President Bush declared forty-six major disasters (8).

Primary agencies included in the Federal Response Plan were the Departments of Agriculture, Defense, Energy, Health and Human Resources and Transportation, the National Communications System, General Services Administration, Environmental Protection Agency, FEMA itself, and the American Red Cross (FEMA 1993, 11). Other federal agencies often also provide resources: Florida received thirty-five million dollars from the Department of Labor under the Job Training Partnership Act.

Report recommendations included mobilizing resources and repositioning them prior to the event, assessing damage more quickly after, clarifying federal authority to move without specific state requests, easing standards to waive state cost-sharing requirements, better coordinated chains of command, and improved communication with the public (FEMA 1993, 2–4). FEMA's OIG was not the only reviewer of federal emergency responses.

If there are multiple agencies involved in a disaster response and therefore coordination is an issue, the problem is compounded at a local level. The National Association of Public Administration (1993) studied the responses to Andrew and noted that, because our emergency response system is bottom first, "there are tens of thousands of 'first responder' organizations," and they are poorly coordinated at best (2). In major emergencies, city, county, then state and National Guard, and finally federal assistance comes in (2). Clearly, this makes it difficult to place blame politically, especially when elections are a long way off. Policy actions taken after problematic responses may alleviate blame-placing. Besides, Americans are never supportive of long-range planning and mitigation efforts (17), so the policy window of opportunity opens and closes quickly.

Another of the national adjustments after Andrew began with seventeen governors signing the Southern Region Emergency Assistance Compact, a mutual aid system initiated through the Southern Governors Association (Kapucu, Augustin, and Garayev 2009). In 1996, the enactment of Public Law 104–321 by Congress established requirements for states to enact their own enabling legislation so they could join the Emergency Management Association Compact (EMAC), thus expanding the

Southern Region Association to a national assistance network. This effort was spearheaded by Lawton Chiles after his experience with Hurricane Andrew as Florida's governor.

Nearly every state sent personnel to help through EMAC after Hurricane Katrina, with National Guard troops predominating among the over sixty thousand personnel responding. Yet the response to Katrina, the largest ever in the United States, was inadequate. Most responders had not been through any emergency training within two years of deployment (Kapucu, Augustin, and Garayev 2009).

Hurricane Andrew hit in 1992; Katrina hit in 2005. Responses to both disasters were seen as inadequate. Is it simply that the U.S. government— or Americans in general—cannot learn from such events? Although the argument might be made convincingly, in this case there was another intervening focusing event that taught a new lesson. The terrorist attacks of September 11, 2001, caused significant adjustments to American public policy, including major reorganizations of the federal government, one of which was the creation of the Department of Homeland Security.

The Federal Emergency Management Agency was moved into the new department, as were various other existing agencies, and the focus of the department was on preventing and responding to terrorist attacks. The Federal Response Plan was replaced by the National Response Plan, which added new expectations for states and localities that focused on terror threats (McGuire and Schneck 2010; see also Birkland 2006, who finds that the homeland security domain corroded natural disaster domains of influence). By 2005, FEMA's top political appointees in the central headquarters and the ten regional offices were mostly people with little or no emergency management experience or expertise. Regions interpreted policies from headquarters as they deemed locally appropriate, and conflicts among the different offices occurred. The FEMA system was not prepared to respond adequately to Katrina; in her wake, studies have resulted in numerous reports and recommendations for reform (McGuire and Schneck 2010).

Should we need periodic disasters to refocus our attention on planning and preparation? Many of the recommendations offered by studies and analyses after Andrew were the same raised after Hurricane Hugo and other disasters (Lewis 1993). The perceived threat of terror attacks may have risen after September 11, 2001, but government leaders should have added it to the continuing threats of hurricanes, earthquakes, and other natural disasters. Sadly, with limited resources and short memories, policy makers are more likely to shift to new problems and ignore old ones, regardless of the persistence of the latter.

Mileti (1999) argued that longer-term mitigation policies are needed and disasters should spur policy makers to accomplish this. He suggested we shift the way we think about disaster mitigation: "1. Adopt a global systems perspective. . . . 2. Accept responsibility for hazards and disaster. . . . 3. Anticipate ambiguity, constant change, and surprise. . . . 4. Reject short-term thinking. . . . 5. Take a broader, more generous view of social forces and their role in hazards and disasters. . . . 6. Embrace the principle of sustainable development" (26).

However, as Birkland pointed out, public officials' interests may "lie more in the provision of disaster relief than in mitigation" (2006, 103). Rapid relief and recovery benefit everyone, but mitigation efforts are usually costly and subject to competition with different interests. Further, mitigation can be done most easily during rebuilding after a hurricane, but is less likely to be on anyone's mind at that hectic time. This is partly because, Birkland suggested, there is no organized advocacy group for hurricane preparedness and less local news coverage about mitigation after hurricanes compared to earthquakes.

Outsiders as Insiders

Community conflict is often minimized after a disaster because the disaster agent is an outside force and thus struggles to highlight existing conflicts (Dynes 1970). A natural disaster is an "attack from outside"—easily identified, creating easily understood priorities (such as rescue)—and this community-wide problem makes community identification and participation stronger than usual (Quarantelli and Dynes 1976, 141).

Activities benefiting others or the community take precedence over particularistic interests—there are urgent, readily apparent needs on which competing interests tend to agree. There is an orientation on the present situation rather than on past problems, social distinctions are reduced, and community identification is heightened. "The presence of extra-community aid need not imply local inadequacies; it may simply reflect the magnitude of the disaster event" (Dynes 1970, 108). Andrew's severity meant local officials needed help; this was perfectly understandable to voters and not something a challenger could successfully use to defeat the overwhelmed local incumbent.

Where normal conditions exist, local autonomy works. Where the situation is abnormal, standard decision-making guidelines may not apply, and some local or outside authority must take charge and create a new action plan (Moore et al. 1963). Although conflict within the community is reduced temporarily, conflict with outsiders is likely. The special bond developed among victims "also creates a wall around them to exclude the outsiders" (Dynes, Quarantelli, and Kreps 1972, 28). Yet after Andrew, outsiders (such as statewide elected officials) became local heroes.

Even those who have come from outside to help are resented, excepting those who give "the appearance that they share the sentiment of the insiders" (Quarantelli and Dynes 1976, 144). Insiders will complain if outsiders are on committees to distribute aid during the relief period, because such appointments are seen as political. "Even in the allocation of blame, the attempt to attribute it to local officials is resisted and resented" (148). Cabinet officials, the governor, and the lieutenant governor came to South Florida after Andrew and stayed long enough—visibly sharing the tragedy and the outrage of the victims about the damage, the vulnerability, and the abuses of price gougers and construction charlatans—to be seen as insiders.

The "rednecks from Lakeland and Ocala" grew comfortable with South Florida culture, and South Floridians accepted them as their own. The statewide officials brought with them many resources and made an all-out effort to provide relief, guide local efforts, and mediate—not cause—local disputes. In the grand scheme of disaster response, it is exactly these state officials who are supposed to provide substantial backup and support to local governments. "If the city is the creature of the state, the logic of that relationship is that the parent assumes responsibility for the child" (Winter 1973). Top state officials came to South Florida and did their jobs, according to their own perceptions. The support they received in south Dade County ballot boxes seems to indicate that the voters felt they did their jobs well.

People who hold power in the formal and informal structures before a disaster need to be involved and should not be placed in subservient positions in disaster relief and recovery operations (Bates et al. 1963). Otherwise, conflicting instructions and authorities will cause problems. Initially after a disaster, new forms of leadership may develop, but that is usually because normal authorities are incapacitated and communications are disrupted. We Will Rebuild involved a preexisting power structure (the Non-Group) and prior economic, governmental, and social elites, and thus was immediately accepted locally, but the ongoing changes in the population brought some existing conflicts into play. State officials helped smooth out those conflicts and helped legitimize the interim structure to others outside the local area, who were asked to contribute to the local relief and rebuilding efforts. These outsiders were necessary and proper to effect relief, and became part of the local scene enough to mediate in local issues.

Intentionally or not, that intervention may have helped bring about an overdue sharing of power within the local community. "A disaster population suffers a temporary sense of incapacity, vulnerability, and confusion. The collapsed social structure renders traditional authority relationships less effective and traditional statuses less meaningful" (Barkun 1974). Andrew may have served as a timely catalyst for the change in that aspect of the local unelected power structure.

A common phenomenon in disaster situations is the formation of a citizen group to direct or assist with aspects of relief and/or recovery (Barton 1970). Such groups are usually heavily represented by business interests and social and economic elites. Authority is frequently diffused, with different groups or persons taking over different tasks and new levels of coordination and interdependence occurring. Community structure seems disorganized, but must disorganize in order for new structure to develop: "This 'disorganization' is a natural process, even though unanticipated, and it is only indirectly related to the unnatural event itself" (Dynes, Quarantelli, and Kreps 1972, 41). Thus, after Hurricane Andrew, as tends to happen after disasters generally, a seemingly chaotic situation became more organized and a private sector group formed to assist in recovery.

A Different Result: The 1992 Presidential Election

One cannot leave the possible political effects of Hurricane Andrew without at least a brief discussion of its putative impact on the 1992 presidential campaigns, especially in Florida, of not only George H. W. Bush and Bill Clinton, but also Ross Perot. Presidential elections are, after all, comprised of statewide elections for electors who later cast ballots in the electoral college, and therefore they have much in common with the statewide elections just discussed. George H. W. Bush's 1992 bid for re-election was interrupted by disasters: Hurricane Andrew in Florida (August 24) and Louisiana (August 26), followed in short order by Hurricane

Omar in Guam (August 28) and Hurricane Iniki in Hawaii (September 11). Andrew's visit in South Florida was the worst of the four.

In South Florida, President Bush's response was initially seen as slow and inadequate, although federal efforts grew to record levels quickly (Slevin and Maass 1992; Silva 1992b). The president's first photo op was alongside a large tree toppled over within the moderate damage zone. Although he did then go into the harder-hit area, he was in and out quickly. The effort he directed to Andrew-related processes from Washington, D.C., was insufficient to make up for the initial perception of limited involvement and attention.

Even the *Wall Street Journal* noted the political importance of the president's response. A front page headline on August 28, 1992, four days after Andrew, read: "Florida and Louisiana Urge Faster Relief in the Wake of Andrew." Bush needed both Florida and Louisiana in his corner in November, and he was trailing in the national polls. The *Wall Street Journal* told the nation, "This is a hurricane George Bush can't afford to blow—and one that's going to cost the government plenty" (Davis 1992).

Republican president Bush presented a request for $7.2 billion in hurricane relief to Congress on September 8, 1992; immediately, Florida's Democratic governor Chiles announced the real need to be more—$9 billion (Anderson, Lim, and Merzer 1992). Congress, too, apparently found Bush's request less than fully adequate, and approved $8 billion (Anderson 1992d). A study of FEMA disaster payments from 1991 to 1999 found that presidential declarations of disaster and FEMA expenditures are statistically correlated to presidential election years and the electoral importance of the recipient states (Garret and Sobel 2003). The political importance of support for Florida, a critical swing state, was not lost on many. A contentious and ultimately unsuccessful part of both requests was the rebuilding of Homestead Air Force Base, destroyed by the storm, though at the same time other bases around the country were being closed after the demise of the Soviet Union and the end of the Cold War (Anderson 1992b; Long, Anderson, and Merzer 1992; Epstein, Maass, and Merzer 1992; Anderson, Epstein, and Merzer 1992; Fiedler and Thompson 1992).

Democratic presidential challenger Bill Clinton not only visited the area and voiced his support for the reconstruction of Homestead Air Force Base, he also proposed to view the devastation, as reported in the *Miami Herald*, "not only as a challenge to the community, but also as an opportunity," one he would meet as president with massive aid and job

Table 5.1. Presidential election result comparison, 1988 and 1992, Dade County, Florida (by percentage and damage zone)

Damage zone	1988 Bush	1992 Bush	Clinton	Perot	Bush change
North	48.58	42.17	47.33	7.72	-6.41
Middle	58.56	48.61	37.31	12.61	-9.95
South	50.08	36.49	45.75	15.7	-13.59
Absentee	56.14	39.62	46.28	10	-16.52
Average for county	**50.89**	**43.19**	**46.73**	**9.91**	**-7.7**

Note: Includes precincts that overlap damage zones, affecting average figure.
Source: Compiled from Miami-Dade County Elections Department data.

training programs (Fiedler 1992e). Visits to south Dade, proposals, and actual aid efforts were seen by all camps as political maneuvering (Anderson 1992a).

To determine whether all this politicizing of the disaster situation had any electoral effect, an analysis of election results similar to those shown in chapter 4 was conducted (table 5.1). George H. W. Bush won the national presidential contest in 1988 as an incumbent vice president seeking a political promotion following two terms under the remarkably popular Ronald Reagan. Bush took the state of Florida and Dade County, losing only in the northern, heavily Democratic, section of the county.

November elections in 1992 came ten weeks after Hurricane Andrew. Bush lost nationally, took Florida, but lost Dade County. The economy was a major campaign theme for Clinton; economic mismanagement was a theme of Ross Perot's independent initiative. Bush's response to Andrew may also have played a part in the results. Clinton, however, was not in Dade County directing the response, although he did visit the area.

Incumbent Bush lost support in every region of the county in 1992. This is clearly not the same pattern of extreme south Dade support for the incumbent seen in the governor's and cabinet races. Nor is it the exact opposite, with extraordinary support in the south for the Democratic challenger. In this case, the independent candidacy of Ross Perot gave voters an alternative to the two major parties, and some voters took it. In Dade County, voters gave more support to Perot the further south in the county they lived.

This may further indicate that the south Dade support for incumbents in statewide races in 1994 was based on the incumbents' efforts after the hurricane and not on partisanship. In the 1992 presidential contest, south Dade voters rejected the incumbent but did not automatically throw their support behind the Democratic contender. If the one had failed in his responsibilities to south Dade hurricane victims, the other had not been in a position to do anything worthy of gaining support lost by the incumbent.

Perot, on the other hand, was in an unusual position for a challenger. As a somewhat viable alternative to the two major parties—he was at times ahead of the two major party candidates in 1992 opinion polls—Perot was an extremely wealthy individual able and willing to support his own presidential campaign. He dropped out of the race in July, during the Democratic National Convention, and reentered in October. In the interim, Hurricane Andrew hit in late August, and in late September Perot announced that he was donating money to the Salvation Army to help buy a small shopping center in south Dade for use as a distribution center (Fields 1992e).

Incumbent Bush had the institutional resources and responsibility to respond to the disaster. He did respond, but in a manner perceived as slow and clumsy, although eventually his effort was certainly significant. Clinton postured, offered rhetoric about what he would do if he were president, visited the area to commiserate with victims, and explored ways to improve federal disaster response capabilities (a thinly veiled accusation of existing failures).

Perot also visited the area, but he put his money where his mouth was and made a significant investment in a nongovernmental organization heavily involved in the disaster relief activities. He also gave his personal endorsement to, and guarantee of, the Salvation Army. Perot was quoted in the *Miami Herald* as saying, "If anybody ever finds a case where they feel their money was wasted, call me and I'll write a check and give the money back, because that is my level of confidence in the Salvation Army" (Fields 1992e).

Politics may be seen as positive (for example, powers that act to enable relief or aid) or negative (such as competitive or conflicting processes that obstruct relief) (Davis 1978). The vast response and personal involvement of elected officials in south Dade County after Hurricane Andrew, as well perhaps as one billionaire challenger, virtually assured positive perceptions from the hardest-hit victims.

*   *   *

We Will Rebuild sprang up from local business and political leaders and got to work quickly, raising eleven million dollars within four weeks of Andrew (Satterfield 1992h). This caused some resentment from existing agencies. But relief organizations frequently exhibit competition and resent new agencies raising funds and doing what they perceive as their jobs, although service is not usually affected by this competition (Barton 1970). To maintain support, existing agencies need to receive recognition for their work. Big disasters enable such organizations to collect funds they may need for less dramatic events (Deutscher and New 1961). Credit for work after disasters helps agencies in other ways—moving into new areas (geographical or functional), proving their value, or defining their role (for example, the Red Cross as appropriate for disaster relief and not government).

Change and conflict were present after Andrew, yet elected officials were generally not adversely affected by turmoil and resentment. Continuity seems to be another norm after disasters (Quarantelli and Dynes 1977). Post-disaster conflict is frequently similar to pre-disaster cleavages (Quarantelli and Dynes 1976; Stalling and Schepart 1990). In cases where change is occurring prior to a disaster, the change may be accelerated afterwards, or where forces protect the status quo beforehand, these protections may be temporarily weakened such that change may occur. Even disaster relief programs may be oriented to return people to the status quo ante, including the relative status of the haves and have-nots (Feld 1973).

In the words of Quarantelli and Dynes (1976), "In general, there is continuity from the pre- to the post-disaster state, but under particular conditions certain major changes can occur, and these may be functional or dysfunctional, depending on the evaluative stance taken" (36). Change continuing or accelerating after an event is in fact a form of continuity—the change itself continues.

Accordingly, it might be expected that a disaster will not change much in the community, outside of physical damage and event-related casualties, which are of course significant in their own right. We should then predict that elected officials would be relatively immune from retributive voting after a disaster, unless their hold on office was tenuous before. Victims pull together, become a more close-knit, cohesive community, and appreciate leadership provided. They feel optimistic about their future, and they continue to support the officials they have previously elected.

Florida officials saw the need to make a number of organizational changes due to Andrew so that the state would be better prepared to respond to future disasters. William Anderson (1973) studied organizations after a major Alaskan earthquake in 1964, determining that some combination of four factors were present wherever long-term organizational changes occurred. In Andrew's case, at least two of those factors were present: (1) New external demands were generated by the hurricane; and (2) new or different structures and authorities were determined to be important. Organizational changes were made by state leaders; there was no parallel perceived need to change the state leaders themselves.

Former Utah governor Scott Matheson dealt with a variety of crises during his term in office, including both a major drought and a major flood (Matheson 1986). He found that even bad mistakes "created a learning opportunity. You can become a more effective governor by learning from your mistakes. . . . If you're fortunate, and the mistakes are not too disastrous, you can recover" (195). Matheson advised that the visibility of the governor after a significant event must be high and that the governor is expected to take charge: not to work miracles, but to be a competent leader.

Governor Chiles and the other incumbents included in this study appear to have done just that—demonstrated competent leadership. The devastation of Hurricane Andrew may have uncovered faults, but systematic analysis enabled the state to learn from its shortcomings and strengthen its ability for future governors to do better.

Matheson also held that a governor must—and after a disaster uniquely can—marshal the forces of all levels of government and the private sector to follow his lead. Florida's elected leadership followed another of Matheson's recommendations: "the governor is responsible for doing whatever is reasonably necessary in the public interest in a crisis situation, allowing the public and the legislature to later judge whether that course of action was correct" (1986, 201).

After Andrew, the Florida legislature worked with the governor and cabinet, supporting actions taken, finding new resources for Dade County recovery, providing state officials more authority and better resources for future disasters, and attempting to alleviate lasting problems. The public did not find incumbent responses lacking, and there is no evidence of any retributive voting or negative/attack campaigning due to this storm. On the contrary, there was renewed support and appreciation for those incumbents from the south Dade County area, which was hardest hit by the storm. For these statewide candidates, however, that spike in support was helpful but probably not decisive.

Now we turn to the third and final level of elected officials: city mayors and council members in Dade County. Elections for state and federal offices are regularly scheduled so that voters go to the polls in November of even-numbered years, incorporating positions with terms of two, four, or six years in length. Dade's municipalities typically avoid November elections. This complicates the study, since each of the seven municipalities included held elections at different times after the hurricane. The following chapters shift the focus to disaster zones—south, middle, and north. We begin with the hardest-hit southern zone where Homestead and Florida City are located.

6

In The Eye

Incumbents from Severely Damaged Cities

Local government is the cornerstone of our democratic society, which is based on the concept of self-rule. This chapter explores the elections for city council and mayor, from 1980 through 2002, in the two cities hit hardest by Hurricane Andrew in order to identify trends of incumbent success and any changes to these trends after Andrew. Next, the incumbents' perception of the impact Andrew had on their political careers is analyzed. Subsequent chapters will explore the same issues for municipalities further from the fury of this powerful storm's eye wall.

Not every incumbent seeks to stay in office, but most do. Few challengers throw their hats into the ring, but some do. When both incumbent and challenger enter the contest, the incumbent has advantages, as outlined in the first chapter. There are mixed indications of changes in incumbency advantage in local elections after Hurricane Andrew: southern-zone mayors appear to have gained support, whereas commissioners fared slightly worse at the polls.

This chapter, as well as chapters 7 and 8, draws on interviews with municipal incumbents who were in office when Andrew struck and who ran for reelection against competition in the first elections after the hurricane. The incumbents provided the primary interviews for the research, but interviews were also conducted with persons the incumbents identified as important to them and to their campaigns.

The study originally sought to interview campaign managers, campaign treasurers/fund-raisers, and/or key aides. These municipalities, however, are small. Many of the incumbents interviewed ran their own campaigns, raised their own funds, and sometimes provided much, if not all, of the funds themselves. One municipal incumbent never asked for or accepted funds for her campaign because she saw campaign donations as similar to lobbying, a practice with which she did not agree. This may be an extreme position, but many small city races do not require much fund-raising.

The Florida Constitution grants the Dade County Commission power to create and abolish municipalities under its home-rule authority (Article VIII, Section 11). Municipalities, once created, establish their own governmental structures, determine eligibility for elected officers, and set election rules. The city clerk administers elections, hires precinct workers, and manages candidate eligibility issues and campaign financial reports. Municipal clerks contract with county election departments to prepare ballots and use voting equipment. A municipal canvassing committee, frequently made up of members of the city council, resolves questions over such issues as absentee ballots and certifies the official results.

Candidates for municipal office in Florida are required to file a form designating a campaign treasurer or deputy treasurer and providing information about the campaign's bank account, which must be established before they can qualify to run. It turns out that many local candidates serve as their own campaign treasurers, or list a spouse or other family member as the nominal treasurer. If the treasurer is not the candidate, she or he may have assisted only in filling out reporting forms and/or keeping track of contributions and expenditures—with little or no involvement with fund-raising or the campaign.

Most of the incumbents interviewed stated that they ran their own campaigns or had key advisers who had since died or were otherwise unavailable. Three offered one secondary referral, and two provided two. That is, the limited number of secondary referrals was not a result of any lack of cooperation by the primary subjects, but rather an artifact of "small campaigns for small positions." As one incumbent stated:

> Well I really did my own thing. But this is grassroots politics here, you realize that? . . . The turnout for the election is three or four thousand votes. And if you don't shake those four thousand people's hands, they're not going to vote for you. It's that simple. If you don't go to their doorstep they don't vote. . . . I had a treasurer . . . a woman, but I used her only because I thought I should have one. Actually I used her only for the name. Because she was big with one of the churches here, so I let her be my treasurer. . . . The psychology of it, you know.

Subjects interviewed provided insights into campaigns in small cities, as well as into their victories and losses. They also provided valuable information about what they saw as the effects of a natural disaster on their election chances.

The South Zone

Florida City and Homestead were the two cities subjected to Andrew's most severe winds (see figure 4, chapter 1). Damage within these municipalities was worse than in any other incorporated jurisdiction of Dade County. Homestead, with an elected mayor-councilman and six council members, was the first of the two devastated cities to hold elections after Andrew, having a November election cycle in odd-numbered years. Tables 6.1 and 6.2 depict incumbent trends from 1981 through 2001, for mayor and for city council, respectively.

Homestead's mayor serves a two-year term. Four mayoral transitions have occurred in Homestead in these twenty-one years. In 1981 and 1987,

Table 6.1. Homestead mayoral incumbents, 1981–2001

Year	Incumbent running	Incumbent won	Incumbent unopposed
1981	Yes	No	No
1983	Yes	Yes	No
1985	Yes	Yes	No
1987	No	N/A	N/A
1989	Yes	Yes	Yes
1991	Yes	Yes	Yes
Subtotal	5 of 6 (83%)	4 of 5 (80%)	2 of 5 (40%)
ANDREW			
1993	Yes	Yes	Yes
1995	Yes	Yes	Yes
1997	No	N/A	N/A
1999	Yes	Yes	No
2001	Yes*	Yes	No
Subtotal	4 of 5 (80%)	4 of 4 (100%)	2 of 4 (50%)
Total	**9 of 11 (82%)**	**8 of 9 (89%)**	**4 of 9 (44%)**

*Incumbent became mayor from council vice mayor position when the mayor at that time resigned to become county manager.
Sources: Miami-Dade County Elections Department; *Miami Herald*, 1981c, 1983c, 1987g, 1987h, 1991f, 1995b; Kollars, 1983a, 1983b; Ulrich, 1985a, 1985b, 1985c; Rowe, 1989; de la Cruz, 1991; Acle and Hartman, 1993; Hartman, 1993b; Musibay, 1995; Etheart, 1997b; Martinez, 1999; Figueras, 2001a, 2001b, 2001c.

Table 6.2. Homestead city council incumbents, 1981–2001

Year	Incumbent running	Incumbent won	Won four-year term
1981	4	0 (0%)	N/A
1983	3	2 (67%)	1 (50%)
1985	3	3 (100%)	1 (33%)
1987	2	2 (100%)	2 (100%)
1989	3	3 (100%)	2 (67%)
1991	4	4 (100%)	2 (50%)
Subtotal	**19**	**14 (74%)**	**8 (57%)**
ANDREW			
1993	3	3 (100%)	1 (33%)
1995	4	3 (75%)	1 (33%)
1997	2	2 (100%)	1 (50%)
1999	3	3 (100%)	2 (67%)
2001	5*	2 (40%)	0 (0%)
Subtotal	17	13 (76%)	5 (38%)
Total	**36**	**27 (75%)**	**13 (48%)**

*Mayor Steve Shiver was appointed to the county manager position for Miami-Dade County early in 2001. Vice Mayor Roscoe Warren then became acting mayor, and Cheryl Arroyave-Sweeney was appointed to fill his vacant council seat on an interim basis. Warren's term would have been up in 2003; the special election to fill his term was held with the regular election.

Sources: Miami-Dade County Elections Department; Miami Herald, 1981b, 1981c, 1983c, 1985c, 1987h, 1989c, 1991f, 1995b; Kollars, 1983a, 1983b; Ulrich, 1985a, 1985b, 1985c; Rowe, 1989; de la Cruz, 1991; Acle and Hartman, 1993; Hartman, 1993b, 1993c; Musibay, 1995; Etheart, 1997b; Martinez, 1999; Figueras, 2001a, 2001b, 2001c.

and after the hurricane in 1997 and 2001, new mayors came from the ranks of elected council members, and the only case of an incumbent defeat occurred before Hurricane Andrew (1981). The only mayoral candidate in 1997 was Steve Shiver, who had been elected to a four-year council term in 1993.

Incumbents in Homestead ran for reelection about as often after the storm (four of five elections) as before (five of six). The increased time commitment required by the job after the hurricane was noted, however, as a key reason that Tad DeMilly, the mayor at the time of the storm, did not seek reelection in 1997 (Etheart 1997a)—a full five years, and in the third election cycle, after Hurricane Andrew.

In the six Homestead elections before Andrew, incumbent mayors won reelection most of the time (four of five elections) and were unopposed less than half of the time (two of five elections). In the five elections after the hurricane, incumbents who sought reelection were always successful (four of four elections) and were unopposed half of the time (two of four elections).

The lack of opposition may reflect a stronger incumbency advantage for Homestead's mayor because of Andrew. Perhaps the position became less desirable—thus resulting in fewer challenges—because the job required more effort and time, but its rewards did not increase. As with most of the municipalities studied, Homestead's city manager is responsible for the day-to-day operation of the city, and the mayor and council members serve, if not as volunteers, on a part-time basis. For example, from 1992 through 2003, Homestead commissioners received an annual salary of $4,800; the mayor received $6,000 (Rowe 1989; Ousley 1992; Auxier 2003).

Candidates for city council in Homestead ran as a group for open seats, with four open in a normal election. Municipal elections in Dade County are nonpartisan. The two candidates with the highest number of votes won four-year seats; the two next-highest won two-year seats. The number of candidates determined whether a primary election was to be held. Homestead has since changed to district commission seats.

Incumbency is traditionally strong on the Homestead City Council. Twenty-seven of thirty-six incumbents who sought reelection from 1981 through 2001 won; four council members advanced to mayor—two before Andrew (1981, 1987) and two after (1997, 2001). There was virtually no difference in incumbency success in the periods before and after the storm: fourteen of nineteen before Andrew and thirteen of seventeen after.

As noted above, candidates won four-year or two-year terms, depending on the number of votes received. Between 1981 and 2001, slightly fewer than half of the successful incumbents won the longer terms. It is interesting to note, however, that half were successful before Andrew, but only one-third were successful after. In 1989 and 1991, only two candidates won four-year terms, and they were incumbents. In no election since the disaster, however, have two incumbents captured the longer term.

In the two Homestead elections immediately before Andrew and in the first three post-hurricane elections there were insufficient numbers of candidates to require a primary election. Thus, Hurricane Andrew was not the cause of the decrease in competition in the elections after it struck, although it may have been a factor in the continuation of that trend. The hurricane was a major factor in the reduced number of voters

Table 6.3. Florida City mayoral incumbents, 1980–2002

Year	Incumbent running	Incumbent won	Incumbent unopposed
1980	Yes	Yes	No
1982	Yes	Yes	No
1984	Yes	No	No
1986	Yes	Yes	Yes
1988	Yes	Yes	Yes
1990	Yes	Yes	No
1992	Yes	Yes	Yes
Subtotal	7	6 (86%)	3 (43%)
ANDREW			
1994	Yes	Yes	Yes
1996	Yes	Yes	No
1998	Yes	Yes	Yes
2000	Yes	Yes	Yes
2002	Yes	Yes	Yes
Subtotal	5	5 (100%)	4 (80%)
Total	12	11 (92%)	7 (58%)

Sources: Miami-Dade County Elections Department; Florida City Office of the City Clerk; Andrews and Gressette, 1980; Ulrich, 1982a, 1982b, 1984; Gonzalez, 1996a; *Miami Herald*, 1980a, 1986a, 1998a, 2000a.

in November 1993. In Homestead municipal elections, however, it was rare for more than 30 percent of registered voters to participate.

Florida City, the smaller of the two hardest-hit municipalities, has five elected officials: a mayor (two-year term) and four commissioners (staggered four-year terms). Elections are held in January in even-numbered years. The first elections after Hurricane Andrew were held in January 1994, nearly twenty months after the storm, when the mayoral position and two of the commission seats were filled; in January 1996, two incumbent commissioners were up for reelection.

Tables 6.3 and 6.4 show the pattern of Florida City incumbent success from 1980 to 2002. The mayor's office has changed hands only once since 1980, the incumbent having been ousted in 1984. That incumbent had been challenged in both of the previous elections, but had been able to stave off the competition. The mayor in office since the 1984 election has seen opposition only twice, in 1990 and 1996. More generally, prior to Hurricane Andrew incumbents had been unopposed in only three of seven elections, whereas after the hurricane the incumbent was unopposed in four out of five elections. Thus, incumbency strength may have changed after Hurricane Andrew.

Table 6.4. Florida City commission incumbents, 1980–2002

Year	Incumbent running	Incumbent won	Incumbent unopposed
1980	0	N/A	0
1982	1	1	0
1984	1	1	0
1986	1	1	0
1988	1	1	0
1990	2	2	0
1992	2	2	0
Subtotal	8	8 (100%)	0
ANDREW			
1994	2	2	0
1996	2	1*	0
1998	2	2	0
2000	2	1*	0
2002	2	2**	2
Subtotal	10	8 (80%)	2 (20%)
Total	18	16 (89%)	2 (11%)

*Incumbents defeated by former commissioners. In 1992, Commissioner Israel Andrews resigned to run for state legislature. In 1996, he won his seat back, gaining more votes than Commissioner Juanita Smith, who then won in 2000, when Andrews lost the seat.
**No election held as there was no challenger.
Sources: Miami-Dade County Elections Department; Florida City Office of the City Clerk; Andrews and Gressette, 1980; Arthur, 1994; Ulrich, 1982a, 1982b, 1984; Gonzalez, 1996a; Miami Herald, 1980a, 1986a, 1986b, 1988a, 1992a, 1998a, 2000a.

Although this potential change is interesting, because it reflects a pattern similar to that of the Homestead mayor, the consolidation of support for the mayor could be due to other factors, including personal characteristics of the incumbent or the distribution of favors or patronage unrelated to the disaster. In 1990, voters in this small, poor city agreed to change from a strong to a weak mayor system, reducing the position to a part-time job (Rowe 1990). However, the city manager resigned in 1994, and the part-time mayor became acting city manager, increasing his salary from $4,440 to $55,046. In 1996, voters decided to return to the strong mayor system (Gonzalez 1996a). Otis Wallace, first elected Florida City mayor in 1984 after serving eight years on the city commission (Ulrich 1984), was in office throughout these changes and remained mayor in 2009, with his salary increasing to $96,499 in 2003 and to $146,089 by 2009 (Paul 2003; Lyle 2009).

Two of the four four-year seats on the Florida City commission are up for election every two years. A block of candidates runs for the available seats, and the two candidates with the most votes win. With two exceptions, every Florida City incumbent seeking reelection since 1980 has been successful. The exceptions were in 1996, the second election held after the hurricane, when former commissioner Israel Andrews defeated incumbent Juanita Smith, and in 2000, when Smith came back to best Andrews.

The only potentially hurricane-related change evident in Florida City commission elections (based on these data) is that incumbent commissioners became more likely to stand for reelection. It cannot be for the salaries: annual 1992 compensation for commissioners was $3,000, where it remained until 1999, when it increased to $4,400 (as of 2009 it had grown to $10,400).

No campaign finance information was available for Homestead or Florida City for the election prior to Andrew or for the first two elections after the hurricane. In the southern severe damage zone, no consistent hurricane-related trends could be derived from this analysis. Mayors may have fared slightly better since the hurricane, but council/commission members seem to have done slightly worse; Homestead incumbents were less likely to win longer terms.

Incumbents thus continued to fare well in both cities within Dade County's severe damage zone, even if the number of cases is small. In fact, only seven individuals have filled the mayoral posts in the two cities from 1980 through 2002—five in Homestead and two in Florida City. There is only a slight indication that the incumbent strength may have increased for the top job, but it is certainly clear that it has not declined. The possible slight erosion in incumbent success among commissioners apparent thus far comes from defeat by former commissioners in Florida City—in the first of the two cases, a former incumbent who had resigned to run for another position then returned to the commission; in the other case, a former incumbent won her seat back after one term out of office—and shorter terms, not defeats, in Homestead. Other factors that came into play and impacted incumbents' success at the polls will be discussed later.

Seven former incumbent officials (five of whom were currently elected officials at the time of their interviews) and one secondary individual were interviewed from the southern damage zone. Half the subjects interviewed were white non-Latino/a, half were African American, while gender was equally divided. The first post-hurricane election for these incumbents occurred variously in November 1993, January 1994, November

1995, and January 1996, representing a time span of fourteen to thirty-nine months after Hurricane Andrew, given different election schedules for the cities and staggered terms.

Effects of the Hurricane

As noted previously, nearly every building in the southern zone was affected, with taxable property value dropping by 78 percent in Florida City and 61 percent in Homestead (Dash 1995). Incumbent descriptions of the physical damage were brief, blunt, and poignant: "flattened," "destroyed my community," "twenty-four square miles of devastation," "it looked like an atomic bomb went off," and "everyone was affected."

Andrew's destruction wiped out the municipal property tax base, the predominant source of city income in Florida. These losses were offset initially by infusions of funds from the Federal Emergency Management Administration (FEMA), but some incumbents saw this as a source of two types of later problems for Florida City and Homestead: (1) Some grants targeted to specific tasks were insufficient to complete all aspects of a project; and (2) grant funds supported new types of jobs and new employees who, because they had expertise unavailable in the local community, were outsiders—and were consequently resented.

Recovery and rebuilding involved an extraordinary amount of work, much of it funded by federal grants. Staff was hired and expert consultants brought in. Federal grants, however, are temporary, and funds eventually dried up. Homestead resorted to service cuts and personnel layoffs, perhaps the first such cuts in Homestead's history according to the respondent.

Both people and businesses suffered from the nearly total destruction of buildings in the southern zone. Many residents moved away—in Homestead, primarily the middle class. Much of that loss came from the destruction and closing of Homestead Air Force Base, as described by the respondent from the city:

> You don't realize what you have in a military base until you don't have one. That's another city. It's a city with tentacles, because people come for the, retired people come for the hospital and the other benefits of the base. Families move because families are in the service. And when that left, I'm telling you that was one, one of the biggest blows that we've had and still feel the effects, because

we don't, people that we have here now, while we have the same number of people, they don't have the disposable income that those people had.

The base was indeed a major economic engine in south Dade, with some 8,700 employees generating about $152 million in payroll (Provenzo and Provenzo 2002, 132–33). Base amenities also attracted military retirees, some 21,000 of whom lived in the area. The base closure meant an annual loss to the south Dade area of about $430 million.

These losses highlighted the differences between Homestead and Florida City, as well as between different ethnic groups. Homestead respondents, black and white, spoke of the problems associated with the middle- and upper-class flight. Those who left—90 percent of some retirement communities and those associated with the air force base—took away their disposable income, community involvement, and voting habits. In a world of "givers" and "takers," the official explained, those who left were givers. Many who initially replaced them moved into subsidized multi-family dwellings built after the hurricane (see Hartman 1993a), had little disposable income, and exhibited more limited community involvement. They were poorer, less likely to be citizens, and included some who were undocumented.

Florida City was one of the poorest cities in the nation before the storm. When asked about population changes after the hurricane, a white non-Latino/a respondent said, "we had some leave, but not that many," whereas black respondents believed that many left—about 30 percent of the population, one estimated. One of the respondents thought that most who left were poor; another suggested that people from a mix of socioeconomic classes departed. One said that employers from Tampa, Orlando, and Jacksonville came with buses to transport people to new homes and jobs. Many never returned to Florida City.

Given the general perception of a substantial change in the population of these municipalities, it is also important to determine to what extent the voter base changed. After all, the population of the city of Homestead in 1990 was 26,866, whereas the number of registered voters at that time was only 7,482 (Bureau of the Census 1992; Miami-Dade County Elections Department data). Thousands of people could have left without the voter base being affected at all. The voter base, however, was affected by the exodus from both cities (see table 6.5).

Table 6.5. Voter registration pre- and post-Andrew, Florida City and Homestead, Florida

	1990	1992	1994	1998
Florida City	2,612	2,408	1,895	2,722
Homestead	7,482	6,559	5,650	8,047

Note: Since book closing for registration occurs twenty-nine days before the election, the September 1992 primary registration reflects registered voters at the time of the August 24 hurricane.
Source: Data used were from "Voters Who Voted" reports issued by the Miami-Dade County Elections Department for the November general elections in 1990, 1994, and 1998 (when elections for Florida's governor and cabinet as well as U.S. Congress were held) and the September primary in 1992.

Florida City lost over 21 percent of its voters between August 1992 and November 1994; Homestead lost nearly 14 percent during the same period. By 1998, both cities had more than recovered from these losses through a combination of new residents moving in, residents becoming citizens, and newly registered voters. Given the general perception among incumbents from these municipalities that there was a substantial shift in population but that the hurricane did not affect electoral chances, a deeper analysis is needed.

Although the total number of registered voters decreased after the hurricane, the partisan mix (table 6.6) remained virtually the same. After a slight increase (1 percent) in 1994, the percentage of registered

Table 6.6. Voter registration percentage by party pre- and post-Andrew, Florida City and Homestead, Florida

	1990	1992	1994	1998
FLORIDA CITY				
Democrat	78.5	78.6	79.9	74.7
Republican	14.5	13.5	12.5	11.2
Other	6.9	7.8	7.6	14.1
HOMESTEAD				
Democrat	58.1	56.4	57.1	51.6
Republican	31.2	31.7	30.0	27.6
Other	10.7	12.0	12.9	20.8

Source: "Voters Who Voted" reports issued by the Miami-Dade County Elections Department for the November general elections in 1990, 1994, and 1998, as well as the September 1992 primary.

Democrats in Florida City decreased by 1998 (-4 percent) but remained the preponderant group at 75 percent, whereas other registrations, such as those registering with minor parties or with no party affiliation, nearly doubled, increasing to 14 percent. The percentage of Democrats in Homestead also declined (by less than 5 percent) to 52 percent in 1998, and the percentage of registrations with other than the two major parties also nearly doubled, from 11 percent in 1990 to 21 percent in 1998. The decline in the dominant Democratic Party and the rise in independent and minor party registrations were common throughout Dade County and Florida during this period. The only unusual phenomenon seen in the figures for the southern zone cities is the slight decrease in Republican registrations.

In each city, the percentage of non-Latino/a white voters declined by nearly 16 percent, whereas the percentage of Latino/as increased. This is a continuation of a trend throughout the county that seems to have begun before the hurricane. Thus, although the population and the number of registered voters dropped significantly immediately after Andrew, the change in the ethnic mix of the registered voters in these two cities does not appear to be directly hurricane related.

In the early days after the storm, incumbents described working twelve hours a day, seven days a week at city hall, stabilizing the situation (and some people), handing out food and water, trying to stop looting, and making sure that citizens had a place to sleep and something—anything—to wear. The emphasis was on rescuing citizens. Although elected officials were equally impacted by the hurricane in terms of damage to homes and loss of normal working conditions, one respondent noted emphatically that council members asked for no special treatment as public officials.

The incumbents' perception of their constituencies' condition clearly improved with time. When asked what proportion of the constituencies were suffering at the time of the first reelection bid after the hurricane, those in the first wave of reelections (fourteen to sixteen months post-Andrew) used such terms as "most," "very much so," and "85 percent still suffering . . . looking for leadership." By the end of the second cycle (January 1996, approximately forty months after Andrew), however, the typical response was "very little . . . about a quarter."

Did disaster issues play a part in their campaigns? Many incumbents in the first round believed so, but that perception decreased during the three and a half years between the hurricane and the last group of the first post-disaster reelections, as reflected in the issues noted as part of their reelection efforts by the seven incumbents:

- *November 1993*: Rebuilding; campaign centered on the Homestead Economic Rebuilding Organization (HERO) and encouraging citizens to hang in there, stay, and be part of rebuilding effort.
- *November 1993*: "It did not play too much of a part as far as campaigning goes. . . . I don't really believe that the disaster itself proved a positive or negative situation as far as reelection goes."
- *November 1993*: "You know, I really don't remember. I'm sure I spoke about reconstruction and I'm sure I spoke about spending the dollars wisely."
- *January 1994*: What and how of rebuilding—homes, government buildings, tax base to generate business.
- *January 1994*: "I felt like the public knew me; that I was close to them for the whole time, during the storm. Normally most, 50 or 55 percent of them I seen [*sic*] daily. And I really didn't get out and campaign. . . . I didn't change my pattern of helping to run for office."
- *November 1995*: "I don't know if we had any, because there was, we had so much help. We just got so much help, from everybody— We Will Rebuild and all the other agencies. And the city was kind of a go-between . . . a facilitator in helping these other organizations help people."
- *January 1996 (t + 40 months)*: "Not much. Very little. Everyone knew everyone . . . since we'd all been together. We didn't have any new candidates."

One casualty of Hurricane Andrew was the Cleveland Indians' anticipated move from Winter Haven to Homestead for spring training, initially delayed for a year after the new Homestead stadium suffered severe damage. A combination of factors, including efforts by the Winter Haven City Commission to upgrade the facility there and the loss of infrastructure and population in Homestead needed to support baseball, led to the Indians' decision to stay in Winter Haven (Habib and Brennan 1993). One incumbent spoke of sharing outrage with her constituency about this decision.

The earlier analysis demonstrated that few challengers emerged in the Florida City and Homestead elections after Andrew. This point was not lost on the incumbents interviewed. Where new challengers did emerge, few were seen as entering the race because of the hurricane. Steve Shiver, as noted in chapter 1, has given the hurricane as the reason he entered public service, but it appears to have been more of a timing effect, not a fundamentally novel decision. It came as no surprise to his new colleagues that he ran for a commission seat, one stating simply, "Well, of course, Steve did, Steve Shiver did [run after Andrew]. However, I think he would have come anyhow."

Another detailed the predictive evidence:

> No, we all always knew that Steve Shiver was interested in politics and he was going to eventually run because he was sitting on some of the boards, like the planning and zoning board. You'll find in most, most candidates running have served in some capacity in the city, and at some point will take the next step. Steve was one of those. . . . So we had anticipated Steve was going to run. No doubt.

Only one incumbent in the two cities did not run for reelection after Andrew. In retrospect, some of his fellow commissioners believed the hurricane to be the cause. One speculated that that incumbent "didn't want to live here anymore. So that could, that was a contributing factor. . . . He's the only one who left, 'cause he didn't want to live here anymore." Another was certain, stating that the former colleague "did not even seek reelection because based on the remaining population his chances were nil in terms of getting reelected." A third incumbent, however, had a different spin:

> No, no, no, no. He served, I think, two terms on the city council and retired and his health was not that great. So he decided not to run anymore. And they owned five acres of land in Maine. When he was in the Navy he was stationed up in that area. He liked that area so he bought five acres of land. . . . He could have stayed on and won an election again. . . . He was popular; he had no problem about winning elections. He could have won again and if he wanted to he'd be on there today.

Further clarification confirmed the latter explanation. A heart attack had led to heart surgery, then retirement. Retirement property had been purchased long before the hurricane, thus Andrew was not the cause of his relocation.

Overall, incumbents did not see challenger quality as being any different in either of the first two elections after Andrew. In Florida City, only one new face was seen in the political fray in the 1994/1996 round, and she was a well-known person whose family was from the area—a newcomer would have had a harder time entering the contest. In the second round of elections after the hurricane (1998/2000), one additional individual ran for a commission seat, and he was related to an incumbent who considered his own family his primary political asset. Two other challengers entered three of the four elections, but both had previously been on the commission. Thus, no incumbent believed that the hurricane led to new challengers.

Two of the subjects interviewed, however, advised that the election after a disaster would in fact be a good time for a challenger to mount a bid for office. They held that in the aftermath of a disaster there would be a relatively small proportion of available and interested voters, and a challenge could be successful with a small but dedicated constituency, essentially allowing someone to get into office and then build a "real" reelection constituency afterwards.

This advice was not evident in the empirical data reviewed, but is consistent with Fenno's description of "concentric" congressional constituencies (1978, 1). He found congressmen relying on an "intimate" constituency for political advice and emotional support (24), a "primary" constituency of strong partisan supporters (18), a "reelection" constituency of potential/periodic supporters (8), and a geographic constituency of everyone in the district (1), including those who do not support him or who do not even vote.

Since Homestead commissioners may serve either two-year or four-year terms, the first and second elections after Andrew for Homestead incumbents occurred in the 1993, 1995, and 1997 elections. A total of six individuals challenged incumbents in those three elections. In 1993, the three challengers in the race were all civically active, but incumbents saw their own positions as safe, especially because one commissioner's departure left an opening. One noted that, "other than filling that vacancy there wasn't too much of a challenge."

Contemporary news reports depicted the winner of that vacant seat to be supportive of—and supported by—the incumbents running for re-election, whereas the one candidate who suggested a different strategy for the council (concentration on immediate needs rather than "grand designs for the future") was framed as a negative campaigner and defeated in spite of being able to raise substantial funds (Hartman 1993c). That challenger had opposed an incumbent-supported charter amendment that was defeated in a September 1993 primary in which only 279 voters participated (Hartman 1993b, 1993d). The increase to 1,500 voters in the general election two months later, when all incumbents seeking reelection were returned to office, was seen as a vindication of those incumbents' efforts.

The incumbents generally stood together and worked well together, according to their own recollections, although one respondent said, "I think they all [the Homestead Commission] became much more of a cohesive group, you know, after the hurricane," which "carried over into the city as well." One notable post-Andrew division saw a commissioner fight, alone, for the removal of the city manager, only to lose his own 1995 reelection bid some four months later (Musibay 1995). The lone challenger in that election, a building industry business owner who had long included his face in company advertisements, was successful, eliminating the then-controversial incumbent.

In 1997, one commissioner chose not to seek reelection, and another ran (unopposed) for mayor, leaving two vacancies to be filled. One of the three challengers had run before, and the two successful candidates were likely challengers with strong name recognition (one was both well-known and the first Latino/a to run) and/or connections (another had family in the banking industry and a long-time commissioner for a father-in-law).

In only one case did a southern zone incumbent believe that someone had entered a post-Andrew race because of the hurricane. That challenger decided to get involved, the incumbent recalled, because he was frustrated with the council's direction in rebuilding, believed more needed to be done, and was critical of apparent failures of some post-Andrew reconstruction strategies. A former commissioner first elected there in 1989 summed up the general perception: "We have a group of old coots that perennially run. And those are the ones who recycled through then. They were there before and after [Andrew]."

The general sentiment of the incumbents interviewed seems to be summed up in these retrospective assessments offered by two who stood for reelection in Homestead and Florida City, respectively, in the first round of post-disaster reelections. The first:

I think probably it kept some people out of politics because they were so busy trying to reestablish things, and work. And it was not a particularly enviable task, to be caught in the middle of the political arena here, for a long time. People just didn't want to be bothered for a long time. And many of the people who, probably, would have been interested had left, had moved, gone away . . . [the election of 2001] was the first time that people really began to move into that arena.

The second:

At that time there were a lot of struggles . . . a lot of people doing different things in their lives, trying to get their lives, even, back together. So the farthest thing from their minds was running for political office right then.

Incumbents generally did not see any difference in the style or content of opponents' campaigns—in their words—first because "we really didn't have that many opponents," and second, because "there wasn't [sic] a lot of issues you could raise because we really had no control over a lot of things." If anything, the disaster benefited the incumbents, as one who stood for reelection just sixteen months after Andrew discussed:

I think they [the challengers] were affected too, and they understood what it was all about, and they could not have done anything any different from what we did. It was just a difficult time and we all had to pull together. And I think the campaign, the election, was really secondary to our situation, and probably because of the fact that we were in office at the time, and we didn't cause the disaster—nature caused it—and therefore, we were there, we probably did benefit somewhat at the time, the election time, to trying to do some positive things to get straightened out. You know, it just happened that the election time was just around the corner. Had it not been around the corner we would have done exactly the same thing.

Campaign strategies were affected by the severity of the damage, the most drastic adjustment being the incumbent who said that he did not campaign in January 1994 because he was too busy helping people—which could be seen as surrogate campaigning, or campaigning without campaigning. In practical terms, fewer buildings meant there were fewer meeting places and fewer people attending meetings. In addition, there was little or no speaking to community groups because there were fewer groups having meetings. Travel was impeded, and one former council member noted that the "local paper's . . . ability to generate news and distribute their papers was very restricted, which was our primary source of getting the message out."

One elected official had to establish telephone banks as a campaign strategy in lieu of his normal door-to-door canvassing. "There were some areas that were messed up so bad that you couldn't campaign because of fear of crime, violence. And then some . . . homeowners associations had some restrictions on people entering their areas." Yet the strategy adjustments did not harm incumbents. On the contrary, "if you had name recognition, the incumbent had a tremendous advantage," one explained. All candidates had difficulty finding people; mailing and voter lists available from the county election department had become inaccurate because so many people had moved within and outside of the city due to storm damage. Thus challengers would have had a more difficult time developing the same level of name recognition already attained by incumbents.

Funds Flow

With the intense damage, dislocation of residents, and revised campaign strategies, one might expect that campaign fund-raising would also be problematic. It certainly was not for the incumbents. Only one recalled raising substantially less, and that was his decision: because of the condition of the community and its residents, he chose not to solicit funds. He was offered, and accepted, some financial support, but he mostly financed the campaign himself. A more typical response to fund-raising after the hurricane was that in a small city not much money is needed anyway, and so no difference was noted after Andrew.

The explanation from one former commissioner about raising funds was explicit:

> Let me tell you, when you're an elected official and you have all the suppliers that you have from the city, the attorneys, you can almost go down the list of contributors and see that they have something to do with the city. You don't have any trouble raising money. I hate to tell that, but that's the truth."

Personal finances after the storm were also altered in unexpected ways. By the time of the first reelection efforts (fourteen to sixteen months after Andrew), insurance and federal disaster assistance checks had been distributed to a large portion of the hardest-hit populations, including the residents of Homestead and Florida City.

As one former commissioner put it:

It was easy. . . . Remember . . . the infusion of dollars . . . was just tremendous. And to be honest with you, people were getting their insurance proceeds far exceeding the value of the property. Even the poor were getting vouchers and grants from FEMA. So money was plentiful.

Another said: "No . . . there was thirty billion dollars in insurance money that came into south Dade, and most people were not strapped, financially. I've never had problems raising money. I've never raised a lot, but then again it didn't take a lot."

Nicole Dash (1995) found that Florida City residents, the majority poor and black, received far less assistance than Homestead residents in the first year after the storm. Inequality may have lessened in subsequent years. The pecuniary largess seems to have reached its apex by January 1996, in time for the last of the first round of post-Andrew elections. As one officeholder at the time described: "That year I had more money. . . . People that I never heard of . . . contributed. . . . It was flourishing, money was, and I didn't even have to ask for much. . . . I had more money that year than I've ever had in my campaign."

It is interesting that the only two incumbents who lost in this first round of reelection bids after the storm were the last to stand for reelection, in November 1995 and January 1996. The second of these defeated incumbents attributed the loss to the fact that there was more money than normal, so they were busy doing things not normally part of the campaign. More funds allowed the commissioner to rent a car, bullhorn, and coordinate a large number of paid campaign workers—instead of spending the usual time at precincts soliciting votes on Election Day.

Municipal elections in Dade County are nonpartisan. In some jurisdictions and in some elections, however, clear coalitions supporting or opposing certain projects or individuals are formed. Incumbents were asked the extent to which they formed coalitions or worked cooperatively in their campaigns, and whether that changed after the storm. Although the use of coalitions—or the perception thereof—varied somewhat between candidates, all said there was no difference after Andrew.

Contrary to expectations, it appears that Hurricane Andrew did not affect incumbent perspectives and campaign strategies in subsequent elections in the southern municipalities of the county. In fact, as seen above, one incumbent who lost attributed her defeat to changes in campaign activities not because of the hurricane, but because of excessive campaign funding. Although it could be argued that the additional funds were an indirect effect of the hurricane, changes were not made in the campaign explicitly because of hurricane or recovery issues.

A Homestead commissioner noted that winning a two-year rather than a four-year term was again due to the campaign. "I really didn't campaign like I should have. I didn't put as much in the campaign as I had before. And that's why I got a two-year term. So I think I had lost steam by then. . . . Everything was a contributing factor." It is evident from the interview however, that "everything" includes the personalities of the council members at least as much as the hurricane. That incumbent did not seek a subsequent term because of personality conflicts within the council at that time.

Second Time Around

Six out of eight incumbents in office at the time of Hurricane Andrew who ran for reelection after the hurricane with competition were successful. Five of them ran for reelection a second time after the storm, and one incumbent who lost in the first round ran again in the next round, this time successfully. The second round of elections was conducted in November 1995, November 1997, January 1998, and January 2000—roughly thirty-eight, fifty, fifty-two, and seventy-six months after Hurricane Andrew. Predictably, as physical reconstruction progressed, signs of the hurricane faded. Fund-raising and campaigning were back to normal in the second round. New concerns, however, faced public officials. Incumbents from both Florida City and Homestead specifically noted this situation as it related to campaigns—one, for example, said that explaining to citizens why one project began when another remained incomplete became a major aspect of the reelection campaign.

Two noted that disaster issues played little part in opponents' campaigns and were not damaging to incumbents because the officials could not be blamed for things outside of their control, although this lack of control had to be explained to people not accustomed to the workings of governmental bodies. Incumbent candidates found the need to offer justifications for why some projects had not been completed and why few local residents were hired into new jobs. At the same time, though, incumbents could show all the money brought into the city, and residents could readily see many physical improvements.

The first issue, incomplete projects, could be explained by the lack of control over funding processes; visible improvements were coupled with businesses moving into the area—a Wal-Mart, an outlet mall, and new motels. This was generally beneficial for, and used by, incumbents, so that by the 2000 elections, disaster issues played no part in the campaign. As one post-Andrew elected official explained, "during '96 to 2000 was when the city folded in all of the things that had been promised."

One incumbent noted that in 1998, six years after the storm, about half of the population was still suffering, but much of that was "mental suffering due to anxiety, pressure, illnesses, and deaths related to the whole experience." In fact, a study conducted just months after Andrew concluded that health issues, especially stress-related problems, were significantly greater in the severely affected areas. Loss of health insurance due to the storm exacerbated these problems, which increased dramatically from north to south in Dade County (Alvarez 1992d).

This is a common problem after disasters. In addition to the physical stress of coping with difficult living situations, crippled transportation, and employment issues, people typically have lost irreplaceable personal effects and suffer from psychological stress during and after a major disaster (Waugh 2000). Elected officials are wise to arrange for counseling and other mental health services for both responders and victims.

Nevertheless, the incumbent remembered:

At that time we were on a roll. We were in the process of making things happen, and it's kind of hard to fight against that. . . . We were able to show the money that had been brought into the city, the federal, the state governments, all the different grants we were getting, all the things we were trying to do as far as our water, our sewer, and everything.

Homestead, wealthier than Florida City prior to Hurricane Andrew, saw a revitalized downtown, a new community college campus, and considerable physical improvement. "Every year it got better and better for them," the official said. At the same time, negative economic impacts were manifesting: job losses from businesses that had not reopened or had moved away, a movie theater that had closed, and the flight of residents with disposable incomes. The city's financial situation was deteriorating, eventually requiring layoffs and downsizing. Justification and explanation were needed, but sufficed. One incumbent explained:

> And I think that some people were disappointed that we weren't doing enough, quick enough. But I don't think it was that dangerous, the thoughts were that dangerous that it would affect the elections of anyone. It's just that it's hard to explain to, sometimes, to people what the political arena's all about, you know. Because they're not used to it and they don't know anything about what you have to do.

Incumbents' perceptions were nevertheless that Hurricane Andrew did not negatively affect their chances of reelection. Homestead had experienced hurricanes before. Recovery from this one took a long time, but no blame was apparently placed on local elected officials for the storm or for the fact that Andrew caused such a huge upheaval in the residential and business populations. Those upheavals caused new problems that the elected officials tried to address. New economic development was pursued, though the negative news image of a flattened city made it difficult to attract businesses to the area. For example, a motorsports racing complex was built, credit for which one incumbent linked to the disaster:

> I would attribute it to the aftermath of Hurricane Andrew, for several reasons. There were so many commitments made to the community after the hurricane that a lot of folks just did not follow through on. So we had the support of the governor, the support of the county commission, to help us with these rebuilding efforts. The county didn't hesitate to give us the thirty-one million dollars in bed tax [a special local tax on hotels/motels] monies to help build that facility. So I would say so, that we were in a unique position to continue to get the ear of our local and our state politicians to help.

In the aftermath of this major disaster, elected officials did their jobs as best they could without apparent regard to reelection concerns, at least according to their own recollections of those times. Their view of their reelection chances, as a result of those activities, was clear: they did not need to change their campaign strategies, although physical restrictions in the first election after the storm caused some tactical shifts (for example, telephone contact instead of door-to-door canvassing). An experienced and successful campaigner described local campaign strategy as follows:

> Homestead politics have not changed that much in twenty or twenty-two years. . . . Your goal is to get the endorsement of the PBA, to get the endorsement of the IBEW, the two major unions of the area, to get the endorsement of about three major homeowners associations, and also to raise the money you need to get your message out. . . . Once you've got those endorsements you're pretty much halfway there. . . . The strategy has not changed.

It appears that municipal incumbents in the southern zone faced some challenges to campaigning due to the physical destruction of their communities and their own activities as public officials. Those activities, however, supplanted normal campaign activities, perhaps even amounting to surrogate campaign activities—campaigning without campaigning. Incumbents adjusted their normal campaign activities as needed. No negative effects on election outcomes appear to have resulted from these short-lived physical challenges, which receded as reconstruction progressed and life returned to normal. The most negative outcome, ironically, was attributed to *more money being available* for the campaign than normal.

Chapter 1, however, identified cases that indicated negative political impacts were possible, if not probable, after a disaster. Why are these Hurricane Andrew cases devoid of negative impacts? Many anecdotal tales about elections or politics are mentioned within studies focused on other aspects of a disaster. In some areas, controversies existed or changes were in the works before the disaster. The events themselves did not necessarily cause the changes, although additional support for change may have developed as a result of those events. In that light, Homestead and Florida City's substantial population changes need exploration.

Movers and Stayers

Large numbers of people moved from south Dade after Andrew. This was, to some extent, a quickening of a pre-storm process, namely the movement of white non-Latino/as out and Latino/as in. Although the total numbers were substantial, it made little immediate impact on voting constituencies, except, again, as the Latino/as, particularly Cubans, were more often Republican, a trend established before Andrew.

Another aspect of this migration should be noted: Dade County more than doubled in population in 30 years, growing from a 1960 population of 935,047 to 2,006,000 residents in 1992 (Bureau of the Census 1963 and 1992). Many of these new arrivals had never experienced a hurricane in their former homes.

At least half of the population, then, was of "rookie" status as Andrew swept ashore, and their first experience with a hurricane was an unusually bad one. Many were unwilling to experience another. This is significant for the south Dade population. One of the Homestead former elected officials noted the difference between the old-timers, who had seen hurricanes before, even if not as powerful, and the newer residents:

> A lot of people moved out of here. Because a lot of those people who moved had never been in a hurricane before. Never realized it. We were, like, twenty-seven years free of any hurricanes in Homestead, until this hit. And so a lot of these people that came down here had never even been in a hurricane. . . . I don't think they really understood what a hurricane was. . . . And I think that's what these people found out and they left, went inland, more or less in the middle of the state, getting away from the hurricane. . . . The ones that were raised around here basically stayed, a few brave souls that ventured down here before the hurricane stayed. . . . And I think they fully understand what a hurricane's about, now.

Thus, longtime residents who had previous hurricane experience saw Andrew as just another storm, albeit an extremely powerful one. Communities recovered from hurricanes—recovery from this one would just take a bit longer. Studies have shown that people and communities that have been through disasters are more prepared, more likely to follow evacuation orders, and more easily adjust and recover afterwards (Dynes 1970).

*   *   *

In sum, the hurricane did not spoil these incumbents' reelection chances, and the experience supported Abney and Hill's (1965) finding: hurricanes may not be legitimate political issues. In this worst-case scenario of a Category 5 storm, the reactions of the incumbents working out in the community were in keeping with their normal function as public officials, but they were responding to a problem far more severe than any of them, or any of their constituents, had previously experienced. Their increased community activities and their electoral successes support May's 1985 (see table 1.1) finding correlating visibility in disaster response with post-event incumbent success. Similarly, the south Dade incumbents, more active after the storm to bring support to their suffering constituents, demonstrate Wolensky and Miller's (1981) description of custodial versus activist job performance. Thus, incumbent and constituent perceptions of the elected official's proper role changed together in south Dade, continuing the strong support that incumbents enjoyed before the disaster.

Elected officials faced with a post-disaster situation should increase their constituent service activities and place little emphasis on reelection activities.

With this set of findings from the devastated southern zone, attention can now be shifted to post-Andrew incumbent experiences in the middle (moderately damaged) areas of the county.

7

On the Edge

Incumbents from Less Severely Damaged Cities

As might be expected, the campaign strategies of elected officials in the area most affected by Hurricane Andrew were impacted by the storm's physical destruction. This did not, however, alter incumbent perceptions of their reelection chances. Still, the experience seems to have strengthened their advantages as incumbents. Also as expected, the effects of the hurricane on incumbents' campaign management were greatest in the first elections after the disaster, gradually lessening as time progressed.

This chapter explores the experiences of incumbents from the part of Dade County that did not experience the fierce winds of Andrew's eye wall. The city of South Miami and the village of Key Biscayne were the only two jurisdictions entirely within the middle region, which was adjacent to the eye wall. Incumbents in this area predictably experienced few hurricane-related effects on their reelection chances or their campaigns.

The Middle Zone: Moderate Damage

The municipalities (the village of Key Biscayne and the city of South Miami [figure 4]) in this section of the county (that is, the area moderately damaged by the hurricane) also held elections in 1993 and 1994. Key Biscayne, located on a barrier island, is physically separated from the mainland, connected by a single causeway with two bridges. It is unique among the municipalities discussed in this book, having incorporated just before Hurricane Andrew. Long before Hurricane Andrew hit, some residents felt isolated from their government and advocated for their community to have "more of a voice" with the county commission (*Miami Herald* 1987e). They organized an unofficial village council, to which members were first elected in 1987, to develop that voice (McGarrahan 1987). In 1989, a second election for the unofficial council was held, and straw votes about development issues and possible incorporation were taken (Ycaza 1989c).

Members of that unofficial council were incumbent elected leaders when Key Biscayne legally incorporated and held its first municipal elections in 1991 for the new board of trustees—later renamed the village council (Klingener 1990; Faiola 1991a, 1991b, 1991c, 1991d, 1991e, 1991f). The 1993 post-hurricane elections therefore provided the third test of incumbency for Key Biscayne voters. The outcomes were mixed—one incumbent was successful; one incumbent commissioner and the mayor lost.

The 1987 council was used as the first set of elected officials for the village to determine its pattern of incumbency. It should be noted that although the position of mayor was not established before incorporation, both candidates running for the first mayoral seat in 1991 had been members of the unofficial council. The woman who had served as chair of that council for four years lost her bid to become mayor in 1991, but won a seat on the council the following year in a special election to fill a vacancy.

In its short existence, the Key Biscayne mayor's office has been sought after—no candidate has ever run unopposed—although it is strictly a voluntary position (Ousley 1992). No one has been able to retain the post for more than two terms. It is important to understand this unique history since for Key Biscayne no pre- and post-Andrew patterns can be compared as has been done for other entities in this study; the island has no political history before Andrew.

There are differences in council incumbency, however, before and after the hurricane. Fewer incumbents have sought reelection after Andrew, and the success rate for those who have tried to continue on the council has diminished. This may be a matter of structural change, however, not disaster related.

The initial, unofficial council consisted of nine members, who elected their own chairperson (McGarrahan 1987; Ycaza 1989a, 1989b, 1989c; Shukovsky 1989). All seats were up for reelection in 1989. After incorporation, the council was reduced to six members, with a separately elected mayor. After the initial 1991 election—when all seats on the new official council were open—a staggered system was inaugurated.

In order to consider the differences due to structural changes, the percentage of possible incumbents was identified. In 1991, five out of nine incumbents ran for council seats; two of three incumbents whose terms expired in 1993 sought reelection that year.

Key Biscayne's records on campaign finance are complete for the targeted period. Interestingly, neither incumbency nor expenditures is a great predictor of success, nor are the two combined. Of nine incumbents seeking reelection in these contests, five won. Nine of fourteen candidates in the top half of spenders in any election were successful.

Only three of six incumbents who were among the top spenders retained their seat. Three of the incumbents were among the half of the candidates spending the least on campaigns and two of them won. These candidates were, however, competitive spenders in their races. No candidate, incumbent or not, won in any of the races with expenditures less than $3,344. The lone incumbent who spent less than that ($3,330) lost.

Key Biscayne is the wealthiest of the seven municipalities included in this study, and, according to the data obtained for this review, the level of campaign expenditure for Key Biscayne is high compared to other cities. Spending on political campaigns has increased in recent years, but in the years following Hurricane Andrew, campaign expenditures were trivial.

The city of South Miami holds its elections in February of even-numbered years. The first elections after Hurricane Andrew were in February 1994. No incumbents ran in the 1996 election (Gonzalez 1996b). During the twenty-three-year period from 1980 through 2002, there was little difference in the proportion of incumbent mayors seeking reelection: in five of seven cases the incumbent did so before Hurricane Andrew; and in four of five cases after. Incumbent success, however, differed substantially. In the period before Andrew, all five times that an incumbent sought to remain in office she won, three times without opposition. After the storm, only two out of four of those seeking reelection were successful, and there was opposition in every case.

The only two instances of incumbents losing were in 1994, the first election after Hurricane Andrew, and in 1998 when the incumbent had been in office for less than a year. The winner of that 1998 contest was the first Latino mayor in a city making the transition from majority white, non-Latino/a (54 percent in 1980) to a population more evenly proportioned (39 percent white, non-Latino/a and 34 percent Latino/a in 2002). Thus, the incumbent success rate for mayor appears to be different after the storm in South Miami, whether or not the hurricane was the cause of this change.

As in the southern zone, only two municipalities that existed at the time of Hurricane Andrew lay entirely within the middle zone. They experienced moderate damage, although there were numerous pockets of severe damage. Five former elected officials were interviewed from this area, one of whom was a commissioner at the time of the study. In addition, five individuals who served as campaign managers or were otherwise influential in incumbent reelection efforts were interviewed. Eight of these ten subjects were male and two were female; one was Latino and nine were white, non-Latino/a. Five lost or were connected with losing campaigns in their first reelection bid after Andrew, whereas five were on winning sides.

Key Biscayne is unique among the municipalities included in this study. It is different both in the level and type of damage sustained during Hurricane Andrew. It was also newly incorporated at the time of the storm. Andrew's eye wall swept over the southern tip of the barrier island, leveling the state park that borders the south side of the village of Key Biscayne, something that each of the former elected officials noted during interviews. Nearly two hundred homes, both single-family homes and condominium units in high-rise buildings, were rendered uninhabitable by the storm, as were three large hotels, two of which were in operation at the time of the hurricane. The wind damage was less severe than in Homestead and Florida City, but greater than that experienced in South Miami and the other cities studied here. Two Key Biscayne residents interviewed noted that some severe damage on the Key was due to insufficient protection (such as storm shutters).

In addition, the east side of the island was swept with seawater from the storm surge, which then washed up onto the mainland, inundating the west side of the island in a "back surge" as it returned to the Atlantic Ocean. Salt water killed much of Key Biscayne's vegetation not blown over by the wind, and its intrusion into houses caused corrosion of electrical wiring and other problems for residents. One incumbent noted that the water level had been nearly to the front door of his coastal residence, which sat 10.6 feet above sea level.

The county police department originally established a mild damage rating for Key Biscayne, partly due to the ability to limit access to the community and thereby protect it from looting and other crime. In the words of the respondent, "we virtually had a zero-crime situation out here for, for a long period of time . . . we had a crime holiday." The decision to include Key Biscayne in the moderate damage category for this study appears valid. The unique status of the village also created a different type of challenge for elected officials.

Formal votes on incorporation for Key Biscayne occurred in November 1990, when residents agreed to form a municipality, and June 1991, when a new village charter was approved. The first election of a formal, official Board of Trustees followed in September 1991. Hurricane Andrew thus smashed into a municipality with virtually no institutional structure, a village manager—the first for the village—hired only a few months earlier, and almost no governmental employees. The police department had yet to be formed, let alone building or public works departments. The village manager did have experience working with FEMA, in a previous position, to repair tornado damage.

Services were provided by the Metropolitan Dade County government until structures were established by the new municipality, but the county itself faced a Herculean post-disaster task. A huge area of still-unincorporated Dade County, where well over the half the county's population resided (in other words, an area that had no city governments, where all municipal services were provided by the county), was affected by Andrew. The respondent said, "once we looked at our own particular environment we realized that we were alone in this." Key residents spoke of the "infant state" of the government, "this little bumpkin city that we were trying to form," and noted that the experience was "a trial by fire, especially for our manager, and our new council, too."

The city of South Miami saw mostly minor damage to homes and other buildings. Both South Miami and Key Biscayne experienced major problems with downed trees, blocked roads, electrical outages, and the related lack of traffic lights. There was a "tremendous amount of cleanup that had to be done," the respondent noted. Key Biscayne was unique among the municipalities in this study in another respect: it was the only one completely covered by mandatory evacuation orders. Nearly everyone left the island for the storm, and many (including some elected officials and the few village employees) had great difficulty returning for days after. South Miami was not evacuated, although some low-lying areas were under evacuation orders or recommendations, and the police department, public works department, and elected officials were able to immediately begin to react to the storm's aftermath.

Prior preparation was noted as essential for the success candidates felt they had achieved in both municipalities. On Sunday, a state of emergency was declared for South Miami, in advance of the actual event. The mayor spent the night in city hall, as did the police department: "We just said every policeman is on duty. . . . We had battened down the hatches . . . moved our trucks and our equipment . . . taken movies of all of our property, all of our parks, all of our streets, so that we were prepared."

Key Biscayne officials were also able to move quickly. "We were very nimble," the respondent explained, because the village charter "gave the village council superpowers under those conditions to go ahead and make decisions and do things that might take a public hearing and a resolution—we could actually do it and then do that after the fact." The first of many special council meetings was held when enough members to constitute a quorum found each other. "We declared an emergency meeting and immediately proceeded to retain a company to clean the streets of all debris, without any idea of where we were getting any money or whether we had any money," the respondent recalled. The streets had to be cleared, and they were.

Comparison is universal among the subjects interviewed from areas outside of the southern damage zone. Respondents from Homestead and Florida City talked about the horrendous damage and resulting problems for their own cities, while others noted that what they had experienced was not as bad. With the exception of one respondent who thought that Key Biscayne's damage was as bad as that sustained in the southern zone, municipal officials and political elites from the middle and northern zones all noted that they were not as severely affected as the southern parts of the county. Several compared Andrew to other hurricanes they had experienced, and nearly all noted that their municipality had completed its cleanup well ahead of Homestead, Florida City, and unincorporated Dade County. Several stated proudly that their city was first or among the first to complete the task.

In the middle zone, there was also frequent mention of the city communicating with its residents, either through a newsletter or a city cable television channel once electricity was restored to the area. Noted several times was an information center established by the village of Key Biscayne that "served as a nerve center. People had questions, rumor control, that sort of thing, they were popping in and seeing what was going on." A respondent from Key Biscayne declared:

It was the coalescing moment. . . . Suddenly [elected officials] realized that they had a heavy responsibility and that they could help.

And that the people were looking to them for that. . . . They had a help line . . . they manned a counter down at the bank building . . . councilmen sort of came in and sort of took duty.

Nearly all the respondents from Key Biscayne identified Andrew as the pivotal point when residents of that community knew that incorporation had been the right decision. The battle for incorporation had been contentious, with strong pro and con factions. (Each side was supported by about 40 percent of the residents, according to one estimate.) All those interviewed here, it should be noted, both elected officials and political elites, were from the pro-incorporation faction. Having won that battle and having seen how the new government responded to the hurricane, they were convinced beyond any shadow of a doubt that their decision had been the right one.

The first reelection after the storm for the middle zone ranged from November 1993 to February and November 1994, given staggered terms in office and different jurisdictions, or approximately fourteen, seventeen, and twenty-six months post-Andrew. Electricity was restored within a few weeks in the middle zone, and street clearing and debris removal was completed within a few months. Although traffic was still affected in and around South Miami, mostly because of the conditions that caused tremendous and long-lasting traffic pattern adjustments, the hurricane was but a memory for South Miami voters by February 1994. Other issues were the focus of the first post-disaster election.

Key Biscayne was hit harder, and some aspects of Key life were not back to normal by the time of the first election in 1993. Temporary reductions in property values as a result of storm damage were calculated at fifty-seven million dollars (Samuels 1993c). Trees and other plants had not been replaced, but the detritus had been removed. The municipal government had cleared streets, and residents could compare conditions on the mainland to the Key. The respondent declared:

All they had to do was turn on their television to see what was happening in town. And they realized that we were so far ahead of the game, having our own ability to make our own decisions, quickly, and to restore some form of normalcy back into the everyday life out here.

In fact, residents had seen the difference close up, "because the only section on Key Biscayne that was still under county control was . . . the median in Crandon Boulevard [the main thoroughfare through the village] and that was the last to be cleaned up," as noted by a former incumbent.

The state park on the south side of the village was closed, as were the two major hotels, and small businesses that relied on the tourist trade, largely generated by the hotels and the park, suffered (Higham 1992b; Faiola 1992c; Samuels, 1993b, 1993d). Private homes were being rebuilt and repaired. With the state park flattened, an effort was made to install new ball fields near the village so that youth would have a local place to play.

In spite of Andrew's impact on the Key, the phenomenon of people moving away from the area, so well recognized in Homestead and Florida City, was not repeated on the Key. Rather, Key Biscayne was a recipient community, a desirable destination for people escaping the devastation further south. Condominiums filled quickly, property values soared, and Key residents who needed to rebuild or repair because of the hurricane mostly built bigger and better. In fact, Andrew seems to have marked a point in time at which vacant lots began to be, and still are, developed with large, expensive homes, while older dwellings are razed to make room for mansions.

None of the subjects interviewed in either Key Biscayne or South Miami could recall the hurricane being an issue during the first election cycle after the storm. The rapid recovery and the governmental response to the crisis were noted in incumbent campaign literature, along with other accomplishments during their terms. One former candidate, when asked about the impact of the hurricane on campaigning, said:

I think that the incumbents talked about the great job that they did, you know, in cleaning up after the hurricane. . . . What happened after Hurricane Andrew was a positive thing for incumbents here . . . but I'm not sure that sold very much. . . . I think by and large the electorate felt like, that anybody could have done it . . . you see an acrobat do it and it makes it look easy, you know. . . . As it turned out, I don't think it was much of an issue, but your question was: What did I think going into the election? I thought it was a pretty important thing and it would be a definite benefit for the incumbents. Coming out of the election and looking at the results and stuff, I don't think it was a major issue.

Council members met often, as much as twice a week for several months on Key Biscayne. With virtually no aides, their involvement was deeper than simply attending meetings. South Miami elected officials, too, were busy taking care of city affairs, one noting that damage to a personal residence was not dealt with for some time because of the workload. The candidate defeated in the first round of elections recalled exhausting and demanding post-Andrew work.

Given the focus of the questions posed in the interview, the respondent thought her defeat might have been partially attributable to the fact that her campaign was not an all-out effort. In fact, the incumbent had to be convinced to seek reelection:

> And that was a mistake on my part, because unless you really, really want to be elected, you should never run. And I ran halfheartedly, and when I look back . . . I can see that I probably should not have agreed to run again. . . . Because I was tired . . . I don't think any of us who were in government at the time of the hurricane really realized for a long time what it took out of us personally. . . . Anything the hurricane had to do with that election would only be: perhaps I was not as enthusiastic about it as I should have been. . . . But that's from hindsight . . . at the time, I would have said [Andrew] had no effect.

Specific disaster-related issues were not recalled by incumbents or political elites as any major part of campaigns. "The recovery efforts went so well, people could not complain about them," the respondent said. Three of five incumbents, however, said that they perceived their performance and the experience of their municipality after Andrew as improving their own chances for reelection. Only one noted any personal orientation regarding policy at the time of the first post-Andrew reelection effort that can be considered disaster related.

This candidate, who was easily reelected, spoke extensively during his campaign about the financial troubles of small businesses hurting from the hurricane-induced tourist slump. When asked to what extent the constituency was still suffering from hurricane effects during the reelection campaign, he noted, "I believed it was still affected. I don't know what percentage. I made an issue of maintaining status quo on budgets and no increases. My issue was more a conservative approach, in that, you know, we've got to go slow here."

Andrew may not have been an important issue within election campaigns, but it was a public policy issue. South Miami was an established city with an existing infrastructure, police department, and public works department. Its public works department received substantial assistance from a self-contained public works crew donated by the city of Daytona Beach. Four private debris removal contracts were also let, with a competitive proviso in each that "he who finishes cleaning their area first has the right to go into somebody else's area," as the respondent described it. The city was quickly able to move to other issues.

Key Biscayne had a different situation in Andrew's wake. A police department was being established, but lack of communication with the county fire station on the Key after the storm apparently was one of the reasons the new city decided to create its own fire department—unlike most small Dade County municipalities, which utilize the county's fire-rescue services. A new building and zoning department was prioritized, and a new storm water system was installed.

The general denuding of the area created "a bald town," "naked but beautiful," as the respondent described it. This necessitated—and allowed—massive tree planting and the installation of uniform, aesthetically pleasing landscaping, seen as "a blessing . . . virtually a clean slate to start out with . . . a great opportunity to correct some things," in the words of the respondent. Beach restoration was also implemented. Businesses hurting from the lack of tourism "were very, very vocal," successfully lobbying the village council to advertise the Key's attractions, provide funding to the chamber of commerce, and reduce or hold the line on taxes and fees.

Three incumbents lost the first election after Andrew, and neither of the successfully reelected officials in that round ran again, although one defeated candidate did successfully return to politics in a subsequent election. Reasons given for the three defeats were not hurricane-related, except for the possible explanation of being tired after the disaster experience, perhaps leading to a lackluster campaign. The styles of the candidate or campaign were seen as the reason for the defeats, not anything clearly related to the disaster. One judged the defeat his own doing, brought about by not controlling his temper at commission meetings. "I just blow my stack." Another referred to himself as "a hotheaded Irishman" who says what he thinks. "And you know that's not the key to being a successful politician."

Other respondents, too, saw personal qualities and campaign tactics as key. One defeat "just had to do with [the incumbent's] personality and the issues he engaged in." Comparing two incumbents in the same election who achieved different outcomes, the respondent explained, "people would not have distinguished them based upon the hurricane issue. One of them ran a better campaign than the other, pure and simple." Several respondents suggested that the electorate has a short collective memory, unless the memory is negative.

For example, "I think people soon forget. . . . If you ask an elected official for something ten times and nine times they agree with you, they are more apt to remember the one time they don't." From another respondent:

> To be a successful, long-term politician you need to stay below the radar and not make decisions, because when you make controversial decisions, by definition of them being controversial, you irritate the side you're not on. So if you have a controversial decision and . . . you support 80 percent of the people; that means 20 percent of the people are now opposed to you. You do one more of those and now you've got 40 percent, and one more and you're out.
>
> Regardless of what may or may not be an issue six or eighteen months before an election cycle . . . so much just depends on how a campaign is run. And, you know, issues, particularly if they affect everyone, then it kind of negates that as a factor. I mean, there were no major policy decisions that were made where someone could say, "Oh my God, we just spent X million dollars after the hurricane." . . . I think in terms of people winning or losing it has more to do with the campaigns that they ran, or didn't run [and the actual work to get the vote out].

*　*　*

I expected that the further away from the hurricane—both geographically and temporally—the less effect the hurricane would have on elections. In the southern zone, the storm seemed to have some effect, which apparently diminished as the years went by and recovery progressed. The middle zone appears to have experienced small effects, less dramatic than those further south. The first round of elections in areas which were farther away from the severe winds of the eye wall seems to have exhibited a reduced level of electoral impact, as expected. Before turning to the northern zone, however, another electoral factor that was repeatedly mentioned by subjects of this study bears highlighting.

Nearly everyone interviewed from Key Biscayne discussed divisions that had developed in the island community prior to Hurricane Andrew.

Political factions had formed in the battle over incorporation, with pro- and anti-incorporation components. Those who had favored incorporation generally believed, as one elite explained, "the village had been neglected by Unincorporated Dade County for years and years and years, and we had a tremendous amount of catch-up to do." Their solution was to maintain the level of taxes, which generated more than was needed for basic village operations, and spend the excess on capital improvements, which have included a new park complete with ball fields and restroom facilities, new police and fire stations, a new city hall complex, and a new community center (in the planning stages as this was written).

Each new project has been fought by a vocal group of former anti-incorporationists, certain that each new undertaking would push the village finances over the breaking point, necessitate higher taxes, and prove to be a wasteful boondoggle. Tax rates have in fact been reduced, and increasing property values have bolstered tax receipts. Petitions circulate throughout the community regularly to stop the initiation of a project, or, failing that, to reduce its size and therefore its cost. Individuals interviewed for this study were all associated with the pro-incorporation, progressive faction. The research design targeting elected officials in office at the time of the hurricane coincidentally omitted any representatives from the opposing faction. Whether individuals from that group, who have a different philosophical orientation, would have any different perceptions of the incumbents' hurricane-related activities is therefore an open question.

8

Out of the Eye

Incumbents from the Least Severely Damaged Cities

The northern section of Dade County escaped most of Andrew's fury, suffering only mild damage. Three cities were selected for review in this relatively unscathed area—Hialeah Gardens, Miami Springs, and West Miami. Miami Springs' population was between those of Homestead and South Miami; Hialeah Gardens' population was between those of Florida City and Key Biscayne. West Miami's population in 1990 was closest to the selected small cities (see table 1.2).

Twenty other municipalities existed in Dade County in 1992. Most had larger populations than Homestead, the most populous of the severely affected cities, or smaller than Florida City, the smaller of the hardest-hit cities. Miami Springs, Hialeah Gardens, and West Miami are located completely within the northern zone and are roughly comparable in size, although Homestead's population is nearly three times that of South Miami's. Given this study's interest in elections, the key was the number of registered voters in these jurisdictions, and they were roughly comparable at the time of Hurricane Andrew.

Again, elections were analyzed in this damage zone as in the other zones. The details and tables from these remaining cities are not included here, but are highlighted below.

The Northern Zone (Mild Damage)

The city of Hialeah Gardens now holds its elections in March of odd-numbered years. Prior to 1997, however, elections were held each year. Council members were elected for two years, except the winner in any election receiving the fewest number of votes among the winning candidates, who earned only a one-year term. Terms were staggered under this system, but some seats were up for election every year. The mayor was elected for a two-year term. In September 1996, voters approved four-year terms for the mayor; in March 1997, they approved doubling the council terms to four and two years (Camacho 1997).

The mayor's seat in Hialeah Gardens was contested in each of eleven elections from 1981 through 2001, including the 2000 special election (to fill a vacancy caused by the removal of a mayor convicted of criminal charges). The incumbent was successful in reelection bids only half of the time. Incumbent success during the period before the hurricane—three wins out of five incumbent bids for reelection—was better than post-Andrew—when only two of five won. Hialeah Gardens, however, provides examples of the give-and-take of politics.

In 1987, Daniel Riccio, a two-term incumbent, drew two challengers and lost in a runoff to Greg Read. Read drew three challengers in the next (1989) election and came in dead last in the general election. Riccio came back to finish first in that election, only to lose to Gilda Oliveros in the runoff. Oliveros was the first Cuban-American woman to be elected mayor in the United States (Smith 1989). Oliveros, the two-term mayor in office at the time of Hurricane Andrew, was defeated when she ran for reelection in 1993, but she won her seat back in the next (1995) election.

The other post-Andrew instance of incumbent loss came in 2000. The incumbent in that special election, Fátima Morejón, was selected by the city council in December 1999 to temporarily fill the vacancy left by the removal of Oliveros following her felony arrest. Morejón had been on the council for three years but had not run for, or been elected to, the mayor's post. She had initially been appointed to the council to fill a vacancy, and had not drawn a challenger when she stood for reelection in 1997. Thus, of five incumbents who failed at reelection attempts, two lost to former incumbents, and one was only in office for about six months and had never previously campaigned.

It is important to note that the mayor of Hialeah Gardens is considered a full-time city employee and is paid as such. In 1992, the mayor received a $20,000 annual salary (Ousley 1992); council members then made $190 (Joffee 2003). The council pay was increased to $2,400 in 1994 (Camacho 1998). An attempt in 1995 to raise council salaries to $5,200 was voted down, but in 1998, city voters (78 voting out of 4,507 registered) gave council members limited authority to increase compensation for the mayor and for themselves (Camacho 1998; *Miami Herald* 1995a, 1998e). In 2000, the mayor's compensation was $23,000, but by 2003, the mayor made $45,000 with a $57,000 expense account, whereas the council members received $2,760 in salary with a $13,800 expense account (Taylor 2000b; Joffee 2003).

Council incumbents have better track records than the aforementioned mayors, perhaps partly due to their lower salaries, which make their seats less desirable. The pattern here changes after the hurricane as well, because 77 percent of incumbents (24 of 31) won before Andrew, but 89 percent (17 of 19) succeeded afterwards. Only 26 percent of incumbents (8 of 31) before Andrew ran unopposed, but 63 percent (12 of 19) afterwards did so. The special referenda that lengthened the terms of the mayor and council members also occurred after the 1992 disaster, but if residents of Hialeah Gardens were more satisfied with their elected representatives, there is no indication of the hurricane being a factor.

The city of Miami Springs, also in the northern zone, holds its elections in April of odd-numbered years. The mayor and four council members hold two-year terms, and candidates for city council run for separately designated seats. Individuals are limited to eight years in office as either mayor or council member. The first post-Andrew election was held less than eight months after the hurricane.

Incumbent mayors were successful every time they sought reelection during our period of review. In six of eight of those elections the incumbent ran unopposed. Nonetheless, the incumbents ran unopposed in all five cases before the hurricane, whereas they were unopposed only one of three times afterward. In five out of six elections from 1981 through 1991, the incumbent mayor sought reelection; after Andrew (1993–2001), the incumbent sought reelection in three out of five elections. The incumbent at the time of Hurricane Andrew did not run for reelection in 1993. The mayor's salary in 1992 was only $1,800 (Ousley 1992).

Council incumbents in Miami Springs were nearly as successful, with 29 wins out of 31 reelection attempts. Again, the pattern is different pre- and post-Andrew, with all incumbents (18 of 18) before the hurricane successful and 11 of 13 successful after. Overall, 17 of the incumbent reelection attempts were unopposed, 11 of 18 before Andrew, and only 6 of 13 post-disaster.

The last of the seven municipalities is the city of West Miami, which holds municipal elections in April of even-numbered years. The mayor is elected for two-year terms, whereas the four commissioners serve staggered four-year terms. Prior to the elections in 1986, however, the mayor and commission seats were elected together, with the top vote-getter winning a four-year term on the commission, serving the first two as mayor.

No apparent difference in patterns of incumbent success before and after Hurricane Andrew exists. Incumbents running for reelection won 100 percent of the time. Incumbents not only won, they rarely had opposition, with challengers standing for election only one time during the period before and one time during the period after. West Miami's mayor receives minimal annual compensation—$1,680 in 1992 (Ousley 1992).

As with the post of mayor, West Miami's council elections show no evidence of any difference in pre- and post-disaster incumbent success. Fully 80 percent of the incumbents who sought reelection were successful, both before and after Andrew. Except for one election, there has been opposition consistently. The exception was nearly ten years after the hurricane, and multiple appointments to replace resigning mayors may have depleted the small city's candidate pool that year.

Four incumbents from the northern zone were interviewed for this study, including one female and three males; one Latino and three white, non-Latino/as. None provided secondary referrals to key campaign aides, having largely conducted such activities themselves. The first round of elections for these incumbents after the hurricane took place in March and April 1993 (seven and eight months post-disaster, respectively) and in April 1996 (forty-four months after the storm).

Hurricane damage in these municipalities consisted of downed trees and debris on the roadways, along with some peripheral building damage (such as missing roof tiles and torn awnings). One former elected official noted that a tornado associated with the storm had significantly damaged some mobile homes within his city. Electricity was out in some areas for three or four weeks.

Demographics changed little in these cities, because West Miami and Miami Springs were older, developed communities. Some people moved into the area from the severely affected south, and an increase in police activity was noted in West Miami, which was attributed to an influx of people temporarily moving in with relatives in the city and surrounding areas. Hialeah Gardens was undergoing a substantial growth period, begun well before Andrew, and no disaster-related demographic change was perceived there. Tree and debris removal was the most significant issue for these cities, and that was completed within a matter of weeks. It was a significant undertaking, requiring West Miami to borrow funds, but FEMA reimbursements resolved that temporary financial setback.

Elected officials were responsive to the situation and to constituents. Two recalled special council meetings to deal with hurricane-related issues. One official remembered walking the city checking on residents to ensure that health needs were addressed. Another spoke of waiving city ordinances, such as noise ordinances, which would otherwise not have permitted generators to run at night—a necessity for refrigerating insulin and other medicines. Special meetings and workshops were also held in at least one city to address planning—seeing the severity of the situation further south, residents and officials wanted to address issues in advance of the next storm.

In every case, Andrew was only a memory well before the next election cycle. The only related issues discussed were, in the respondent's words, "positive reinforcement" notations of how well incumbents had responded to the crisis, how they had taken care of constituents, and, for one city, how they had obtained funds to retrofit a community center into a Red Cross–approved hurricane shelter. The respondent said, "I don't think the opposition was attacking it, so it just became something else that the incumbents were doing to work for your community." She noted that an existing contingency fund had allowed her city to move quickly to clear streets and remove debris:

> The economic impacts for our community and the businesses around in this area were probably on the plus side, because we received a lot of added business from the people who lived in the south that were dislocated. . . . I would say the citizens . . . really had no complaints. . . . We took care of the problem and we dealt with it immediately . . . because we had the money. . . . Money is an evil thing, but when you have it, you're king. . . . We never agreed on anything five to zero except to take care of that, but when the time came, the elected body of this city was one team. . . . Nobody could use the hurricane as a fault-finder . . . for me it was a good thing to posture from, because we were quite successful. . . . In three weeks, I mean, we cleared the place out, I mean, it was just like the place we lived before, without trees. So I used that. . . . Citizens were still living in fear there was one going to come again. You know, people hadn't gotten over the fear factor, right at that time.

Interestingly, all four former elected officials from the northern zone noted flooding problems within their cities, although Andrew is generally considered to have been a relatively dry hurricane. One respondent noted flooding with Hurricane Andrew and "any storm that comes through" because of poor construction practices that cause drainage problems. Two noted flooding as a comparison, because a major storm later in 1992 caused more flood-related problems than the hurricane. The other respondent stated, "Andrew was a dry storm and it did not flood us. We've had some floods afterwards that have almost cost people elections, but not from Andrew." That city has since obtained federal funds to improve its storm drainage system.

*   *   *

To identify patterns emerging from this review, table 8.1 summarizes the mayoral incumbent success across jurisdictions, while table 8.2 does the same for council/commission incumbents, with municipalities grouped by damage zone. The beginnings of a pattern emerge in table 8.1, which summarizes mayoral success. In the southern zone, which suffered severe damage, incumbent mayors were less likely to have opposition in their reelection bids after Hurricane Andrew, when 67 percent were unopposed, as opposed to before, when only 42 percent ran unopposed. Of course, with less opposition, incumbents won more often. Before Andrew, incumbent reelection efforts boasted a respectable 83 percent success rate, but this increased to 100 percent afterwards.

In the northern and middle zones, however, electoral challenges increased and incumbent mayors were less successful. There may be several reasons for this. With tremendous district damage and significantly increased responsibility, mayoral jobs in the south may have been less appealing, thus generating less opposition. Moreover, incumbents who sought to remain may have benefited from their leadership roles in severely stricken communities. Their visibility in reconstruction, relief, and redevelopment efforts could have chased off competition, thus consolidating their hold on office. Outside of the severe damage zone, mayoralties did not become less appealing, and similar leadership may have neither reduced competition nor provided any additional enhancement to the incumbent advantage.

The pattern is only partially repeated with council/commission incumbents in the same jurisdictions. Incumbents from the southern zone faced slightly less opposition—with the incidence of unopposed

Table 8.1. Mayoral incumbent success across seven jurisdictions, by hurricane damage zones

	Incumbent ran		Incumbent won		Incumbent unopposed	
Jurisdiction	Pre-	Post-	Pre-	Post-	Pre-	Post-
Homestead	5/06 (83%)	4/05 (80%)	4/05 (80%)	4/04 (100%)	2/05 (40%)	2/04 (50%)
Florida City	7/07 (100%)	5/05 (100%)	6/07 (86%)	5/05 (100%)	3/07 (44%)	4/05 (80%)
South zone	12/13 (92%)	9/10 (90%)	10/12 (83%)	9/09 (100%)	5/12 (42%)	6/09 (67%)
Key Biscayne	—	3/04 (75%)	—	2/03 (67%)	—	0/03 (0%)
South Miami	5/07 (71%)	4/05 (80%)	5/05 (100%)	2/04 (50%)	3/05 (60%)	0/05 (0%)
Middle zone	5/07 (71%)	7/09 (78%)	5/05 (100%)	4/07 (57%)	3/05 (60%)	0/08 (0%)
Hialeah Gardens	5/06 (83%)	5/05 (100%)	3/05 (60%)	2/05 (40%)	0/05 (0%)	0/05 (0%)
Miami Springs	5/06 (83%)	3/05 (60%)	5/05 (100%)	3/03 (100%)	5/05 (100%)	1/03 (33%)
West Miami	3/03 (100%)	4/05 (80%)	3/03 (100%)	4/04 (100%)	2/03 (67%)	3/04 (75%)
North zone	13/15 (87%)	12/15 (80%)	11/13 (85%)	9/12 (75%)	7/13 (54%)	4/12 (33%)

Note: # actual / # possible (%)

Sources: Miami-Dade County Elections Department; Florida City Office of the City Clerk; Hialeah Gardens City Clerk's Office; Miami Springs City Clerk's Office; South Miami City Clerk's Office; Village of Key Biscayne Village Clerk's Office; West Miami City Clerk's Office; Acle and Hartman, 1993; Andrews and Gressette, 1980; Batista, 2002a, 2002b, 2002c, 2002d, 2002e, 2002f; Cauvin, 1996; Davis, 1993a, 1993b; de la Cruz, 1991; de Valle, 1995a, 1995b; de Valle, et al., 1997; Etheart, 1997b; Faiola, 1992a; Figueras, 2001a, 2001b, 2001c; Garcia, 1999; Gonzalez, 1996a, 1996b; Hartman, 1993b; Kollars, 1983a, 1983b; Marquez-Garcia, Winsor, and Branch, 1998; Martinez, 1999; Martinez, Fernandez, and Batista, 2000; McClure, 1981; McGarrahan, 1988; *Miami Herald*, 1980a, 1980b, 1981a, 1981c, 1982a, 1982d, 1983a, 1983c, 1984a, 1984c, 1985a, 1986a, 1986d, 1987a, 1987b, 1987c, 1987d, 1987g, 1987h, 1988b, 1988e, 1989a, 1989b, 1990a, 1990c, 1991a, 1991b, 1992d, 1992f, 1993a, 1993b, 1993d, 1993i, 1994c, 1995a, 1995b, 1996b, 1997a, 1997b, 1998a, 1998b, 1998c, 1998d, 1999, 2000a, 2000b, 2000c, 2001a; Musibay, 1995; Rejtman, 1995; Rivas-Vazquez, 1985; Rothaus, 1993b; Rowe, 1989; Salazar, 2000a, 2000b; Samuels, 1994a; Smith, 1986, 1989; Taylor, 2000b; Ulrich 1982a, 1982b, 1984, 1985a, 1985b, 1985c.

Table 8.2. Council/commission incumbent success across seven municipalities, by hurricane damage zones

Municipality	Incumbent ran Pre-	Incumbent ran Post-	Incumbent won Pre- (%)	Incumbent won Post- (%)	Incumbent unopposed Pre- (%)	Incumbent unopposed Post- (%)
Homestead	19	16	14/19 (74%)	12/16 (75%)	0/19 (0%)	0/16 (0%)
Florida City	8	10	8/8 (100%)	8/10 (80%)	0/8 (0%)	2/9 (22%)
South zone	27	26	22/27 (81%)	20/25 (80%)	0/27 (0%)	2/25 (10%)
Key Biscayne	12	7	10/12 (83%)	4/7 (57%)	0/12 (0%)	0/5 (0%)
South Miami	8	6	6/8 (75%)	4/6 (67%)	4/8 (50%)	2/6 (33%)
Middle zone	20	13	16/20 (80%)	8/13 (62%)	4/20 (20%)	2/11 (18%)
Hialeah Gardens	31	19	24/31 (77%)	17/19 (89%)	8/31 (26%)	12/19 (63%)
Miami Springs	18	13	18/18 (100%)	11/13 (85%)	1/18 (6%)	6/13 (46%)
West Miami	15	10	12/15 (80%)	20/25 (80%)	0/15 (0%)	4/10 (40%)
North zone	64	42	54/64 (84%)	48/57 (84%)	9/64 (14%)	22/42 (52%)

Sources: Miami-Dade County Elections Department; Florida City Office of the City Clerk; Hialeah Gardens City Clerk's Office; Miami Springs City Clerk's Office; South Miami City Clerk's Office; Village of Key Biscayne Clerk's Office; West Miami City Clerk's Office; Acle and Hartman, 1993; Andrews and Gressette, 1980; Arthur, 1994; Batista, 2002a, 2002b, 2002c, 2002d, 2002e, 2002f; Betancourt, 1982; Camacho 1997; Cauvin 1996; Cummings, 1984; Davis, 1993a, 1993b, 1994a, 1994b; de la Cruz, 1991; de Valle, 1995a, 1995b; Etheart, 1997b; Faiola, 1991d, 1991e, 1992a; Figueras, 2001a, 2001b, 2001c; Gonzalez, 1996a, 1996b; Hartman, 1993b, 1993c; Kollars, 1983a, 1983b; Martinez, 1999; Martinez, Fernandez, and Batista, 2000; McClure, 1981; McGarrahan, 1987, 1988; *Miami Herald*, 1980a, 1980b, 1980c, 1981a, 1981b, 1981c, 1982a, 1982b, 1982c, 1982d, 1983a, 1983c, 1984a, 1984b, 1984c, 1985a, 1985b, 1985c, 1986a, 1986b, 1986c, 1986d, 1987b, 1987c, 1987d, 1987e, 1987f, 1987h, 1988a, 1988b, 1988c, 1988d, 1988e, 1989a, 1989b, 1989c, 1990a, 1990b, 1990c, 1991a, 1991b, 1991e, 1991f, 1992a, 1992b, 1992c, 1992d, 1993a, 1993b, 1993d, 1993h, 1994a, 1994b, 1994c, 1995a, 1995b, 1996a, 1996b, 1997a, 1997b, 1997c, 1997d, 1998a, 1998c, 1999, 2000a, 2000b, 2000c, 2001b, 2001c; Musibay, 1995; Rejtman, 1995; Rivas-Vazquez, 1985; Rothaus, 1993b; Rowe, 1989; Samuels, 1993a, 1993b, 1993d, 1994a, 1994b; Smith, 1986, 1989; Ulrich 1982a, 1982b, 1984, 1985a, 1985b, 1985c; Ycaza, 1989a, 1989b.

Table 8.3. Average number of candidates pre- and post-Andrew: selected municipalities by damage zone, 1980–2002

Zone	Jurisdiction	Average number of commission/ council candidates	
		Pre-Andrew (1980–92)	Post-Andrew (1993–2002)
South	Homestead	9.5	7.6*
	Florida City	6.3	3.2
Middle	South Miami	4.4	5.4
	Key Biscayne	14.0**	6.8
North	Miami Springs	6.7	8.2
	Hialeah Gardens***	6.7	4.4
	West Miami***	5.4	4.4

*Includes fifteen candidates in 2001 election, the first time there were ten or more candidates in a Homestead municipal election since 1987.

**Only one election used before Hurricane Andrew, the first election for the newly formed village council. The structure of the new council was changed from that which had led the area to incorporation.

***Structural changes to councils occurred: terms of office were lengthened for Hialeah Gardens after Hurricane Andrew, while the mayor's position was separated from West Miami's council beforehand.

candidates increasing from zero before Andrew to 10 percent after—but virtually the same success rate—81 percent before and 80 percent after. In the middle zone, the rate of council/commission incumbents without opposition decreased slightly—from 20 percent to 18 percent—after Andrew. But in the northern zone, the rate increased from 39 percent to 56 percent.

Table 8.3 displays the average number of candidates in pre- and post-disaster commission/council contests for the various included municipalities. In the southern zone, the average number of candidates is lower after Hurricane Andrew. In the less severely damaged areas, however, no clear pattern is evident. Incumbents faced opposition in the southern zone, but there were fewer challengers, possibly supporting the suggestion that elected office was less attractive after the storm.

A possible erosion of support for commissioners and an increase for mayors are indicated in the southern zone, whereas no pattern of change is evident in less severely affected areas. Do the changes in the southern zone reflect a change in attitude toward elected officials, or simply the fact that the hurricane turned people's lives upside down? The officials themselves perceived no change in their incumbent advantage after Andrew.

There has been no evidence of storm-related negative effects (such as blaming of elected officials) that could lead to electoral damage, while there is some indication of an enhancement of the incumbency advantage. Municipal incumbents appear to have somewhat benefitted from Hurricane Andrew—with the strongest evidence being found in those areas most severely affected by Andrew—though this effect subsided as time passed. Municipal incumbents in the northern, mildly damaged areas of the county appear to have had experiences similar to those in the moderately damaged area, adding credence to this observation.

*   *   *

From this review of municipal elections and municipal elected officials it appears that there was in fact a political effect from Hurricane Andrew—a positive one that helped strengthen, albeit minimally, the already strong advantage that incumbents had before the disaster. No negative effect related to this particular disaster has been observed.

In the southern zone, severely affected municipalities' elected officials were not blamed for any condition that may have led to severe damage. For one thing, the existing building code (established by the county commission) was the strongest in the country, regardless of how inadequate it may have proven. Also, city elected officials were affected by the disaster as much as their constituencies, so Andrew could not be perceived as a distant problem for them. Finally, the hurricane was an act of nature over which local elected officials had no control, and therefore the storm was not a legitimate political issue, as Abney and Hill (1966) determined in their previous study.

Elected officials' response was apparently seen as appropriate, and citizens rallied to support those who led the charge to rebuild and recover. As with the disaster itself, the response was too big for local officials, and their ability to work with state and federal resources played in their favor. This is especially evident in the few cases of nonincumbents seeking public office after the storm, because the one who clearly differed with incumbents lost, while those who won supported or were accepted by the incumbents.

In the middle and northern zones, Andrew had little electoral effect. Because the damage was relatively quickly remedied, the timing of elections outside of the severely damaged areas allowed officials and voters alike to move on to other matters before reelection efforts began. Hurricane response was one of a number of retrospective actions noted by incumbents in campaigns, but was itself insufficient to make or break reelection chances. Prospective plans for the city, personal characteristics, and/or campaign styles helped or hindered candidates more than anything related to Andrew.

Incumbents in all regions of the county talked about the reasons for defeat—before and after the hurricane—or reduction in voter support (such as winning a two-year rather than a four-year term). Not wanting to run, no longer enjoying public life, overconfidence, and personal actions (such as losing one's temper) were reasons given—never preparation for or response to Hurricane Andrew. This is important for elected officials: if one seeks office, be sure to run—not walk—for election or reelection. Less than an all-out effort does not ensure victory. An all-out campaign may still be defeated, but a half-hearted effort almost certainly will fail.

Even though no evidence of negative effects from Hurricane Andrew has surfaced, there have been indications that disasters can potentially be problematic for elected officials. Elected officials in the less severely affected zones more than once referenced other events that caused greater damage than Hurricane Andrew. Even in the southern zone, there were comments about how nobody could have done any better than the incumbents, so their efforts could not be used against them.

Whether or not to frame Hurricane Andrew as a natural disaster has even been an issue. Significant events may be seen as disasters—or not—by different actors because of political issues or because of different sets of responsibilities and criteria (Davis 1978). In our case, structural engineers showed how building practices were inadequate, resulting in more severe damage than necessary. Experts cited by Ted Steinberg (2000) even argued that Andrew's worst winds were little over 130 mph., maybe gusting to 160–65 mph. Steinberg maintains that, given the officially designated wind speeds, the catastrophe was beyond man's (and therefore elected officials') control. It was something to be taken in stride, then forgotten. A return to routine, to the status quo ante, was desired.

Several elected officials in the southern zone believed the negative publicity about Andrew posed local problems. News images always show the worst—rumors get reported as facts, compounding the image of disaster (Quarantelli and Dynes 1972). "A disaster is a dramatic event and editors think it should be reported as drama. The camera lens focuses on destruction and despair" (70).

Managing perceptions of an event is important and is achieved through framing and ritualistic actions (t'Hart 1993). Municipal officials from south Dade framed Andrew as another hurricane and used the rituals of solidarity and reassurance. Further north in the county, municipal officials framed their own cities as lucky and better-off, having the southern reference handily available. Whether done consciously to further their positions or not, incumbents at all levels almost uniformly legitimized their positions, seizing the opportunity to take control and exercise leadership, in essence campaigning without campaigning. T'Hart maintains this is common after disasters, and in the chaotic situation after Andrew, there were opportunities aplenty to be so seized.

Outside of the hardest-hit southern portions of the county, the hurricane was a short-term inconvenience. With the huge infusion of people (government officials and their staffs, insurance representatives, construction workers, and so forth) and money into the area, however, businesses in northern areas of the county flourished. People repaired homes and added a little more than was there before, increasing property values and local tax bases, a phenomenon referred to as "the Jacuzzi effect" (Pearl and Brannigan 1992). This rebuild-and-improve mode was noted especially in Key Biscayne, but was probably more widespread. People bought new cars, furniture, and other big-ticket items, mostly from local dealers. Hotels and rental housing filled up. The south Dade economy may not have ever fully recovered, but this lag was not felt in the rest of the area. There were, then, many positive effects of the storm.

9

Disasters as Political Challenges
and Opportunities

This book set out to explore the question of Hurricane Andrew's possible impact on Florida's elected officials, from local to statewide. In particular, it focused on post-disaster campaigns and electoral outcomes in Miami-Dade County, with a special eye on three geographic zones representing differing levels of damage from the 1992 event. Although the working hypothesis was that Andrew was politically problematic and that any problems would be most noticeable in the more severely damaged southern zone, alternative theories indicated at least the possibilities of no effects or even advantageous effects for incumbents.

Because disasters such as Hurricane Andrew present both challenges and opportunities to incumbents, the findings are interesting and subtle. Thus, a three-tier approach is offered in this chapter. After summarizing the findings from the previous chapters, a "step back" will allow reflections on them from a more general perspective, then yet another step back will discuss this study's theoretical implications (and draw some additional comparisons from outside South Florida). Finally, it will explore possibilities for future research in this area and attempt to draw some overall lessons.

First-Tier Conclusions

There are five principal findings. First, and most important, Andrew had no apparent negative electoral effects for the incumbents examined in this study. That is, the officials fared no worse in reelections in the aftermath of a major disaster. Incumbents adjusted their activities to include more, and more visible, hurricane-related duties and emphasize their roles as elected officials, so the disaster served to reinforce the incumbency advantage. Indeed, many incumbents campaigned less, or not at all, but were nonetheless unusually active and visible within their constituencies as a result of providing storm relief in one form or another. Some northern legislators even directed their efforts at southern relief (that is, outside their districts), but this seemed to have no negative repercussions. Cases peripheral to this study, however, indicate that the potential for negative effects of disasters on incumbents should not be discounted just yet, a point to which we will return below.

Second, and unsurprisingly, Hurricane Andrew did have a profound effect on the "process" of elections in Dade County. The disruptive effect was seen most clearly, and lasted longest, in the hardest-hit areas of southern Dade County. As one moves away from the severe damage zone (geographically speaking), one sees reduced hurricane-related effects. In the middle and northern zones, the relief and recovery periods lasted only a short time, a few months at most, and campaigns and elections beyond that initial period were affected minimally, if at all. Legislative elections were held soonest after the actual event, and the greatest impact on campaign strategies was experienced in those elections, even in the north, although voting outcomes were apparently unaffected.

Likewise, as one moves away from the hurricane temporally, the disruptive effects are reduced. After the first several months, the hurricane only affected the southern zone, where its physical effects lingered.

Third, campaigns and voting were especially affected because citizens moved out of the severely affected areas—some permanently—and were thus (at least temporarily) less involved in "normal" politics. Sensitive to the problems of their constituents, incumbents adjusted both their requests for campaign funds and their action profiles, increasing official constituent services while decreasing overtly political campaign activities, especially during the early stages of the relief and recovery periods, and especially in the hard-hit southern zone. For their part, municipal and legislative incumbents from the middle and northern zones of the county could—and did—use their experience and activities after the storm in campaigns, citing this work as one of the good things accomplished during their terms in office.

Fourth, neither municipal nor legislative incumbents received any blame or suffered any decrease in electoral support, except some that was self-inflicted (for example, incumbents restricting or eliminating fund-raising appeals and/or campaigning because their constituents were suffering from the disaster). In two legislative cases incumbents saw decreased vote shares, but not enough to compromise their victories. For example, one of these legislators had five challengers, but won in the primary without being forced into a runoff. His vote share decreased from the previous election, but new district boundaries in 1992 brought out many new challengers.

Fifth, and surprising at first glance, Andrew affected statewide races despite the fact that the disaster-ravaged area encompassed only a small part of the electorate. A significant number of statewide incumbents, led by the governor, radically adjusted their actions in response to the hurricane and later somewhat adjusted their campaigns. In the end, several statewide incumbents clearly benefited politically within the most damaged southern zones of Dade County. Although such support was insufficient to decide the final outcome of the elections—the area and population where this benefit is apparent are relatively small—this is very important. Although most statewide officials did not recall perceiving any political effects of Hurricane Andrew at the time, certain advantages became obvious to them upon reflection when interviewed for this study.

Second-Tier Conclusions

Let us now step back and reflect on two apparently opposing theoretical perspectives on how a disaster may affect the fortunes of incumbent elected officials. According to one perspective, a disaster could bring blame, in one manner or another, to an elected official, causing electoral loss, if not outright defeat. Inadequate preparation, poor or ineffective response, unnecessarily severe damage, or other catastrophic disaster consequences are among the types of blameworthy conditions that might result in voters turning against those perceived as responsible. On the other hand, disasters could bring praise to, and increased support for, an incumbent because of a strong/dedicated/competent/caring (choose one or more) response.

Conditions at the time of Hurricane Andrew could have resulted in blame of public officials. Thomas White (2001) identified three necessary conditions for blame to be placed in technological disasters (blame so placed, White also noted, may be on the most convenient—but not the most culpable—individuals): 1) A terrible event "could have been prevented by one or more persons"; 2) those persons were morally obligated "to undertake measures to prevent the disaster"; and 3) they "had no legitimate reason for not doing so" (White 2001, 25).

Inadequate building codes, noncompliance by builders, and lax enforcement of existing codes were often correlated to the severity of the damage south Dade County sustained from Hurricane Andrew. The county commission was primarily responsible for establishing and overseeing the local code, although municipal officials could have established stronger codes themselves. Note, however, that the county officials were not included in this study because the county implemented a major reorganization of its commission shortly after Andrew, based on a court decision handed down just two weeks before the storm. A nine-member at-large election system was transformed into a thirteen-member commission elected by district. This structural change would have affected elections at least as much as the hurricane, and the causal relations would have been virtually impossible to determine, thus the focus on municipalities and statewide races, where any hurricane effects could be isolated with greater certainty.

To be fair to Dade County, however, Andrew packed more powerful winds than the typical hurricane, and building codes were not designed to withstand 200 mph winds. Municipalities that adopted the Dade County code adopted the strongest in the country at the time. The fact is, mitigation practices frequently prove inadequate in an extraordinary event, and this was the case for Andrew. The winds in south Dade were fiercer than those against which the strongest codes were intended to protect.

The flawed pre-Andrew South Florida building codes, noncompliance with existing codes, and lax enforcement (Soto and Getter 1992; Silva 1992a; Finefrock 1992c) were nothing new. Similar problems had been identified after Hurricane Donna in 1960 (Getter 1992); thirty-two years later the problem still existed (or existed again), and people were still vulnerable as a result. No one may have gone to jail for faulty construction, but civil suits were brought against various contractors (Finefrock 1992d; Morgan 1992; Finefrock 1993). The term "Mickey Mouse construction" took on new dimensions after Hurricane Andrew, when the Walt Disney Company agreed to an out-of-court settlement to help rebuild condominiums inadequately constructed by its former subsidiary company (Finefrock 1993).

A few of the respondents spoke of the pre-storm building code issue. More, however, spoke of the inadequacy of the state's preparation to *respond* to disaster, and these were mostly the officials and political activists involved with statewide campaigns. This was a major lesson learned, and the improved system and new emergency command bunker in Tallahassee are seen as giving the state a much higher level of preparedness. In the event of another major disaster on the scale of Andrew anywhere within Florida, former officials and their supporters were convinced, the state government would respond well.

In sum, the impact of Hurricane Andrew was not totally apolitical, in the sense that no incumbent or challenger made any political issue out of it, or that any incumbent response was performed or framed in a potentially political manner, although the cases explored here were remarkably devoid of such positioning. One case peripheral to this study, however, indicates a possible negative political repercussion of Andrew: the case of the county mayor.

The Dade County mayor (in a weak mayor, strong county manager system) at the time of Hurricane Andrew avoided any public appearances in the first several days after the hurricane, staying out of the way of the county manager, the professionally trained emergency responders, and the media. Two respondents in this study mentioned this lack of action as a problem for the mayor, who did not seek to remain on the commission in the next election, at which point they temporarily eliminated the mayoral position as an interim step toward a new governmental system. One respondent said that the mayor:

> Never even showed up at the command post, which is a foolish thing to do. Because the public elects the mayor. He's their image of the person running the city even though it may be a strong manager form of government. . . . [Officials are] measured by that, you know. . . . [He] didn't do that. He probably, technically, was correct. So nothing was happening because county government was so slow in getting to the federal government and all the other things. The bureaucrats don't do anything that isn't in a straight line. That's why they elect citizens that are willing to go a little bit off campus.

Note that the former county mayor later was elected mayor of the city of Miami, the largest municipality within the county. This one case notwithstanding, and reflecting on all the incumbents examined in this study, we might want to transcend the post-disaster political blame versus post-disaster political credit dichotomy, viewing them less as opposites and more as two sides of the same theoretical coin. Moreover, the ability to "bounce back" may be at least partly within the control of the incumbent officials themselves. Although the incumbents were not fully prepared for the severity and related consequences of the disaster, their work with relief and recovery, their presence for an extended period, and the staff and resources they brought to Dade compensated for prior inadequacies.

This argument should be good news for elected officials, because cities frequently find that their existing disaster plans have little relevance to actual disaster situations (Kartez and Lindell 1990). It is also why "a public official will ordinarily say, 'Hey, whatever [is] the most politically protective rule [that] exists, that's the one we'll follow,'" in the words of one respondent.

Further reassurance can be had from the fact that voters appear to be discerning about what is or is not within the control of the elected officials to whom they look for leadership. Blame is not placed just because an individual is in an official position. Even the best plans can go—or be led—astray. For example, New York City had developed "a state-of-the-art command center" from which to manage emergency situations (Giuliani 2002)—much like that created in Florida after Andrew and described with pride by several of the statewide incumbents and their supporters (discussed in chapter 5). Former New York City mayor Rudy Giuliani (2002, 4) described his city's command center:

It was packed with computers and television screens to monitor conditions all over the city and beyond. It had generators in case the power failed, sleeping accommodations in case we had to stay overnight, storage tanks with water and fuel, and stockpiles of various antidotes.

On September 11, 2001, the day of its greatest need, the bunker was worthless: it was located in one of the five buildings within the World Trade Center complex that collapsed after the twin towers were hit by terrorist-hijacked commercial airliners. Early on that critical day, the command center was wisely evacuated and abandoned.

Local Government Expectations

One must consider the level of authority and responsibility of the respondent to develop a good understanding of the electoral impact of Andrew on a given incumbent. Many of the incumbents included in this study were officials of small municipalities; most were from small constituencies—cities or state legislative districts. Wolensky and Wolensky (1990; 1991) pointed out that local governments, especially of small cities, are—and according to the American concept of limited government should be—limited in capacity. Newton (1976) suggests that private interests want governments to be weak so that private goods and services will be used by governments and the status quo can remain entrenched. Incumbent elected officials are supported by private interests and easily re-elected in a mutually beneficial system. Elites, pluralism theory suggests, are involved with issues or causes in which they have special interests, expertise, and therefore legitimacy (Polsby 1963).

The core value of people after a disaster is helping victims; a second tier of values includes maintaining public morale (Dynes 1970). People in a disaster area are frequently optimistic about rebuilding and the future of their cities and neighborhoods (Dynes, Quarantelli, and Kreps 1972). Municipal officials in the southern zone were out in the community, helping where they could, and some recalled that in their campaigns they urged people to stay the course; keep hope alive and remain in the community to get past Andrew's terrible blow. This message was well-received because morale is typically high after a disaster—people feel good about surviving and helping others, and accordingly pull together as a community more than normal (Quarantelli and Dynes 1972; Dynes, Quarantelli, and Kreps 1972). The image of neighborliness and community cohesion was conveyed by several of this study's respondents.

Elections in Andrew's wake do not appear to have had unique results (Twigg 2009). A more recent review of elections after the busy 2004 Florida hurricane season showed similar results—in August, Tropical Storm Bonnie struck the panhandle and Hurricane Charlie smashed into Punta Gorda in Charlotte County; in September, Hurricane Frances hit Florida's east coast, Hurricane Ivan tore into the Pensacola-Escambia County region in the panhandle, and Hurricane Jeanne struck on the east coast at almost the identical spot that Frances had just hit. The paths of Charlie, Frances, and Jeanne all crossed through Polk County in central Florida.

Municipal and county incumbents from Polk, Charlotte, and Escambia Counties seeking reelection after the storms were generally successful. With a few notable exceptions, incumbents won or were defeated because of non-hurricane-related issues. Hurricane Charley struck shortly before primary elections; turnout was substantially reduced, and candidates adjusted campaign tactics. Six months after Charlie, two challengers for the Punta Gorda Commission defeated incumbents who were seen as too passive in the disaster's wake—remaining in the pre-disaster custodial roles Abney and Hill (1966) identified as potentially problematic. In another case, a Pensacola commissioner was out of town in June 2005 when Tropical Storm Arlene hit an area still living under blue tarps ten months after Hurricane Ivan slammed into the area. His extended unavailability was noted in the local media; he was soundly defeated in the next election.

George W. Bush stood for reelection in 2004. The season's first presidential debate, held at the University of Miami in Coral Gables, was considered a win for Democrat John Kerry. Bush appeared tired and perhaps inadequately rehearsed. Earlier in the day he had been in hurricane-ravaged Stuart, near the landfall site of both Hurricane Frances and Hurricane Jeanne weeks before. President Bush increased his margin of victory in Florida—razor thin in 2000—to over three hundred and eighty thousand that year, and although the disaster responses cannot be seen as the sole reason for his victory, his visibility (often with his popular brother, Florida governor Jeb Bush) after each storm certainly did not hurt his standing in the state.

Third-Tier Conclusions: Theoretical Implications

The idea that disasters are political has been stated often, but their effects on elections and campaigns have not been systematically studied to the extent that any theory has been tested and corroborated (or rejected). To that end, the following theory is offered for further consideration: A disaster will be electorally beneficial or harmful to an incumbent official to the degree that the event demonstrates (or a challenger uses the event to demonstrate) adequacy or inadequacy on the part of the elected official before and/or after the occurrence. In other words, the electoral environment is one in which actors (incumbents, challengers, voters, and so forth) operate. The environment itself is to some extent shaped by the actors themselves. The actors may operate to change the environment to a greater or lesser extent and in ways that are more or less beneficial to themselves.

Along this line, Niccolo Machiavelli wrote of a combination of *virtu* (ability and preparedness, in the original Roman meaning of the term:

"military courage and intelligence combined with civic responsibility and personal integrity" [Ebenstein 1969, 287]) with unique or historical opportunity, generally provided by *fortuna* (luck), that enables a leader to be great (Bondanella and Musa 1979). Although Machiavelli wrote in a different context, Hurricane Andrew provided an opportunity for leadership that rarely comes to elected officials. Subjects interviewed for this study often used that language—opportunity for leadership—when speaking of their own actions or those of officials with whom they were associated. This leadership opportunity has presented itself in other venues as well.

For example, the national election campaign season was well under way in 2002 when major floods hit parts of eastern Germany. Incumbent chancellor Schroeder was behind in the polls. In the previous election, Schroeder had campaigned on his party's ability to improve the economy, maintaining that he should subsequently be turned out of office if he failed. He was failing, and trailed his challenger in opinion polls "until the floods in August gave Schroeder an unanticipated opportunity to profile himself, especially in eastern Germany, as the 'man in charge'" (Roberts 2003, 59). He won.

The Machiavellian philosophical explanation may be instructive, but proves inadequate in the case of South Florida. There may in fact be a certain aura associated with some incumbents in a disaster's aftermath that goes beyond leadership-heroism. One former statewide elected official noted that incumbents were treated as heroes in south Dade after Andrew. And this phenomenon is not new. Landrum Bolling (1940) similarly described a businessman in Dayton, Ohio, as becoming a local hero after major floods in 1913: the owner of a cash register company located on high ground somehow managed to turn his factory into a producer of boats for the rescue efforts, as well as a relief center with dormitories, kitchens, and infirmaries for evacuees, and followed these efforts up by compiling crews to repaint neighborhoods and repair a government facility. In ensuing elections this local hero's cause—a new city charter—was approved overwhelmingly; he was himself then elected to the new city commission with the highest number of votes of any candidate.

More recently, after the September 11, 2001, terrorist hijacking that resulted in the destruction of the World Trade Center towers and outlying buildings as well as thousands of innocent civilian deaths, New York mayor Rudy Giuliani became something of a local—and national—hero; his approval rating soared, and he was even referred to as "a civic saint"

(Barry 2001; see also Murphy 2001a; Newfield 2002). . Though he was term limited in 2001, Giuliani was able to pass that support on like a relay runner.

A contentious Democratic primary weakened that party's candidate, Mark Green, and Republican Michael Bloomberg substantially outspent him, but in a largely Democratic town, the coup de grace for Green was the late endorsement of Bloomberg by incumbent—and local hero— Rudy Giuliani (Barry 2001; Cooper and Barbanel 2001; Greenhouse 2001; Murphy 2001a; Murphy 2001b; Nagourney 2001a; Nagourney 2001b; Purnick 2001; *New York Times* Editorial Board 2001). Leadership was an important frame of that campaign. Of course, the spotlight dimmed and moved on, and Giuliani was unable to capitalize on that civic sainthood seven years later in his bid for the White House.

Related to hero status is the war analogy that came out of several interviews. Heroes arise in times of war. In the aftermath of Hurricane Andrew, the far southern part of the county, subjected to looting and other crimes and then protected by a mass military effort, was frequently referred to as a war zone. Other war symbolism was used as well, such as referring to a major east–west thoroughfare, normally called Kendall Drive or Southwest 88th Street, as the "88th parallel." Some interviewees compared the disruption to campaigning in Andrew's immediate aftermath to holding an election after a war; people had more immediately important things on their minds.

Thus, whether perceived as heroes or simply as leaders, incumbents face both opportunities and challenges in disasters. Numerous subjects interviewed for this study noted that no challenger did—or could—use the disaster to their benefit. In the few cases where negative issues surfaced, either they were not incorporated into campaigns (such as pet- or livestock-related issues), they did not catch on as campaign issues (for example, that no one went to jail, or that insurance rates increased), or voters backed incumbents and their supporters (for example, the Homestead Commission).

To the Future

This study has identified phenomena for further exploration. Disaster may affect campaigns and voter turnout, but these effects are short-lived and associated with disaster-related physical barriers. An incumbent elected official involved with relief and recovery activity is not likely to experience retributive voting, according to the cases included in the present study, simply because of the disaster itself. Hurricane Andrew, however, hit an advanced, wealthy, industrialized nation. The response to this disaster included tremendous resource allocation to aid the affected communities.

Nevertheless, the theory needs to be modified. First, voter perception of their elected officials *before the event* becomes part of the post-event analysis. In addition, resources brought into the community after the disaster by, for, or on behalf of incumbents may be a factor in the electorate's perception of incumbent adequacy and worth.

Thus, a disaster will be electorally beneficial or harmful to an incumbent elected official: (1) to the extent that the event demonstrates (or a challenger uses the event to demonstrate) adequacy or inadequacy on the part of the elected official before and/or after the occurrence; (2) to the extent to which pre-disaster perceptions of adequacy or inadequacy exist in the minds of the electorate; and 3) to the extent to which incumbents and challengers can and do bring resources to the affected community.

Alternatively, the electoral environment is one in which actors operate. This environment is to some extent shaped by preexisting perceptions of the actors. The actors may operate to change, or bring additional resources to, the environment in ways that are more or less beneficial to themselves.

This points to new directions for future study. The current research should be replicated or similar studies should be undertaken to explore changes in campaign tactics or strategies, perceptions of incumbents about their chances of reelection, and any adjustments to campaigns or perceptions resulting from disaster. Another aspect that should be incorporated into future studies is whether, and to what extent, resources are brought into an area as a result of a natural or man-made catastrophe.

This would be an important element to consider, especially in comparative studies. In a wealthy country such as the United States, resources can be heaped on devastated communities and recovery—although oriented toward private recovery—is substantially enhanced by government largess. Does the availability of resources affect political actors differently in developing countries or regions? Is there any correlation of size or amount of relief on incumbent success in retaining office? If the private sector is weak, do domestic governmental relief efforts or international assistance have any effect on incumbents' reelection chances?

In light of the findings of this study, the 1992 Dade County Commission also remains an intriguing subject for future study. Hurricane Andrew hit in late August 1992. In January 1993, less than five months later, candidates began filing paperwork with the county elections department to run for a commission seat. When the qualifying period ended for the special election to fill the thirteen new seats, the record ninety-one candidates included seven incumbents (Filkins and Strouse 1993). Appeals challenging the new structure were filed, and candidates, unsure whether the election might be canceled or postponed, tempered their campaigns until the appellate court upheld the district court's plan—less than three weeks before the March general election (Filkins and Kidwell 1993; Filkins and Samuels 1993). Incumbents, however, used their still-considerable advantage in the meantime to gather campaign contributions—seven of the top eight campaign war chests were held by incumbents a month before the election (Tanfani and Filkins 1993).

Less than seven months after Andrew, confusion and apathy were noted preceding the election, resulting in a turnout of only 22 percent—the problem was apparently strongest among White non-Latino/as, only 17 percent of whom voted (Filkins and Kidwell 1993; *Miami Herald* 1993e). This may be partly due to the lingering disruption of normal life in south Dade following the hurricane. Ethnicity and opportunity also significantly factored in: the new system was intended to dilute the voting power of non-Latino/a whites and they knew it.

Other issues were also factors in reducing voter turnout. The only incumbent to be defeated in the general election was denying allegations of sexual trysts with a prostitute and cocaine use. An ongoing corruption investigation involved this incumbent, who disappeared from Dade County after his defeat and later surfaced in Australia.

Three other incumbents were forced into runoffs. Two of these were defeated in the April runoff, both non-Latinos in largely Latino districts (Garcia 1993; Rubin 1993; Tanfani 1993b; Tanfani 1993; Filkins and Branch 1993). Moreover, they were defeated by Latinos, one a state senator who had attempted a 1992 run for Congress, the other the mayor of the city of West Miami. One of the four successful incumbents was defeated in 1994 while fighting allegations of sexual harassment and ethics violations. Another retired from politics in 1994 at the age of seventy-one, and the other two remained on the commission until 1996, when they both ran for the newly reinstated office of county mayor.

*　*　*

An individual U.S. community is only rarely affected by an extreme event. A region, state, or set of communities is affected more often, and the United States as a whole often sees between fifty and a hundred major disasters declared annually. Thus, in exploring the effects of an extreme event on elections and election campaigning, one can take a final step back from Hurricane Andrew and South Florida, attempt to see the larger picture, and draw some broader lessons for U.S. disasters generally. One can also point to questions that merit further study.

Hurricane Andrew was an unusually severe event in south Dade County, but less so in the middle and northern zones. For most of the incumbents, there was no apparent electoral effect. Where an effect was discernible, however, the incumbents actually benefited from their involvement in relief, recovery, and rebuilding efforts.

At the statewide official level in particular, the various incumbents' decisions to go to the hardest-hit areas—in effect to relocate themselves, their offices, and their staffs—plus the significant amount of resources they brought to bear enhanced their reelection efforts. Some moved because they believed they should, but at least one moved because a politically astute governor led the way—and thereby set a symbolic commitment and performance bar for others. Upon reflection, not a single statewide elected incumbent expressed doubts about the wisdom or appropriateness of moving to and becoming involved in post-Andrew South Florida.

Apparently unconsciously, the various incumbents' decisions to be personally involved in south Dade recovery efforts and to give psychological reassurance to the local victims, as well as to provide significant resources for the recovery, constituted a type of "campaigning without campaigning." That is, constituency service substituted for campaigning, especially for those incumbents whose reelections were closest in time to the event (facing voters within two and a half months of Andrew) and those whose constituencies were physically disrupted for longer periods. This included legislators in the northern parts of the county, whose constituency service included enabling their less-affected constituents to aid the devastated victims of south Dade. Amounting to surrogate campaigning, these efforts provided incumbent visibility, free of charge, in a manner that few campaigns can match.

Thus, a nuanced interaction appears between: (1) an extreme event for which incumbents incurred little or no blame; (2) resources to support enhanced constituent service when that service was of unusual importance; (3) visible official activity that constituted surrogate campaigning without the appearance of campaigning; and (4) low-key campaign activities where that appeared feasible/acceptable. This four-element interaction, however, required a fifth component: intelligent incumbents who could see constituent needs and respond (with or without authority) and adjust their service (surrogate campaign) activities in an unprecedented post-disaster environment.

It must be emphasized that incumbents interviewed for this study did not adjust constituent service activities because of election considerations, but rather to meet constituent needs. The electoral effects of those activity adjustments were considered only after the fact—in most cases, in reflective responses to questions raised by this study.

An extreme event affects both elected officials and their constituencies. The elected officials continue, and increase, ongoing constituent service, perhaps bringing additional resources to the table. Some resources go directly to the constituency, whereas others are used to enhance the official's service capabilities. To reiterate the second-tier reflection: with sufficient resources aiding constituents and enhancing constituent service, formal "campaigning" becomes superfluous.

An interesting comparison also emerges from this study: where incumbents were from Andrew's middle or northern damage zones and reelection campaigns were several months or years after the event, few additional resources were used to increase constituent service. Thus, the interaction between event impact, resources, and constituency service as surrogate campaigning was reduced—and more traditional campaigning was the norm.

Can incumbents in other parts of the United States draw political lessons from Hurricane Andrew? The answer is "yes." First, the more severe a disaster's impact, the more elected officials must work to ensure that resources are provided to victims, and the greater constituent service activities should become. Second, and almost a corollary to the first, formal or typical campaign activities should be (publicly) suspended or reduced in disaster environments, allowing enhanced constituency service activities to (quietly) replace them. Third, where disaster effects are less severe or where actions are taken to quickly ameliorate them, incumbents should not count on the event to enhance reelection chances. In those situations, normal campaigning should be resumed quickly.

Future research on the disaster-election nexus should seek to further elaborate the five-element interaction (event characteristics, resources, constituency service/surrogate campaigning, regular campaigning, and incumbent acuity) to see how it changes in different geographic and electoral environments. Only through a better understanding of this interaction may the impact of a disaster on incumbent reelection chances be fully understood.

Appendix: Methodology

Hurricane Andrew's legacy of significant damage in and social disruption to Dade County, Florida, is well documented, as is the widespread perception of slow and sloppy government response (Peacock, Morrow, and Gladwin 2000; Provenzo and Provenzo 2002). This study focused on the following questions:

1. What were the electoral outcomes for the incumbents in the first and second post-Andrew elections? Did any lose, or receive less (or more) support? Did any patterns established before the hurricane change after the event?
2. How did the hurricane affect incumbent perceptions of their own reelection chances? Did incumbents believe at the time that they were more or less vulnerable, or unaffected?
3. Why?
4. Based on those perceptions, how did incumbents respond in their campaigns?

Questions 2–4 are inherently qualitative in nature. Only the first set of questions is potentially conducive to any quantitative analysis. The stories of the incumbents presented within this volume are instructive and important; for those more numerically oriented, this appendix provides a more detailed explanation of the methodology and may therefore provide a modicum of solace.

Any of several power relationships in a community may be affected by a disaster. Hurricane Andrew affected several political jurisdictions, each with multiple officials, both appointed and elected. Although both appointed and elected officials might be affected by a disaster, this study focuses on elections and multiple incumbent elected officials. A sample of municipal governments was included in the study, beginning with the only two cities in the most severely affected area.

Election results and campaigns in three regions of the county were identified. Hurricanes have some common characteristics: Intense winds circulate around an eye of calm; the strongest winds are found in the area in and immediately around the eye, the eye wall; winds gradually weaken out to the edge of the storm system. Andrew moved rather quickly across South Florida, dropping little rain but spawning a sixteen-foot-high storm surge at landfall. (At impact, Hurricane Katrina's winds were less severe, but the storm surge was about twice as high and much more destructive.)

Andrew's eye wall and strongest winds covered an area twenty to twenty-five miles across, throughout the area south of Southwest 112th Street (Clifford 1992, 23A; Mann 1993, 4; Morrow 2000, 4). Large portions of that area suffered severe damage, and the remaining area suffered moderate damage. Most residential damage occurred south of Southwest 112th Street (Haag Engineering 1992). The midsection of the county adjacent to the hardest-hit area, north of Southwest 112th Street but south of Southwest 40th Street, suffered predominantly moderate damage, with numerous small pockets of severe damage. The area north of Southwest 40th Street experienced only mild damage.

I examined three levels of elected officials, beginning at the municipal level with city commissioners and mayors. Florida City (five elected officials) and the city of Homestead (seven elected officials) were, in 1992 when Hurricane Andrew struck, the only municipalities completely within the southern/severe damage section of the county affected by the worst of Andrew's winds. The city of South Miami (five elected officials) and the village of Key Biscayne (seven elected officials) were the only two municipalities entirely within the middle/moderate damage zone at the time of Hurricane Andrew.

Key Biscayne is an island community that experienced coastal flooding as well as substantial wind damage. Businesses on Key Biscayne were affected significantly. Popular Bill Baggs State Park, adjacent to the village, and two major resort hotels in the village were closed for long periods due to hurricane damage (Faiola 1992b; Samuels 1993b). Some 128 housing units were determined to be uninhabitable (MDC Planning Department 1993, 1994); additional homes were badly damaged.

Key Biscayne was assessed by the county police department as having predominantly mild damage, an assessment apparently based partly on

Table A.1. 1990 population of selected municipalities, Dade County, Florida

South zone		Middle zone		North zone	
Homestead	26,866	South Miami	10,404	Miami Springs	13,268
Florida City	5,806	Key Biscayne	8,854	Hialeah Gardens	7,713
				West Miami	5,727

Source: Bureau of the Census, 1992, pp. 5–9 (1990 Census data).

susceptibility to crime. Access to the island is through only one road that traverses bridges and a tollbooth—a setup that can be easily restricted to limit any potential crime problems. The physical damage on Key Biscayne was at least as bad as, if not worse than, that of South Miami.

Two additional cities, Miami Springs (five elected officials) and Hialeah Gardens (five elected officials), from the northern, mildly damaged section of the county were initially included for comparison with those suffering more severe damage. Limiting the study to these six municipalities provided a manageable scale. During field research, unexpected difficulties in obtaining interviews from representatives of the northern area were experienced, however.

Few incumbents sought reelection with opposition after Hurricane Andrew, the focus of the study, and not all of those were available at the time this study was undertaken. One had moved from the area, and one was deceased. Another had been convicted of conspiracy to commit murder and faced election fraud charges, legal battles that had not concluded at the time of the study. Yet another qualifying incumbent was arrested on election fraud/bribery charges and was unavailable for interview. The city of West Miami, a third small municipality from the northern part of the county, comparable in size to Hialeah Gardens, Key Biscayne, and Florida City, was added to the study to compensate.

Table A.1 reflects the populations of the seven cities included in this study as of 1990. Only two municipalities lay entirely within each of the southern and middle zones. The cities selected from the northern zone are comparable in size; Hialeah Gardens and West Miami are similar in size to Florida City and Key Biscayne, creating a smaller city group, and the population of Miami Springs falls between those of Homestead and South Miami for a larger city group.

Given varying systems of staggered terms, the first reelection opportunity for incumbents stretched over several years. Table A.2 reflects the number of incumbents, across all seven jurisdictions, running for

Table A.2. Number of municipal incumbents seeking reelection and first post-Andrew election opportunity

	1993	1994	1995	1996	Total
Florida City		2		1	3
Homestead	3		2		5
South Miami		2			2
Key Biscayne	3	2			5
Hialeah Gardens	3				3
Miami Springs	2				2
West Miami		1		1	2
Total	11	7	2	2	22

reelection with competition in the first opportunity for reelection after the hurricane—which ranged between March 1993 and April 1996.

State legislative elections were also included in the analysis to determine the effects on legislators whose districts included the damaged areas. Twenty districts of the state House of Representatives and seven districts of the state Senate were completely or partly located within Dade County in 1992. Eight incumbents from districts located from the southern to the northern damage zone were challenged in their 1992 reelection bids. Other districts had unopposed incumbents or the incumbents did not seek reelection.

Most of the population in the hardest-hit area lived in unincorporated Dade County; the county government provided all municipal services and was therefore "closest" to that population. Therefore, the Dade County Commission might appear to be an important set of elected officials for this study. However, the county metamorphosed after the hurricane: the emergency management function was reformed and moved into the fire and rescue department, the building code was rewritten, movements to create new municipalities formed or energized in several parts of the county, and a new system of elected regional zoning boards was established, among other changes. An even more fundamental change occurred that was not caused by the hurricane.

Just before the hurricane, a federal district court decision, the result of a lawsuit initiated in 1986, required a new election system for the county commission (Krog 1993). The judge decided that the then-existing countywide elections discriminated against minorities by diluting their voting strength. The court-determined district election system replaced eight commission districts with thirteen. Commissioners had been required to live within the districts they represented, although elections were held countywide; now they were to be elected from smaller districts that differed in ethnic composition. Seven of the new districts had majority Latino/a populations, three were majority black (Filkins and Samuels 1993).

This major change in the election system, as intended, affected who was elected to the county commission. The systemic change and the hurricane coincided, and as such separating their effects on county commission incumbents would be nearly impossible, so they were excluded from this study.

Nor were congressional seats included in the study. Four congressional seats included portions of the south Dade area as of the 1992 election. However, Florida had gained four seats after the 1990 census, resulting in significant constituency adjustments and the carving out of majority-minority districts. Only one of the south Dade seats had an incumbent running in 1992, Congresswoman Ileana Ros-Lehtinen. First elected to the House in a special election in 1989, Ros-Lehtinen, a Cuban-American, was running in a newly created, heavily Latino/a district. Videos surfaced showing the challenger at a conference in Cuba, greeting, kissing, and gushing over Fidel Castro, the nemesis of most Cuban-Americans in South Florida, who were incensed at this outrage. Her challenge was easily defeated, regardless of activities or perceptions related to Hurricane Andrew.

Finally, four statewide races were reviewed to assess any impact of the hurricane on wider constituencies. The targets for interview included the governor/lieutenant governor and three cabinet positions—all incumbents who sought reelection in contested races in 1994. Hurricane-affected south Dade was only a small part of the statewide electorate, but the analysis of these races provided important and unexpected results.

To establish trends/patterns regarding incumbency, election results and voter turnout were reviewed at each level from 1980 through 2002. Beginning this review with 1980 allowed for the identification of post-hurricane pattern changes. Focusing not on the hurricane, but rather on incumbent officeholders, twenty-six interviews with these incumbents were completed. Key campaign supporters (campaign managers or other key staff/supporters) were also interviewed. Because the study focused on multiple cases (incumbent campaigns) after one event, it is best classified as an "imbedded case study" (Yin 1994, 41–42; 2003, 42–45). Given the nature of local politics, many of the incumbents ran their own campaigns and did their own fund-raising, but seventeen individuals connected to the incumbents were identified and interviewed.

The interviews probed various aspects of reelection efforts, including challengers, the degree to which fund-raising was altered (and how), the hurricane's effect on campaign style, adjustments made because of the hurricane, and changes in issues addressed. Finally, Andrew's impacts on constituencies and, most important, its effects on campaigning and reelection chances were explored with respondents. Of course, challengers could also have been interviewed, but they would not know *why* incumbents did what they did, even if they knew full well *what* they did. And few challengers opposed incumbents both before and after the disaster, making it difficult to compare pre- and post-disaster campaigns.

This study uses *multiple* incumbents and thus expands on the approach of Abney and Hill, who analyzed only *one* race and compared heavily flooded precincts with precincts where no flooding occurred. The inclusion of incumbents from less severely affected areas is also similar to May's comparison of counties affected/not affected by his selected disasters.

By the Numbers

The initial review of elections after Hurricane Andrew had as its central research purpose an examination of incumbents in order to determine whether the disaster had any impact on their reelection success. There were subsets of incumbents running for reelection with opposition, but the wider the net was cast, the more dissimilar the elections became—in terms of timing, the types of seats contested, and their partisan nature. In short, incumbents did not stand for reelection on the same day (or in the same year), there was a mix of single-seat districts and multiple-seat contests, and some were nonpartisan, while others fit into the typical Republican-versus-Democrat model. Further, in some cases the only contest for incumbents was in intra-party primary contests. This is not an issue of comparing apples and oranges; it is a fruit bowl with limited comparative potential.

Correlation analyses were attempted on subsets of municipal incumbents within damage zones, and on Dade County–based legislators. Nothing of any statistical significance appeared through these analyses. This was unsurprising, since incumbents and others close to their reelection bids saw little or no connection between their successes, or lack

Table A.3. Incumbent success (won)

	Municipal		Legislative	
	Correlation	Significance	Correlation	Significance
South zone	.311	.160	.062	.532
Middle zone	-.492*	.020	.050	.612
Months after Andrew	-.187	.406	.118	.230
Previous margin	.179	.425	.202	.110
Previous contest	-.025	.912	-.049	.620
Party	NA	—	-.026	.789

*Correlation is significant at the 0.05 level (2-tailed).
Sources: Statistical analysis of data derived from Division of Elections; Florida City Office of the City Clerk; Hialeah Gardens City Clerk's Office; Lilly, DeFranco, and Diefenderfer, 1994; Miami-Dade County Elections Department; Miami Springs City Clerk's Office; South Miami City Clerk's Office; Village of Key Biscayne Clerk's Office; West Miami City Clerk's Office.

thereof, and the hurricane, at least until prodded to think about such a connection during the interview process. Further, with the extremely small populations of these subsets of incumbents, it is unsurprising that no conclusive statistical results appeared.

Enlarging the size of the population included in the analysis does not substantially alter the results. Within the subset of incumbents from the seven municipalities there are an unusually high number of losses in the first round of elections after Hurricane Andrew (table A.3), but only for incumbents from the middle, moderately damaged area. Although this is significant at the 95 percent confidence level in point bi-serial correlation analysis, incumbents generally refuted the notion that the hurricane or their responses to it were important factors contributing to their losses. Thus, the statistical significance is not causally meaningful.

A simple Crosstabs analysis shows that 20 percent of the middle-zone incumbents won reelection after Andrew, while 76.5 percent of other incumbents won reelection in their first opportunity to run after the storm. An Odds Ratio risk estimate indicated that middle-zone incumbents were thirteen times more likely to lose than other incumbents.

Similarly, a Logistics Regression analysis determined that geographic area was a significant predictor of winning (p=.05) when controlling for the length of time (number of months) between the storm and when the election was held as well as the previous margin of victory in the election immediately prior to Andrew. The Logistics Regression showed incumbents in the middle, moderate damage zone were 9.7 times more likely

Table A.4. Incumbent vote margin

	Municipal		Legislative	
	Correlation	Significance	Correlation	Significance
South zone	.154	.494	.266*	.021
Middle zone	-.497*	.019	.078	.507
Months after Andrew	-.006	.979	.035	.767
Previous margin	.100	.657	.583**	.000
Previous contest	.017	.940	-.116	.321
Party	NA	—	.038	.748
(Number of cases)	(22)		(75)	

*Correlation is significant at the 0.05 level (2-tailed).
**Correlation is significant at the 0.01 level (2-tailed).
Sources: Statistical analysis of data derived from Division of Elections; Florida City Office of the City Clerk; Hialeah Gardens City Clerk's Office; Lilly, DeFranco, and Diefenderfer, 1994; Miami-Dade County Elections Department; Miami Springs City Clerk's Office; South Miami City Clerk's Office; Village of Key Biscayne Clerk's Office; West Miami City Clerk's Office.

to lose than incumbents from other areas. As noted above, however, interviewed incumbents generally refuted the notion that the hurricane or their responses to it were important factors contributing to their losses, indicating no causal relationship.

The legislative subset was expanded to all incumbents in the Florida Legislature standing for reelection after Andrew, (80 of 120 House seats and 25 of 40 Senate seats) for a total of 105 incumbents. Neither representation of hurricane-damaged constituencies nor timing of elections correlated with incumbent victory; nor did vote margins in the election prior to Andrew, opposition in the incumbents' prior election, or political party.

Similarly, when the Pearson test was run for the incumbent vote margin variable (table A.4), there is a negative correlation for municipal incumbents in the middle/moderate damage zone, significant at the 95 percent confidence level, but we have seen that this is probably not causally related to Hurricane Andrew. Legislative incumbents whose districts were totally or partially in the southern, severely damaged areas of Dade County enjoyed stronger victory margins than other legislators throughout the state, significant at the 95 percent confidence level. However, a stronger correlation existed with the vote margin for the election prior to Andrew, and the two incumbents from the south zone were popular in their districts before the storm.

Table A.5. Florida legislative incumbents, 1992 elections

	Incumbent won		Vote margin	
	Correlation	Significance	Correlation	Significance
Latino/a	.052	.599	.272*	.019
African American	.114	.248	.101	.387
College-educated	-.148	.133	-.020	.868
District income	-.077	-.049	.054	.643
South zone	.062	.532	.266*	.021
Middle zone	.050	.612	.078	.507
(Number of cases)	(105)		(75)	

*Correlation is significant at the 0.05 level (2-tailed).
Sources: Statistical analysis of data derived from Division of Elections; Florida City Office of the City Clerk; Hialeah Gardens City Clerk's Office; Lilly, DeFranco, and Diefenderfer, 1994; Miami-Dade County Elections Department; Miami Springs City Clerk's Office; South Miami City Clerk's Office; Village of Key Biscayne Clerk's Office; West Miami City Clerk's Office.

Using election results data from the Division of Elections of the Florida Department of State and legislative district data from *The Almanac of State Legislators* (Lilly, DeFranco, and Diefenderfer 1994), the success rate (won the election) and margins of success (vote margins) were also tested (table A.5) against district demographics—ethnicity, education levels, income, and geographic location. No significant relationship appeared with success as the dependent variable. However, when the relative level of success (vote margin) was used as the dependent variable, two variables indicated significance at the 95 percent confidence level—the level of Latinos/as in the district population and the location of the district in the southern part of Dade County, which was most impacted by the storm. Indications were seen earlier in this volume that ethnicity is an extremely important factor in politics.

Finally, because the number of incumbents from the southern and middle Dade County zones was small (3 and 2, respectively, out of 105 cases statewide), the two areas were combined into a zone of hurricane-impacted districts. As with the previous analysis, no interesting success correlations were indicated using the slightly largely "impacted" zone. The margin of victory (vote margin) did correlate at the 95 percent confidence level with the percentage of Latinos/as in the constituency and with location of the incumbents' districts, with those from affected areas having high margins of victory.

Two additional correlations were indicated in this analysis, both significant at the 99 percent confidence level: the percentage of constituents that were white non-Latinos/as and the margin of victory in the election prior to Hurricane Andrew. A higher Latino/a percentage and a lower percentage of white non-Latinos/as are flip sides of the same coin. Statewide, the expected incumbency advantage is consistent, with high vote margins in the election prior to the hurricane correlating with high vote margins in the first post-Andrew election.

We have also seen that the voters most impacted by Hurricane Andrew were very supportive of incumbent officeholders, who were perceived after the disaster as being accessible and working hard to help affected constituents. This further supports Peter May's 1985 study indicating that visibility of the incumbent was related to the incumbent's reelection chances. Thus, although this study was qualitative in structure, it is clear that more quantitative assessments support its qualitative conclusions.

Bibliography

Abney, F. Glenn, and Larry B. Hill. 1966. "Natural Disasters as a Potential Variable: The Effect of a Hurricane on an Urban Election." *American Political Science Review* 60 (December): 974–81.

Acle, Ana, and Todd Hartman. 1993. "NMB OKs Tax to Build New Police Station." *Miami Herald*, November 3: 13A.

Adams, Marilyn. 1992. "Community Banks Face Uncertain Future: Losses in Storm May Hurt Ability to Make Loans." *Miami Herald*, September 7: 7BM.

Alvarez, Lizette. 1992a. "Job-Seekers Flood S. Dade, Seek Gold Amid Ruins." *Miami Herald*, September 10: 1B.

———. 1992b. "Tenants, Landlords Feud After Andrew: Renters Refuse to Abandon Units." *Miami Herald*, October 2: 1A.

———. 1992c. "Housing Loss Imperils Harvest in S. Dade." *Miami Herald*, October 15: 1A.

———. 1992d. "Storm's Invisible Toll: Depression, Anxiety, Stress-Related Illness." *Miami Herald*, December 8: 1A.

Anderson, Paul. 1992a. "Politics Mixes with Aid Policy." *Miami Herald*, September 1: 17A.

———. 1992b. "Emergency Agency is Under Fire: FEMA Efforts Called 'Pathetically Sluggish.'" *Miami Herald*, September 6: 26A.

———. 1992c. "Florida Officials Lobby for Aid: AB Funding Faces a Fight." *Miami Herald*, September 9: 17A.

———. 1992d. "$8 Billion On Way to Florida." *Miami Herald*, September 19: 1A.

Anderson, Paul, Gail Epstein, and Martin Merzer. 1992. "Setback for Homestead: Relief Bill Excludes Money for Air Base." *Miami Herald*, September 11: 1A.

Anderson, Paul, Grace Lim, and Martin Merzer. 1992. "Chiles Seeks $9 Billion in Aid: Bush Will Urge $7.2 Billion Package." *Miami Herald*, September 9: 1A.

Anderson, William A. 1973. "Disaster and Organizational Change in Anchorage." In *The Great Alaska Earthquake of 1964: Human Ecology Volume*, 96–115. Washington, D.C.: National Academy of Sciences.

Andrews, Patricia, and Felicia Gressette. 1980. "Fasulo Wins; Runoffs Set in Mayor, Commission Races." *Miami Herald*, January 24: 3N.

Arthur, Lisa. 1994. "Voters in Florida City Return 2 Incumbents to Positions." *Miami Herald*, January 30: 3N.

Associated Press. 1994. "Turnout Could Be the Key for GOP." *Miami Herald*, October 29: 12A.

———. 2004. "Spread of Citrus Canker Blamed on Storms." *The Ledger*, October 17. B6.

Auxier, Sharon. 2003. Personal correspondence from Homestead city clerk, Sharon Auxier, to author. January 10.

Averch, Harvey, and Milan J. Dluhy. 2000. "Crisis Decision Making and Management." In *Hurricane Andrew: Ethnicity, Gender, and the Sociology of Disasters*, edited by Walter Gillis Peacock, Betty Hearn Morrow, and Hugh Gladwin, 75–91. Miami: International Hurricane Center.

Balmaseda, Liz. 1994. "Non-Group's Appointment Far from Democracy." *Miami Herald*, April 16: 1B.

Barkun, Michael. 1974. *Disaster and the Millennium*. New Haven: Yale University Press.

Barnhart, John D. 1925. "Rainfall and the Populist Party in Nebraska." *American Political Science Review* 19 (August): 527–40.

Barry, Dan. 2001. "An Election in a Shadow: Attempting to Follow an Outsized Giuliani." *New York Times*, November 7: A1.

Barton, Allan H. 1970. *Communities in Disaster: A Sociological Analysis of Collective Stress Situations*. Garden City, N.Y.: Anchor Books.

Bates, F. L., C. W. Fogleman, V. J. Parenton, R. H. Pittman, and G. S. Tracy. 1963. *The Social and Psychological Consequences of a Natural Disaster: A Longitudinal Study of Hurricane Audrey*. Disaster Research Group Disaster Study Number 18, Publication 1981. Washington, D.C.: National Academy of Sciences—National Research Council.

Batista, Elysa. 2002a. "Mayor Tenders Resignation, Is Leaving Area." *Miami Herald*. January 6: 3W.

———. 2002b. "Mayor Gives Resignation, Is Leaving Area: Diaz-Padron Served Since June." *Miami Herald*. January 10: 3E.

———. 2002c. "At Least Four Commission Seats Will Be Open." *Miami Herald*. February 7: 3E.

———. 2002d. "Zoning Chairman Elected to W. Miami Commission." *Miami Herald*. February 10: 3E.

———. 2002e. "W. Miami Incumbents Get Free Pass." *Miami Herald*. February 24: 6W.

———. 2002f. "Mayor, Commissioners Retain Seats: No One Challenges Incumbents." *Miami Herald*. February 28: 3E.

Betancourt, Marie. 1982. "Campaigning Continues for Riccio, Sereik." *Miami Herald*, March 4: 3N.

Birger, Larry. 1992. "Business Leaders Hammer Out Plan for State's Recovery." *Miami Herald*, August 28: 1B.

Birkland, Thomas A. 2006. *Lessons of Disaster: Policy Change after Catastrophic Events*. Washington, D.C.: Georgetown University Press.

Black, Earl, and Merle Black. 1987. *Politics and Society in the South*. Cambridge, Mass.: Harvard University Press.

Bolling, Landrum R. 1940. "City Manager Government in Dayton." In *City Manager Government in Seven Cities*, edited by Frederick C. Mosher, Arthur Harris, Howard White, et. al., 257–322. Chicago: Public Administration Service.

Bondanella, Peter, and Mark Musa, eds. and trans. 1979. *The Portable Machiavelli*. New York: Penguin Books.

Bousquet, Steve, and Ron Ishoy. 1992. "Storm May Mess Up Primaries." *Miami Herald*, August 25: 5A.

Branch, Karen. 1992a. "A Sea Change Washing Over Dade Politics." *Miami Herald*, May 31: 6B.

———. 1992b. "In a Lackluster Year, Some Dade Legislators Shine." *Miami Herald*, July 12: 1B.

———. 1992c. "Casting about for Ballot Locations: Replacements for Blown-Away Polling Places Hard to Pin Down." *Miami Herald*, September 4: 8B.

———. 1992d. "Incumbents Fight Newcomers' Bids for House Seats." *Miami Herald*, September 6: 4B.

———. 1993. "A Coup for Ander Crenshaw: No-Tax-Hike Budget Could Propel Run for Governor." *Miami Herald*, April 5: 11A.

———. 1994. "The Vote Got Out: Off-Year Turnout Sets Record." *Miami Herald*, November 12: 1B.

———. 1995. "Dade Retains its Legislative Clout; Rookies Fare OK." *Miami Herald*, May 14: 1B.

———. 1997. "Big Races, Big Changes for Dade: Miami, Hialeah, Beach Face Crucial Decisions." *Miami Herald*, November 3: 1A.

Branch, Karen, and Steve Bousquet. 1995. "Legislative Scorecard: The House." *Miami Herald*, May 14: 6B.

Brennan, Fran. 1992a. "Low Enrollments after Storm Worry South Dade Educators." *Miami Herald*, October 15: 2N.

———. 1992b. "Sea of Renters Left Homeless and Adrift." *Miami Herald*, October 15: 6N.

———. 1993a. "South Dade Lawmakers Focus on Rebuilding." *Miami Herald*, January 28: 3N.

———. 1993b. "Homestead Seeks to Expand City: Affected Residents Reportedly Agree." *Miami Herald*, June 17: 3N.

———. 1993c. "Business Recovery Bogs Down: As Many as 1,900 Haven't Reopened." *Miami Herald*, October 7: 3N.

Brennan, Fran, Tom Fiedler, and Martin Merzer. 1992. "A National Appeal: Bush Asks 'Nation of Neighbors' to Help: Vows to Rebuild Homestead Air Force Base." *Miami Herald*, September 2: 1A.

Brennan, Fran, Dexter Filkins, and Martin Merzer. 1992. "The War Zone: Flurry of Action but Still Few Beds: Bush, Clinton Both Plan Visits." *Miami Herald*, September 1: 1A.

Brennan, Fran, and Todd Hartman. 1993. "Boosting Status of Area a Priority for Candidates." *Miami Herald*, January 31: 3N.

Bullard, Robert D., and Beverly Wright. 2009. "Race, Place, and the Environment in Post-Katrina New Orleans." In *Race, Place, and Environmental Justice after Hur-*

ricane Katrina: Struggles to Reclaim, Rebuild, and Revitalize New Orleans and the Gulf Coast, edited by Robert D. Bullard and Beverly Wright, 19–47. Boulder, Colo.: Westview Press.

Bureau of Archives and Record Management, Division of Library and Information Services, Florida Department of State. May 1999. *General Records Schedule GS3 for Supervisors of Elections*. Tallahassee: Florida Department of State.

Bureau of the Census, U.S. Commerce Department. 1963. *U.S. Census of Population. Volume 1: Characteristics of the Population; Part 2: Florida*. Washington, D.C.: U.S. Government Printing Office.

———. 1973. *Census of Population. Volume 1: Characteristics of the Population; Part 2: Florida, section 2*. Washington, D.C.: U.S. Government Printing Office.

———. 1982. *1980 Census of Population. Volume 1: Characteristics of the Population, chapter A: Number of Inhabitants; Part 2: Florida, section 1–2*. Washington, D.C.: U.S. Government Printing Office.

———. 1992. *1990 Census of Population, General Population Characteristics; Florida, section 1 of 2*. Washington, D.C.: U.S. Government Printing Office.

———. 1997. "U.S. Metropolitan Area Data." *1997 Statistical Abstract of the United States*. Washington, D.C.: U.S. Government Printing Office.

———. 2002. "State and County Quick Facts." Data derived from *Population Estimates, 2000 Census of Population and Housing*. http://quickfacts.census.gov/qft/states/12/12025.html (October 29, 2003).

Camacho, Maria. 1997. "Gardens Voters to Decide on Mayor, Terms." *Miami Herald*, March 2: 3N.

———. 1998. "Hialeah Gardens to Vote on Mayor's Powers." *Miami Herald*, February 26: 3N.

Carver, Joan, and Tom Fiedler. 1999. "Florida: A Volatile National Microcosm." In *Southern Politics in the 1990s*, edited by Alexander P. Lamis, 343–76. Baton Rouge: Louisiana State University Press.

Cauvin, Henri E. 1996. "Key Biscayne Mayor Elected to Second Term: 2 Council Seats Still Up for Grabs." *Miami Herald*. October 2: 6B.

Chardy, Alfonso, and Cynthia Corzo. 1992. "Dade Leaders Consider Plans for the Future." *Miami Herald*, August 31: 23A.

Clifford, Dan. 1992. "Assessing Andrew's Damage." *Miami Herald*, August 31: 23A.

Colburn, David R., and Lance deHaven-Smith. 1999. *Government in the Sunshine State: Florida since Statehood*. Gainesville: University Press of Florida.

Cooper, Michael, and Josh Barbanel. 2001. "Gains Among Hispanic, Black and Liberal Voters helped Push Bloomberg to Victory." *New York Times*, November 10: D3.

Cox, Gary W., and Scott Morgenstern. 1993. "The Increasing Advantage of Incumbency in the U.S. States." *Legislative Studies Quarterly* 18 (November): 495–511.

Crockett, Kimberly. 1992. "Long-Term Rebuilding Plan Pledged." *Miami Herald*, September 4: 2B.

Cummings, Valerie. 1984. "H. Gardens Campaign Winds Down Quietly." *Miami Herald*. March 4: 2N.

Dacy, Douglas C., and Howard Kunreuther. 1969. *The Economics of Natural Disasters*. New York: Free Press.

Dahl, Robert Alan. 1961. *Who Governs? Democracy and Power in an American City*. New Haven, Conn.: Yale University Press.

Dash, Nicole. 1995. *Inequality in Disaster: The Case of Hurricane Andrew and Florida City*. Unpublished master's thesis. Florida International University.

Davis, Ann. 1993a. "Growth, Rights on Agenda." *Miami Herald*, January 28: 3N.

———. 1993b. "Mayoral Runoff Hinges on Absentee Vote." *Miami Herald*, March 11: 3N.

———. 1993c. "City Council Members are Sworn in." *Miami Herald*, March 21: 4N.

———. 1994a. "Council Race Contributions Vary Widely: Hialeah Gardens Will Vote Tuesday." *Miami Herald*, March 3: 3N.

———. 1994b. "Hialeah Gardens Puts 3 Newcomers on Council." *Miami Herald*, March 10: 3N.

Davis, Bob. 1992. "Bush Response to Hurricane Is Viewed as Important to Re-Election Campaign." The *Wall Street Journal*, August 28: A12.

Davis, Morris. 1978. "A Few Comments on the Political Dimensions of Disaster Assistance." *Disasters* 2/3: 134–36.

de la Cruz, Ralph. 1991. "Incumbents Coast to Victories in Homestead." *Miami Herald*, November 6: 2B.

Deutscher, Irwin, and Peter Kong-Ming New. 1961. "A Functional Analysis of Collective Behavior in a Disaster." *Sociological Quarterly* 2, no. 1 (January): 21–36.

de Valle, Elaine. 1995a. "Springs Spells Election Issue CRA." *Miami Herald*. April 2: 3N.

———. 1995b. "Two Challengers Vow to Keep Fighting Redevelopment Group." *Miami Herald*. April 9: 2N.

de Valle, Elaine, Ivonne Perez, Charles Rabin, and Debra Franco. 1997. "Lots of Familiar Faces Win in Four Municipal Elections." *Miami Herald*. April 9: 2B.

Division of Elections, Florida Department of State Web site. http://election.dos.state.fl.us (October 13, 2007).

Donnelly, John. 1992. "Fear Invades South Dade's Dark Night." *Miami Herald*, August 28: 19A.

Donze, Frank, and Jeffrey Meitroit. 2006. "Many Nagin Donors Switch on Him: They're Bankrolling Other Candidates Now." The *Times-Picayune*, April 20: A-1.

Dye, Thomas R. 1998. *Politics in Florida*. Upper Saddle River, N.J.: Prentice Hall.

Dynes, Russell R. 1970. *Organized Behavior in Disaster*. Lexington, Mass.: Heath Lexington Books.

Dynes, Russell R., E. L. Quarantelli, and Gary A. Kreps. 1972. *A Perspective on Disaster Planning*. Disaster Research Center Report Series No. 11, Contract DAHC20-68-C-0117. Washington, D.C.: Defense Civil Preparedness Agency.

Ebenstein, William. 1969. *Great Political Thinkers: Plato to the Present*. New York: Holt, Rinehart and Winston.

Enarson, Elaine, and Betty Hearn Morrow. 2000. "A Gendered Perspective: The Voices of Women." In *Hurricane Andrew: Ethnicity, Gender, and the Sociology of Disasters*, edited by Walter Gillis Peacock, Betty Hearn Morrow, and Hugh Gladwin, 141–70. Miami: International Hurricane Center.

Epstein, Gail, Harold Maass, and Martin Merzer. 1992. "Officials Fight for Homestead: One Idea: Joint Use by Military, Civilians." *Miami Herald*, September 12: 1A.

Etheart, Pascale. 1997a. "Homestead Mayor: 10 Years is Enough." *Miami Herald*, March 6: 3N.

———. 1997b. "Homestead Mayor Earns Kudos as He Bows Out." *Miami Herald*, November 2: 3N.

———. 1997c. "Homestead Elects Two Newcomers." *Miami Herald*, November 5: 4B.

Faiola, Anthony. 1991a. "Key Biscayne Candidates Play Polite Politics." *Miami Herald*, September 2: 1B.

———. 1991b. "Conte to Head Key Biscayne: Ten Go to Runoffs for Spot in this New Government." *Miami Herald*, September 4: 2B.

———. 1991c. "Mayor Pleased with People's Choice." *Miami Herald*, September 5: 3N.

———. 1991d. "10 Candidates in Key Board Runoff Tuesday." *Miami Herald*, September 15: 4N.

———. 1991e. "Key Biscayne Voters Elect Last 5 Trustees." *Miami Herald*, September 18: 3B.

———. 1991f. "Cheers Ring in New Key Biscayne Government." *Miami Herald*, September 26: 3N.

———. 1992a. "Bass Wins as 35 Votes Divide S. Miami Race." *Miami Herald*, February 13: 3N.

———. 1992b. "Storm Deals Heavy Blow to Tourism on Key Biscayne." *Miami Herald*, September 6: 4N.

———. 1992c. "Storm-Swept Image Hurts Key Biscayne." *Miami Herald*, October 1: 3N.

Federal Emergency Management Agency (FEMA), Office of the Inspector General. 1993. *FEMA's Disaster Management Program: A Performance Audit after Hurricane Andrew*. Washington, D.C.: Federal Emergency Management Agency.

Feld, Allen. 1973. "Reflections on the Agnes Flood." *Social Work* 18, no. 5 (September): 46–50.

Fenno, Richard F., Jr. 1973. *Congressmen in Committees*. Boston: Little, Brown.

———. 1978. *Homestyle: House Members in their Districts*. New York: HarperCollins.

Fiedler, Tom. 1992a. "Storm or No, Election Will Be Held: Local Officials' Pleas to Delay Get No Response." *Miami Herald*, August 27: 1B.

———. 1992b. "Remap, Andrew Turn Election into Circus." *Miami Herald*, September 6: 1B.

———. 1992c. "County Is Ready for a Strange Election." *Miami Herald*, September 8: 1B.

———. 1992d. "Topsy-Turvey Predictions Fall Flat." *Miami Herald*, September 9: 1B.

———. 1992e. "Clinton Proposes Jobs Program with South Dade Rebuilding Effort." *Miami Herald*, September 10: 8A.

Fiedler, Tom, and Martin Merzer. 1992. "Relief Bottlenecks Bring Appeals for More Troops." *Miami Herald*, August 28: 1A.

Fiedler, Tom, Tim Nickens, and Terry Neal. 1994a. "Chiles-Bush in Fierce Finale: Both Are Forced to Defend their Attack Ads." *Miami Herald*, November 2: 1A.

———. 1994b. "Chiles-Bush in Fierce Finale: Bush, Chiles Race to the Finish: Contrast in Paces, Places Reflect Moods of Campaign." *Miami Herald*, November 5: 5B.

Fiedler, Tom, and Mark Silva. 1992. "Dade County Will Watch While Others Vote." *Miami Herald*, September 1: 17A.

———. 1994a. "Trail Mix: The Road to the Florida Election: More Floridians than Ever Registered to Vote." *Miami Herald*, November 1: 5B.

———. 1994b. "Trail Mix: The Road to the Florida Election: Graham Lends Support to the 'Cracker.'" *Miami Herald*, November 1: 5B.

Fiedler, Tom, and Mark Thompson. 1992. "Doubts Are Cast on Air Base's Future." *Miami Herald*, September 3: 1A.

Fields, Greg. 1992a. "N. Dade Rents Expected to Rise." *Miami Herald*, September 1: 9A.

———. 1992b. "South Dade's Recovery: How Long & How Strong?" *Miami Herald*, September 28: 21BM.

———. 1992c. "Andrew Scared Business Away, Survey Finds." *Miami Herald*, October 15: 1C.

———. 1992d. "A Post-Storm Windfall: Temporary Jobs Abound; Economy Still Weak." October 22: 1C.

———. 1992e. "Perot to Buy Center for Salvation Army." *Miami Herald*, September 20: 16N.

———. 1993. "Dade's Job Exodus: Labor Force Has Shrunk since Storm." *Miami Herald*, January 1: 1C.

———. 1996. "Civic Leadership: A Decade of Change." *Miami Herald*, January 1: 16BM.

Figueras, Tere. 2001a. "Colorful Slate of Candidates in Homestead." *Miami Herald*, October 2: 3B.

———. 2001b. "Warren Will Face Sovia in Run-Off: Homestead to Pick Mayor Next Week." *Miami Herald*, October 31: 1B.

———. 2001c. "Warren is Reelected in Homestead." *Miami Herald*, November 7: 5B.

Filkins, Dexter. 1992. "Metro Asks Army to Set Up Vote Sites: Storm Destroyed South Dade Polls." *Miami Herald*, September 3: 1B.

———. 1994a. "District 8 (South Dade)." *Miami Herald*, September 5: 2B.

———. 1994b. "Bad Construction: Who to Hold Accountable?" *Miami Herald*, September 4: 2B.

———. 1994c. "Hawkins Forced into a Runoff; Margolis Wins Commission Seat." *Miami Herald*, September 9: 4B.

———. 1994d. "Battered Hawkins Goes on Offensive: Metro Commissioner Refocuses." *Miami Herald*, September 10: 1B.

———. 1994e. "District 8 Metro Race: Ethics vs. Experience." *Miami Herald*, September 25: 1B.

Filkins, Dexter, and Karen Branch. 1993. "New Majority Reigns at Metro: Blacks, Hispanics Forge Dramatic Change in Dade's Politics." *Miami Herald*, April 21: 1A.

Filkins, Dexter, and David Kidwell. 1993. "Dade Voters Bewildered as Election Nears." *Miami Herald*, February 24: 1A.

Filkins, Dexter, and Christina Samuels. 1993. "Judges Clear Way for Elections: Court Upholds Dade District Plan." *Miami Herald*, February 27: 1A.

Filkins, Dexter, and Charles Strouse. 1993. "Rush Is On: Metro Races Draw 91." *Miami Herald*, January 27: 1B.

Finefrock, Don. 1992a. "OK, This Is A Test: How Many Nails Per Shingle?" *Miami Herald*, November 26: 2B.

———. 1992b. "Volunteers May Get OK to Fix Homes." *Miami Herald*, November 26: 1B.

———. 1992c. "Experts Urge Tougher Wind, Window Codes." *Miami Herald*, October 22: 1B.

———. 1992d. "Lawsuit Seeks to Block Rebuilding." *Miami Herald*, September 11: 4B.

———. 1993. "Disney Agrees to Pay for Repairs of Ravaged Country Walk Condos." *Miami Herald*, May 29: 1A.

———. 1994a. "Scarcity, Prices, Top Insurance Problems." *Miami Herald*, September 2: 1B.

———. 1994b. "Another Insurance Rate Hike? May Hit Homes in State Pool." *Miami Herald*, October 29: 1A.

———. 1994c. "Insured by Pool? Your Rates May Go Through the Roof." *Miami Herald*, November 2: 1A.

———. 2001a. "Top Officials Passed up Manager's Job: Miami-Dade's Penelas Denies Claims that He Set Conditions for Candidates." *Miami Herald*, January 21: 1B.

Florida Democratic Party. 1998. "Senator Darryl L. Jones." Campaign mailer paid for by Florida Democratic Party. Tallahassee: Florida Democratic Party.

Florida House of Representatives. 1980–2002. *Journal[s] of the Florida House of Representatives*. Tallahassee: Florida Legislature.

Florida Senate. 1980–2002. *Journal[s] of the Senate: State of Florida*. Tallahassee: Florida Legislature.

Florida, State of. 1968. *Constitution*. As amended. Tallahassee: Florida Department of State.

Garcia, Manny. 1992a. "3 Challenge Incumbent GOP Lawmaker." *Miami Herald*, July 30: 23N.

———. 1992b. "House 117: GOP Primary Will Decide Who Gets Job." *Miami Herald*, August 23: 3N.

———. 1992c. "Mobile Banks Help Put S. Dade Back in Business." *Miami Herald*, September 2: 19A.

———. 1992d. "Voters Go to Polls Thursday in 5 Legislative Runoffs." *Miami Herald*, September 27: 3N.

———. 1992e. "Three Newcomers Win Jobs in State House." *Miami Herald*, October 2: 3B.

———. 1993. District 6: Reboredo Cooks a Victory Paella." *Miami Herald*, April 21: 2B.

———. 1999a. "Vote Fraud Probe Targets Gardens Mayor." *Miami Herald*. November 20: 1A.

———. 1999b. "Mayor Says She's a Victim of Her Style." *Miami Herald*. December 7: 1B.

Garcia, Manny, and Angela Muhs. 1993. "Lawmakers to Discuss Health, Andrew." *Miami Herald*, January 28: 3N.

Garret, Thomas A., and Russell S. Sobel. 2003. "The Political Economy of FEMA Disaster Payments." *Economic Inquiry* 41, no. 3 (July): 496–509.

Giuliani, Rudolph W., and Ken Kurson. 2002. *Leadership*. New York: Miramax Books.

Godschalk, David R. "Rebuilding After Hurricane Frederic." In *Crisis Management: A Casebook*, edited by Michael T. Charles and John Choon K., 199–212. Springfield, Ill.: Charles C. Thomas.

Gonzalez, Jennifer. 1996a. "Florida City Voters Give Powerful Mayor's Job to Wallace." *Miami Herald*, January 28: 3N.

———. 1996b. "Newly Elected Officials List Youth as Top Priority." *Miami Herald*, February 18: 3N.

Greenhouse, Steven. 2001. "At the End, Labor Made Little Effort for Green." *New York Times*, November 8: D4.

Haag Engineering Company. 1992. *Hurricane Andrew Storm Damage Survey*. Miami. Miami: The Company.

Habib, Hal, and Fran Brennan. 1993. "W. Haven Courting Indians: Homestead Calls Effort 'Pathetic.'" *Miami Herald*, February 20: 1D.

Haner, Jim. 1992. "Lawsuits Planned to Delay Tuesday Vote." *Miami Herald*, August 28: 12A.

Hartman, Todd. 1992a. "Base Closing Hurts Retirees—They Can't Afford to Stay or Go." *Miami Herald*, October 8: 23N.

———. 1992b. "Army Corps Patched Roofs for Free: Homeowners Feared They Were Crooks." *Miami Herald*, October 15: 4N.

———. 1992c. "The Curfew Blues: South Dade Still Grinding to a Halt at 10 p.m." *Miami Herald*, October 15: 1B.

———. 1993a. "Low-Profile Group Plans 1,000 Homes for Homestead Poor." *Miami Herald*, January 10: 3N.

———. 1993b. "Election Revamp Is Put on Ballot Sept. 14." *Miami Herald*, July 18: 3N.

———. 1993c. "Homestead Voters Stand by Incumbents." *Miami Herald*, November 7: 3N.

———. 1993d. "Voter Turnout of 279 People Dismays Homestead Officials." *Miami Herald*, September 19: 4N.

Hill, Kevin A., Susan A. MacManus, and Dario Moreno, eds. 2004. *Florida's Politics: Ten Media Markets, One Powerful State*. Tallahassee: Florida Institute of Government.

Hill, Kevin A., and Dario Moreno. 2004. "South Florida (Fort Lauderdale, Miami, and the Keys): Florida's 'Melting Pot.'" In *Florida's Politics: Ten Media Markets, One Powerful State*, edited by Kevin A. Hill, Susan A. MacManus, and Dario Moreno, 255–90. Tallahassee: Florida Institute of Government.

Holly, Dan. 1992a. "Minorities to Gain Clout Across the U.S." *Miami Herald*, July 30: 1A.

———. 1992b. "Candidates Try to Take Visible Relief Role." *Miami Herald*, August 28: 12A.

———. 1992c. "Dade Suit Asks Delay of Tuesday Elections: County: Right to Vote Jeopardized." *Miami Herald*, August 29: 8A.

———. 1992d. "Thought Dade Roads Couldn't Get Any More Frustrating? Think Again." *Miami Herald*, September 1: 18A.

———. 1992e. "Turnpike Tolls Turn a Bad Traffic Jam into a Nightmare." *Miami Herald*, October 2: 4B.

Holly, Dan, and Steve Bousquet. 1992. "Dade's Election Postponed a Week: Judge Riv-
kind Orders Results Withheld in Multicounty Contests." *Miami Herald*, August
30: 9A.

Holly, Dan, and Karen Branch. 1992. "Redistricting Dust Settles; Races Are Set." *Miami
Herald*, July 23: 1B.

Huckshorn, Robert J. 1991. "Political Parties and Campaign Finance." In *Government
and Politics in Florida*, edited by Robert J. Huckshorn, 58–76. Gainesville: University of Florida Press.

Icardi, Kelley L. 2004. "Peace River Rages: Homes Flooded at Cracker Lake RV Park."
Highlands Today, September 9: 1A.

Jewell, Malcolm E., and David Breaux. 1988. "The Effect of Incumbency on State Legislative Elections." *Legislative Studies Quarterly* 13 (November): 495–514.

Joffee, Maria. 2003. Personal correspondence from Maria Joffee, Hialeah Gardens
city clerk, to author. January 14.

Kapucu, Naim, Maria-Elena Augustin, and Vener Garayev. 2009. "Interstate Partner-
ships in Emergency Management: Emergency Management Assistance Compact
in Response to Catastrophic Disasters." *Public Administration Review* 69, no. 2
(March/April): 297–313.

Kartez, Jack D., and Michael K. Lindell. 1990. "Adaptive Planning for Community
Disaster Response." In *Cities and Disaster: North American Studies in Emergency
Management*, edited by Richard T. Sylves and William L. Waugh Jr., 5–31. Spring-
field, Ill.: Charles C. Thomas.

Katy Sorenson Reelection Campaign. 2002. "Reelect Katy Sorenson Our County Commissioner." Campaign mailing paid for by the Campaign and approved by Katy
Sorenson. Miami: Katy Sorenson Reelection Campaign.

Keating, Dan. 1993. "Inspectors Put Stop on Work at Ocean Reef." *Miami Herald*, January 8: 5B.

Key, V. O., and Alexander Heard. 1949. *Southern Politics in State and Nation*. New York:
Vintage Books.

Kidwell, David. 1991. "Legislators Have Clout but Little to Work With." *Miami Herald*,
May 12: 1B.

———. 1993. "Lawmakers to Push Development, Health Care." *Miami Herald*, January 28: 3N.

Kingdon, John W. 1995. *Agendas, Alternatives, and Public Policy*. 2nd edition. New York:
HarperCollins.

Klingener, Nancy. 1990. "Key Biscayne Votes to Create New Dade City." *Miami Herald*,
November 7: 1B.

Kollars, Deb. 1983a. "Election with Few Issues Becomes Race of Faces." *Miami Herald*,
December 4: 22N.

———. 1983b. "Homestead Elects 3 Incumbents." *Miami Herald*, December 14: 2D.

Krasno, Jonathon S. 1994. *Challengers, Competition, and Reelections: Comparing Senate
and House Elections*. New Haven, Conn.: Yale University Press.

Krog, Kathleen. 1993. "He Fought for Right—And Changed the Face of Politics." *Miami Herald*, April 26: 13A.

Krupa, Michelle, and Frank Donze. 2006. "Mayoral Forum Is Deja Vu All Over Again: Front-Runners Tiptoe Around Tough Issues." The *Times-Picayune*, April 21: A-1.

Lapham, Lewis H. 2007. "Slum Clearance." In *What Lies Beneath: Katrina, Race, and the State of the Nation*, edited by South End Press Collective, 7–14. Cambridge, Mass.: South End Press.

Lewis, Ralph G. 1993. "Intergovernmental Relations and Coordination." In *Lessons Learned from Hurricane Andrew*, edited by Phillip H. Mann, 63–69. Miami: Florida International University.

Lilley, William, III, Laurence J. DeFranco, and William M. Diefenderfer III. 1994. *The Almanac of State Legislators*. Washington, D.C.: Congressional Quarterly Press.

Logan, John R. 2009. "Unnatural Disaster: Social Impacts and Policy Choices After Katrina." In *Race, Place, and Environmental Justice after Hurricane Katrina: Struggles to Reclaim, Rebuild, and Revitalize New Orleans and the Gulf Coast*, edited by Robert D. Bullard and Beverly Wright, 249–64. Boulder, Colo.: Westview Press.

Long, Phil, Paul Anderson, and Martin Merzer. 1992. "'We Will Stay.' Powell Boosts Efforts for Base, Recovery: State's Leaders Take Plea to D.C." *Miami Herald*, September 10: 1A.

Lyle, Cindy. 2009. Correspondence from Florida City Personnel Director, Cindy Lyle, to author.

Maass, Harold, and David Kidwell. 1993. "Lawmakers to Push Hurricane Issues." *Miami Herald*, January 28: 3N.

MacManus, Susan A. 2004. "Florida Overview: Ten Media Markets—One Powerful State." In *Florida's Politics: Ten Media Markets, One Powerful State*, edited by Kevin A. Hill, Susan A. MacManus, and Dario Moreno, 1–64. Tallahassee: Florida Institute of Government.

Mailander, Jodi. 1993. "Slowly, School is Getting Back to Normal." *Miami Herald*, October 6: 1B.

Mann, Phillip H., ed. 1993. *Lessons Learned from Hurricane Andrew*. Miami: Florida International University.

Mann, Thomas E. 1987. "Is the House of Representatives Unresponsive to Political Change?" In *Elections American Style*, edited by A. James Reichley, 261–82. Washington, D.C.: The Brookings Institution.

Marquez-Garcia, Sandra. 1998. "Voters in 3 Miami-Dade Cities Elect New Leadership." *Miami Herald*. November 4: 1B.

Marquez-Garcia, Sandra, Morgan Winsor, and Karen Branch. 1998. "Few Voters Decide Issues in Four Cities." *Miami Herald*. October 2: 1B.

Martinez, Draeger. 1999. "Homestead Mayor Wins Handily." *Miami Herald*, November 3: 2B.

Martinez, Draeger, Mireidy Fernandez, and Elysa Batista. 2000. "Dade Challengers See Mixed Results in Vote." *Miami Herald*. November 8: 5B.

Matheson, Scott M., and James Edwin Kee. 1986. *Out of Balance*. Salt Lake City, Utah: Peregrine Smith Books.

May, Peter J. 1985. *Recovering from Catastrophes: Federal Disaster Relief Policy and Politics*. Westport, Conn.: Greenwood Press.

Mayhew, David R. 1974a. *Congress: The Electoral Connection*. New Haven, Conn.: Yale University Press.

———. 1974b. "Congressional Elections: The Case of the Vanishing Marginals." *Polity* 6 (Spring): 295–317.

McClure, Robert. 1981. "Sergeant Gives the Signal that Mayor Had Won Again." *Miami Herald*. March 5: 2NW.

McGarrahan, Ellen. 1987. "Council Wins Vote on Key Biscayne." *Miami Herald*, November 19: 6N.

———. 1988. "Launcelott Wins S. Miami Commission Seat." *Miami Herald*. February 11: 3N.

McGuire, Michael, and Debra Schneck. 2010. "What if Hurricane Katrina Hit in 2010? The Need for Strategic Management of Disaster." Supplement to *Public Administration Review* 70 (December): S201–7.

Metro-Dade County Communications Department. 1993. "Hurricane Andrew Report Card: Recovery Overview Highlights: Post Andrew." *Citizens' Outreach: Important Information for South Dade Residents* 2, no. 14, September 8.

Metropolitan Dade County Planning Department. May 1993. *Population Estimates and Projections Post-Hurricane Andrew, Dade County, Florida, 1993*. Miami: Metropolitan Dade County Planning Department.

———. August 1994. *Housing and Population Recovery Post-Hurricane Andrew, Dade County, Florida, 1994*. Miami: Metropolitan Dade County Planning Department.

Miami-Dade County Elections Department Web site. http://www.miamidade.gov/elections/resources_reg-stats.asp (August 1, 2002).

Miami Herald. 1980a. "Calautti is Elected Florida City Mayor." February 13: 2B.

———. 1980b. "Porter Wins S. Miami Commission Seat." February 13: 2B.

———. 1980c. "Three Reelected in West Miami." April 9: 2B.

———. 1981a. "Grinnell, Morgan Win Springs Seats." April 8: 3B.

———. 1981b. "Homestead Voters Drop 1 Incumbent." December 2: 3B.

———. 1981c. "Homestead Throws Out its Incumbents." December 9: 4B.

———. 1982a. "Mayor Wins Reelection in South Miami." February 10: 3B.

———. 1982b. "Read Wins in Hialeah Gardens." March 3: 2B.

———. 1982c. "Riccio Wins Run-Off in Hialeah Gardens." March 10: 8B.

———. 1982d. "West Miamians Choose First Woman Mayor." April 14: 2B.

———. 1983a. "Hialeah Gardens Elects Five." March 9: 1D.

———. 1983b. "No One Can Win Tuesday, But 2 Hopefuls Will Lose." December 4: 23N.

———. 1983c. "8 Advance in Homestead Race." December 7: 2D.

———. 1984a. "Porter, Schwait Win in S. Miami Election." February 15: 2B.

———. 1984b. "Hialeah Gardens Reelects Three." March 7: 3D.

———. 1984c. "West Miami Elects First Latin Mayor." April 11: 2D.

———. 1985a. "Hialeah Gardens Elects Mayor to Second Term." March 6: 4B.

———. 1985b. "Miami Assistant Waste Director Wins Seat on Springs Council." April 17: 2D.

———. 1985c. "Homestead Voters Pare Council Field." December 4: 2B.

———. 1986a. "Florida City Commissioner Wins Re-Election." January 29: 2B.

———. 1986b. "FPL Mechanic Wins Florida City Run-Off." February 12: 2B.

———. 1986c. "Hialeah Gardens Incumbent Reelected." March 12: 2B.

———. 1986d. "Reboredo Named W. Miami Mayor." April 9: 2B.

———. 1987a. "H. Gardens to Hold Runoff for Mayor." March 4: 2B.

———. 1987b. "Hialeah Gardens Elects Councilman as New Mayor." March 11: 3B.

———. 1987c. "Miami Springs Mayor, Council Candidates Face Runoff Elections." April 8: 2B.

———. 1987d. "Springs Elects New Mayor." April 22: 2B.

———. 1987e. "Key Biscayne: Islanders Approve Village Council." November 18: 2B.

———. 1987f. "Key Biscayne: Village Council Holds First Meeting." November 25: 2B.

———. 1987g. "Homestead: Councilman Wins Mayoral Primary." December 2: 2B.

———. 1987h. "Homestead: Voters Elect DeMilly as Mayor, Return Kirk, Warren to Council." December 9: 2B.

———. 1988a. "Florida City: Police Chief Elected to Third Term." January 27: 2B.

———. 1988b. "South Miami: Launcelott Wins Commission Seat." February 10: 2B.

———. 1988c. "Nengel Would Help Hialeah Gardens." Editorial. March 6: 16N.

———. 1988d. "Hialeah Gardens: Kemp Defeats Nengel for Council." March 9: 3B.

———. 1988e. "West Miami: 3 Newcomers Voted Onto Council." April 13: 2B.

———. 1989a. "Hialeah Gardens Voters Oust Mayor Again." March 8: 2B.

———. 1989b. "Miami Springs: 4 Incumbents, 1 Newcomer Elected." April 5: 2B.

———. 1989c. "Elections Results: Homestead Council." November 8: 2B.

———. 1990a. "South Miami: Cathy McCann Elected Mayor; 3 Win Seats on Commission." February 14: 2B.

———. 1990b. "Hialeah Gardens: Three Re-Elected in Council Race." March 7: 2B.

———. 1990c. "West Miami: Newcomer, Incumbent Win City Seats." April 11: 2B.

———. 1990d. "Ranking the House." June 10: 18A.

———. 1991a. "Hialeah Gardens Re-Elects Oliveros." March 6: 2B.

———. 1991b. "Miami Springs: Five Elected to City Council." April 3: 2B.

———. 1991c. "How the House Ranked." May 12: 16A.

———. 1991d. "Legislative Scorecard: The House." May 12: 2B.

———. 1991e. "Key Biscayne Runoff Election Today." September 17: 3B.

———. 1991f. "Dade Results: Homestead." November 6: 2B.

———. 1992a. "Florida City: Incumbents Lead Commission Voting." January 29: 2B.

———. 1992b. "Hialeah Gardens: Two New Council Members Elected." March 4: 2B.

———. 1992c. "Key Biscayne: Sime Wins Village Board Seat." March 11: 2B.

———. 1992d. "West Miami: Mayor, 3 Commissioners Elected." April 15: 2B.

———. 1992e. "How the House Ranked." July 12: 10A.

———. 1992f. "Legislative Rankings: The House." July 12: 2B.

———. 1992g. "Well Done, Dade Voters: Election Challenge is Met." September 10: 30A.

———. 1992h. "Dade Farms Must Sow Again: After Reaping the Wind." September 28: 14A.

———. 1993a. "Hialeah Gardens: Two Challengers Make Mayoral Runoff." March 3: 2B.

———. 1993b. "Hialeah Gardens Election Up in Air." March 10: 3B.

———. 1993c. "Election '93: Meet the Candidates." March 11: 3N.

———. 1993d. "It's Official: Hameetman Is Gardens Mayor." March 13: 2B.

———. 1993e. "A New Day Dawns." March 17: 26A.

———. 1993f. "How the House Ranked." April 18: 10A.

———. 1993g. "Legislative Rankings: House." April 18: 4B.

———. 1993h. "Retiree Completes M. Springs Council." April 21: 8B.

———. 1993i. "In Brief: Key Biscayne: Festa Wins Mayor's Job in Landslide." October 6: 2B.

———. 1994a. "Hialeah Gardens to Pick 3 for Council." March 8: 3B.

———. 1994b. "Hialeah Gardens: Newcomers Win Three Council Seats." March 9: 4B.

———. 1994c. "West Miami Elects Newcomers to Commission." April 13: 2B.

———. 1994d. "How the House Ranked." April 24: 16A.

———. 1994e. "Election Preview: A Summary of Major Issues on Tuesday's Ballot." November 7: 20A.

———. 1995a. "Hialeah Gardens: Former Mayor, 3 Incumbents Elected." March 8: 2B.

———. 1995b. "Dade Results: Homestead." November 8: 8B.

———. 1996a. "Hialeah Gardens: Council Incumbent Wins Third Term." March 6: 2B.

———. 1996b. "In Brief: Government in Action: W. Miami Re-Elects Mayor and Allies." April 10: 2B.

———. 1996c. "Key Biscayne: Two Newcomers Join Village Council." November 6: 5B.

———. 1997a. "Hialeah Gardens Mayor Re-Elected." March 5: 2B.

———. 1997b. "Two Elected to Council in Springs." April 2: 2B.

———. 1997c. "Attorney Wins Commission Seat." May 28: 2B.

———. 1997d. "Around Dade: Key Biscayne." September 10: 2B.

———. 1998a. "Incumbents Win Florida City Elections." January 28: 2B.

———. 1998b. "Robaina Wins South Miami Mayor's Seat." February 11: 2B.

———. 1998c. "West Miami Fills Two Commission Seats." April 15: 2B.

———. 1998d. "At a Glance: Key Biscayne." November 4: 5B.

———. 1998e. "Hialeah Gardens Empowers Leaders." *March* 4: 3B.

———. 1999. "Springs Mayor Wins Seventh Term." April 7: 2B.

———. 2000a. "Florida City: 2 Incumbent Commissioners Re-Elected." January 26: 4B.

———. 2000b. "South Miami: Mayor Easily Turns Back Challenger." February 9: 4B.

———. 2000c. "Incumbents Win in West Miami." April 12: 2B.

———. 2000d. "Peters Elected in Key Biscayne; Guillen and Garcia Face Runoff." October 4: 2B.

———. 2001a. "Hialeah Gardens: Incumbent Mayor Swept Back into Office." March 7: 3B.

———. 2001b. "Miami Springs: Councilman Wheeler Wins Mayor's Seat." April 4: 3B.

———. 2001c. "Miami Springs: Runoff Determines Two Council Members." April 18: 3B.

———. 2003. "Hialeah Gardens: Prosecutors Weigh Retrial of Former Mayor." March 15: 3B.

Higham, Scott. 1992a. "Boom to Bust: Out-of-Town Truckers Told to Hit the Road." October 15: 1B.

———. 1992b. "Cleanup Starts at Bill Baggs Park." December 8: 1B.Mileti, Dennis S. 1999. *Disasters by Design: A Reassessment of Natural Hazards in the United States.* Washington, D.C.: Joseph Henry Press.

Monroe County Elections Department. 2003. *General Election Canvass Reports, November 6, 1990, and November 8, 1994.* Key West: Monroe County Elections Department.

Moore, Harry Estill. 1958. *Tornadoes Over Texas: A Study of Waco and San Angelo in Disaster.* Austin: University of Texas Press.

Moore, Harry Estill, Frederick L. Bates, Marvin V. Layman, and Vernon J. Parenton. 1963. *Before the Wind: A Study of the Response to Hurricane Carla.* Disaster Study no. 19, pub. 1095. Washington, D.C.: National Academy of Sciences—National Research Council.

Morgan, Curtis. 1992. "Stakes High in Debate over Wind: 'Millions' Rest on Speed." *Miami Herald*, October 8: 1A.

Morrow, Betty Hearn. 2000. "Disaster in the First Person." In *Hurricane Andrew: Ethnicity, Gender, and the Sociology of Disasters*, edited by Walter Gillis Peacock, Betty Hearn Morrow, and Hugh Gladwin, 1–19. Miami: National Hurricane Center.

Morrow, Betty Hearn, and Walter Gillis Peacock. 2000. "Disasters and Social Change: Hurricane Andrew and the Reshaping of Miami." In *Hurricane Andrew: Ethnicity, Gender, and the Sociology of Disasters*, edited by Walter Gillis Peacock, Betty Hearn Morrow, and Hugh Gladwin, 226–42. Miami: National Hurricane Center.

Moss, Dennis. 2002. Interview by author. February 5.

Muhs, Angie, and Manny Garcia. 1993. "Lawmaker Priorities: Rebuild, Reform." *Miami Herald*, January 28: 3N.

Murphy, Dean E. 2001a. "In Homestretch of Campaign, Mayor Endorses Bloomberg." *New York Times*, October 28: A31.

———. 2001b. "Bloomberg Recipe: Luck, Lots of Cash and a Hands-On Role." *New York Times*, November 11: A39.

Musibay, Oscar. 1993a. "It's Not Over Yet: Volunteers Are Still Needed in South Dade." *Miami Herald*, June 17: 4N.

———. 1993b. "All Signs Point to Progress." *Miami Herald*, October 17: 3N.

———. 1995. "Homestead Voters Pick Newcomer, 3 Incumbents: 14-Year Council Veteran Unseated." *Miami Herald*, November 8: 8B.

Nagorney, Neal. 2001a. "Bloomberg Puts Eggs in a Basket: Giuliani's." *New York Times*, October 28: A29.

———. 2001b. "Bloomberg Edges Green in Race for Mayor; McGreevey Is an Easy Winner in New Jersey: City 'Alive and Well and Open for Business,' Says Victor." *New York Times*, November 7: A1.

National Academy of Public Administration (NAPA). 1993. *Coping with Catastrophe: Building an Emergency Management System to Meet People's Need in Natural and Manmade Disasters.* Washington, D.C.: NAPA.

National Oceanic and Atmospheric Administration (NOAA), U.S. Department of Commerce. 2002a. "NOAA Press Release 02-107, August 21." National Hurricane Center, Tropical Prediction Center Web site. http://www.nhc.noaa.gov/NOAA_pr_8-21-02.html (September 18, 2002).

———. 2002b. "The Saffir-Simpson Hurricane Scale." National Hurricane Center, Tropical Prediction Center Web site. http://www.nhc.noaa.gov/aboutsshs.shtml (September 30, 2002).

Neal, Terry, Tim Nickens, and Tom Fiedler. 1994. "Candidates Speed through S. Florida; Jeb's Ride Bump." *Miami Herald*, November 6: 1A.

New York Times Editorial Board. 2001. "Mayor-Elect Michael Bloomberg." *New York Times*, November 7: A22.

Newfield, Jack. 2002. *The Full Rudy: The Man, the Myth, the Mania.* New York: Thunder Mouth's Press/Nation Books.

Newton, Kenneth. 1976. "Feeble Governments and Private Power: Urban Politics and Policies in the United States." In *The New Urban Politics*, edited by Louis H. Masotti and Robert L. Lineberry, 37–58. Cambridge, Mass.: Ballinger Publishing Company.

Nickens, Tim. 1990. "2 Lawmakers Again Named 'Most Effective.'" *Miami Herald*, June 10: 1A.

———. 1991. "2 S. Florida Lawmakers Ranked as State's Tops: Women, Minorities Wielding More Clout." *Miami Herald*, May 12: 1A.

———. 1992a. "S. Florida Lawmakers Lead Class: Survey: Jenne, Saunders Best." *Miami Herald*, July 12: 1A.

———. 1992b. "House Incumbents Rebut Backlash." *Miami Herald*, September 9: 7B.

———. 1992c. "Florida Backs Term Limits for Politicians." *Miami Herald*, November 4: 22A.

———. 1993. "Law and Order: Top Legislators Kept the Peace: Survey: Less Dissension, More Harmony in Capitol." *Miami Herald*, April 18: 10A.

———. 1994a. "Cool Heads Distinguish Top Legislators: Wallace, Kiser Rose Above Emotionality." *Miami Herald*, April 24: 16A.

———. 1994b. "GOP Nominates Smith for Cabinet." *Miami Herald*, September 18: 6B.

———. 1994c. "Agriculture Race Gets Hot in 11th Hour." *Miami Herald*, October 30: 6B.Nickens, Tim, Terry Neal, and Tom Fiedler. 1994. "Politics from the Pulpit." *Miami Herald*, November 7: 1A.

Nickens, Tim, Terry Neal, and Mark Silva. 1994. "Trail Mix: The Road to the Florida Election: Chiles Passes Bush in the Latest Poll." *Miami Herald*, November 5: 5B.

Nickens, Tim, and Mark Silva. 1994a. "Candidate Quits Cabinet Contest, Clearing the Way for Jim Smith." *Miami Herald*, September 17: 5B.

———. 1994b. "Trail Mix: The Road to the Florida Primary: 'Bill' Boards Blossom in House Race." *Miami Herald*, October 21: 5B.

Olson, Richard Stuart. 2000. "Toward a Politics of Disaster: Losses, Values, Agendas, and Blame." *International Journal of Mass Emergencies and Disasters* 18 (August): 265–87.

Ousley, Yvette. 1992. "Small-Town Mayor Earns Big-Time Pay." *Miami Herald*, October 7: 1B.

Palm Beach County Elections Department. 2003. *General Election Canvass Reports, November 6, 1990, and November 8, 1994.* West Palm Beach, Fla.: Palm Beach County Elections Department.

Paul, Sheila. 2003. Personal correspondence from Sheila Paul, Florida City city clerk, to author. January 29.

Peacock, Walter Gillis, Betty Hearn Morrow, and Hugh Gladwin, eds. 2000. *Hurricane Andrew: Ethnicity, Gender, and the Sociology of Disaster*. Miami: International Hurricane Center.

Pearl, Daniel, and Martha Brannigan. 1992. "With Growth Slowing, Florida Faced Clouds Even Before Hurricane: During 1980s Boom, It Failed to Prepare for Downturn and Has Been Hit Hard: A Hope: The 'Jacuzzi Effect.'" The *Wall Street Journal*, August 28: A1.

Platt, Rutherford H. 1999. *Disasters and Democracy: The Politics of Extreme Natural Events*. Washington, D.C.: Island Press.

Polsby, Nelson W. 1963. *Community Power and Political Theory*. New Haven, Conn.: Yale University Press.

Portes, Alejandro, and Alex Stepick. 1993. *City on the Edge: The Transformation of Miami*. Berkeley: University of California Press.

Provenzo, Eugene F., Jr., and Sandra H. Fradd. 1995. *Hurricane Andrew, the Public Schools, and the Rebuilding of Community*. Albany: State University of New York Press.

Provenzo, Eugene F., Jr., and Asterie Baker Provenzo. 2002. *In the Eye of Hurricane Andrew*. Gainesville: University Press of Florida.

Purnick, Joyce. 2001. "No Doubt: Money Wins Elections." *New York Times*, November 7: D1.

Quarantelli, E. L., and Russell R. Dynes. 1972. "When Disaster Strikes." *Psychology Today* 5, no. 9 (February): 67–70.

———. 1976. "Community Conflict: Its Absence and Its Presence in Natural Disasters." *Mass Emergencies* 1: 139–52.

———. 1977. "Response to Social Crisis and Disaster." *Annual Review of Sociology* 3: 23–49.

Rappaport, Ed. 1993. "Preliminary Report: Hurricane Andrew: 16–28 August, 1992." National Hurricane Center Web site. http://www.nhc.noaa.gov/1992andrew.html (October 10, 1999).

Reichley, A. James. 1992. *The Life of the Parties: A History of American Political Parties*. New York: Free Press.

Rejtman, Jack. 1995. "Allegations Dominate Hialeah Gardens Races." *Miami Herald*. March 5: 3N.

Rivas-Vazquez, Ana Gloria. 1985. "Borgmann, Ziadie Meet in Runoff." *Miami Herald*. April 4: 3N.

Roberts, Geoffrey K. 2003. "'Taken at the Flood'? The German General Election of 2002." *Government and Opposition* 38, no. 1 (January 2003): 53–72.

Rossiter, Clinton, ed. 1961. *The Federalist Papers*. New York: New American Library.

Rothaus, Steve. 1993a. "Schooling is Among Priorities: Legislators Ready to Go." *Miami Herald*, January 28: 3N.

———. 1993b. "Ex-Springs Mayor Voted Back into Office." *Miami Herald*, April 8: 3N.

Rowe, Sean. 1989. "Homestead Picks 3 Incumbents and a Newcomer." *Miami Herald*, November 8: 2B.

———. 1990. "Florida City Elects New Police Chief." *Miami Herald*, January 24: 3B.

Rubin, Aaron S. 1993a. "District 10: Dusseau Loses to Ex-Lawmaker." *Miami Herald*, April 21: 10A.

Russell, Gordon, Michelle Krupa, and Michael Perlstein. 2006. "Nagin Backer Softens Stance." The *Times-Picayune*, April 21: B-1.

Salazar, Carolyn, and Judy Odierna. 2000. "Convicted Former Mayor Granted Bond: Oliveros Goes Free While She Appeals." *Miami Herald*. July 29: 1B.

Salokar, Rebecca Mae. 1998. "After the Winds: Hurricane Andrew's Impact on Judicial Institutions in South Florida." *The Judges Journal* 37, no. 4 (Fall): 26–32.

Samuels, Christina A. 1993a. "3 Challenge Incumbent in Key Biscayne Race: Environment, Budget Are Top Issues." *Miami Herald*, September 19: 4N.

———. 1993b. "Souto Says Park Ought to Be Open: Hurricane Battered Key Biscayne Site." *Miami Herald*, June 17: 3N.

———. 1993c. "Tax Bill on Key Biscayne May Drop: But Fire Protection Is Added to Budget." *Miami Herald*, July 18: 3N.

———. 1993d. "Key Biscayne Eager for Return of Sonesta: Renovated Hotel Reopens on Friday." *Miami Herald*, September 26: 1N.

———. 1993e. "Revived Resort, Store Herald Key Biscayne Comeback." *Miami Herald*. October 1: 1A.

———. 1993f. "Council Hopefuls Get Basic: Key Biscayners Stress Efficiency." *Miami Herald*. October 24: 3N.

———. 1993g. "Newcomers Nearly Sweep Key Elections." *Miami Herald*. November 7: 3N.

———. 1994a. "New S. Miami Mayor Plans to Keep in Touch." *Miami Herald*. February 13: 3N.

———. 1994b. "New Faces Will Dot Key Biscayne Council: Taxes Were Among Top Island Issues." *Miami Herald*. November 13: 4N.

Sanyika, Mtangulizi. 2009. "Katrina and the Conditions of Black New Orleans: The Struggle for Justice, Equity, and Democracy." In *Race, Place, and Environmental Justice after Hurricane Katrina: Struggles to Reclaim, Rebuild, and Revitalize New Orleans and the Gulf Coast*, edited by Robert D. Bullard and Beverly Wright, 87–111. Boulder, Colo.: Westview Press.

Satterfield, David. 1992a. "State Warns Against Using Public Adjusters." *Miami Herald*, September 7: 11BM.

———. 1992b. "Thousands Waiting for Adjusters: Insurers Facing Oct. 15 Deadline." *Miami Herald*, September 28: 1A.

———. 1992c. "State Farm Ups Payout Estimate to $2.1 Billion." *Miami Herald*, October 15: 18A.

———. 1992d. "Today is Deadline for Adjusters Handling Storm-Related Claims." *Miami Herald*, October 15: 1A.

———. 1992e. "Andrew Rings Up $10.2 Billion Toll." *Miami Herald*, October 22: 1C.

———. 1992f. "Insurer to End Underwriting in Florida." *Miami Herald*, October 22: 1C.

———. 1992g. "Pulling Up Stakes: Thousands Planning to Relocate Because of Andrew." *Miami Herald*, November 10: 1A.

———. 1992h. "We Will Rebuild Hits $11 Million." *Miami Herald*, September 19: 1A.

———. 1993. "Bill Would Limit Risk of Insurers: Cap a 'Travesty,' State Regulator Says." *Miami Herald*, February 24: 1A.

Schneider, Saundra K. 1995. *Flirting with Disaster: Public Management in Crisis Situations*. Armonk, N.Y.: M. E. Sharpe.

Seline, Rex. 1994. "Homeowners Facing Substantial Rate Hikes in State Insurance Pool." *Miami Herald*, October 11: 1A.

Shiver, Steve. 2002. "Hurricane Andrew 10-Year Anniversary Summit." Conference speech, Florida International University, Miami, May 30.

Shukovsky, Paul. 1989. "Key Biscayne Residents Vow to Block Resort: Evacuation Problems Cited." *Miami Herald*, December 3: 3N.

Silva, Mark. 1992a. "Inspectors, Bad Work at Fault, Report Says." *Miami Herald*, October 5: 1B.

———. 1992b. "Military Helpers Starting to Leave: Units to Head Home as Civilian Firms Take Over Work." *Miami Herald*, September 19: 18A.

———. 1993. "There's More Business to Be Done: Legislature to Deal with Budget, Tolls." *Miami Herald*, April 4: 7B.

———. 1994. "Homespun Legend vs. Young Agent of Change." *Miami Herald*, October 30: 6B.

Silva, Mark, and Dexter Filkins. 1992. "After 10 Years, Simon Artfully Bows Out." *Miami Herald*, July 11: 1B.

Silva, Mark, and Terry Neal. 1994a. "Home is Where the Hurt Is: Gallagher Loses in Dade." *Miami Herald*, September 10: 22A.

———. 1994b. "Trail Mix: The Road to the Florida Elections: Chiles, Bush Running Even Race, Poll Shows." *Miami Herald*, October 28: 5B.

Slevin, Peter. 1994. "Barriers Crumble as Civic Elite Pass Leadership Torch." *Miami Herald*, April 13: 1A.

Slevin, Peter, and Harold Maass. 1992. "Military Machine Gathers Speed: Escalating Effort is Long on Compassion, But Short on Coherence." *Miami Herald*, September 1: 25A.

Smith, Stephen. 1989. "Hialeah Gardens Elects First Cuban Woman Mayor in U.S." *Miami Herald*, March 15: 3B.

Sorenson, Katy. 2002. Interview by author, February 13.

Soto, Luis Feldstein, and Lisa Getter. 1992. "Panels Faulted Dade's Building Inspections." *Miami Herald*, September 13: 1A.

South End Press Collective. 2007. *What Lies Beneath: Katrina, Race, and the State of the Nation*. Cambridge, Mass.: South End Press.

Stalling, Robert A., and Charles B. Schepart. 1990. "Contrasting Local Government Responses to a Tornado Disaster in Two Communities." In *Cities and Disaster: North American Studies in Emergency Management*, edited by Richard T. Sylves and William L. Waugh Jr., 75–90. Springfield, Ill.: Charles C. Thomas.

Steinberg, Ted. 2000. *Acts of God: The Unnatural History of Natural Disaster in America*. New York: Oxford University Press.

Strouse, Charles. 1992. "Some Alleged Gougers Make Amends: Complaints Now Mostly About Rents." *Miami Herald*, October 2: 16A.

———. 1994a. "Dade Lawmakers Dominated Legislature." *Miami Herald*, April 24: 1B.

———. 1994b. "Legislative Scorecard: House." *Miami Herald*, April 24: 2B.

Strouse, Charles, Dexter Filkins, and Patrick May. 1992. "Apathy, Confusion Are Victors in Post-Storm Election." *Miami Herald*, September 9: 1A.

Swarns, Rachel L. 1992. "Swamped Metro Officers Only Handling Emergencies." *Miami Herald*, August 28: 5A.

Sylves, Richard. 2008. *Disaster Policy* and *Politics: Emergency Management and Homeland Security*. Washington, D.C.: CQ Press.

Tanfani, Joseph. 1992. "Political, Civic Leaders Try to Coordinate Help." *Miami Herald*, August 29: 22A.

———. 1993a. "Deering Estate to Close Till 1994." *Miami Herald*, January 28: 2NKE.

———. 1993b. "Dusseau Can't Buy English Radio Ad." *Miami Herald*, April 19: 2B.

———. 1993c. "Incumbents Pull Out Stops in Campaigns." *Miami Herald*, April 19: 2B.

Tanfani, Joseph, and Dexter Filkins. 1993. "New Metro Election a Lot Like the Old Ones: Incumbents' Campaign Chests Bulging." *Miami Herald*, February 18: 1A.

Taylor, Jacqueline. 2000a. "Verdict, like Arrest, Jolts Oliveros' Town.: *Miami Herald*. July 9: 4NW.

Taylor, James, Louis A. Zurcher, and William H. Key. 1970. *Tornado: A Community Responds to Disaster*. Seattle: University of Washington Press.

Taylor, Ronetta. 2003. Correspondence from Ronetta Taylor, South Miami city clerk, to author. January 9.

t'Hart, Paul. 1993. "Symbols, Rituals and Power: The Lost Dimensions of Crisis Management." *Journal of Contingencies and Crisis Management* 1, no. 1 (March): 36–50.

Truman, David B. 1951. *The Governmental Process: Political Interests and Public Opinion*. New York: Alfred A. Knopf.

Twigg, David K. "Florida Elections and Hurricanes." *Florida Political Chronicle* 19 (Winter 2008–2009): 33–54.

Ulrich, Yolanda. 1982a. "Chief of Police Wins New Term in Florida City." *Miami Herald*, January 27: 3B.

———. 1982b. "Florida City Elects Mayor, Picks Two Commissioners." *Miami Herald*, February 10: 3B.

———. 1984. "Florida City Elects Black Mayor; Chief Facing Runoff." *Miami Herald*, January 25: 1D.

———. 1985a. "Eight Win in Homestead Council Primary." *Miami Herald*, December 5: 3N.

———. 1985b. "Mayor Pulls Off Homestead Win." *Miami Herald*, December 11: 1B.

———. 1985c. "Black Voters in Homestead Aid Mayor's Win." *Miami Herald*, December 12: 3N.

Wallace, Richard. 1992a. "Metro-Dade Police Desk Aiding in Search for Friends, Loved Ones." *Miami Herald*, August 28: 16A.

———. 1992b. "How Fast Was Andrew? Engineers, Meteorologists Differ." *Miami Herald*, September 6: 24A.

Warren, Christopher L., John F. Stack Jr., and John G. Corbett. 1986. "Minority Mobilization in an International City: Rivalry and Conflict in Miami." *PS* 19, no. 3 (July): 626–34.

Waugh, William L. 2000. *Living with Hazards, Dealing with Disasters: An Introduction to Emergency Management*. Armonk, N.Y.: M. E. Sharpe.

Weaver, Jay. 2002. "Murder-For-Hire Evidence Ruled Out: Ex-Mayor Could Get New Trial." *Miami Herald*, November 15: 1B.

White, Thomas G., Jr. 2001. "The Establishment of Blame in the Aftermath of a Technological Disaster: An Examination of the *Apollo I* and *Challenger* Disasters." *National Forum: The Phi Kappa Phi Journal* 81, no. 1 (Winter): 24–29.

Winter, William O. 1973. *The Urban Polity*. New York: Dodd, Mead and Company.

Wolensky, Robert P., and Edward J. Miller. 1981. "The Everyday versus the Disaster Role of Local Officials: Citizen and Official Definitions." *Urban Affairs Quarterly* 16 (June): 483–504.

———. 1983. "The Politics of Disaster Recovery." In *Sociology toward the Year 2000: The Sociological Galaxy*, edited by Charles E. Babbitt, 259–70. Harrisburg, Penn.: Beacons Publishing Company.

Wolensky, Robert P., and Kenneth C. Wolensky. 1990. "Local Government's Problem with Disaster Management: A Literature Review and Structural Analysis." *Policy Studies Review* 9, no. 4 (Summer): 703–25.

———. 1991. "American Local Government and the Disaster Management Problem." *Local Government Studies* 17, no. 2 (March): 15–32.

Ycaza, Cindy. 1989a. "13 Candidates Vie for Biscayne Council Seats." *Miami Herald*, November 19: 8N.

———. 1989b. "Biscayne Activists Council Elects 9." *Miami Herald*, November 26: 3N.

———. 1989c. "Key Biscayne Straw Poll Shuns Development." *Miami Herald*, November 26: 18N.

Yin, Robert K. 1994. *Case Study Research: Design and Methods*. 2nd edition. Thousand Oaks, Calif.: Sage Publications.

———. 2003. *Case Study Research: Design and Methods*. 3rd edition. Thousand Oaks, Calif.: Sage Publications.

Index

David Twigg is an adjunct instructor for FIU's Department of Politics and International Relations and is a former director of the FIU Jack D. Gordon Institute for Public Policy and Citizenship Studies and Program in National Security Studies.